Britain's Postwar Dollar Problem

BRITAIN'S
POSTWAR
DOLLAR PROBLEM

by ELLIOT ZUPNICK

Columbia University Press, New York, 1957

Clarke F. Ansley Award

This study, prepared under the Graduate Faculties of Columbia University, was selected by a committee of those Faculties to receive one of the Clarke F. Ansley awards given annually by Columbia University Press.

TO LILLIAN

Preface

DESPITE a general recovery in the economies of Western Europe, the dollar shortage persists as a major problem. This persistence has rendered inadequate the facile explanations that were current in the early postwar period. The tendency at that time was to attribute the dollar problem to transitory developments, faulty policies, or a concatenation of fortuitous adverse circumstances. As the dollar shortage outlasted the particular factors adduced at one time or another to explain it, it became evident that more searching analyses were required. It was not long before these were forthcoming. The ECA's report on the sterling area and the various annual reports of the Economic Commission for Europe may be cited as examples. The absence of a detailed analysis of the position of the United Kingdom— a pivotal country in the world economy—motivated this study.

This study, which was substantially completed in the summer of 1953, emphasizes developments between 1946 and 1951. In preparing the manuscript for publication, some attempt was made to take into consideration more recent developments, though basically the structure of the study remains the same as that of the original dissertation. The underlying thesis of this book, that the postwar dollar problem was the resultant of basic structural changes which adversely affected Britain's position in the world economy, continues to have validity today. An understanding of these structural changes should provide insight into current developments and perhaps point the way to solutions.

I am deeply indebted to a number of people who helped me in the course of this study. I owe my greatest debt to Professor J. W. Angell who, in addition to stimulating my interest in monetary and international problems, supervised the writing of this dissertation and gave unsparingly of his time and knowledge. Professor R. Nurkse provided helpful suggestions at the beginning of the study. Professor J. M. Fleming kindly read and criticized an early draft. Professors A. G. Hart, D. Landes, and J. Mosak read the completed dissertation and made many valuable suggestions, as did my colleague Professor B. Klebaner. My wife, to whom this book is dedicated, was helpful in innumerable ways throughout. Finally, I should like to thank my editor Miss J. Soderman for her aid in preparing the manuscript for publication.

ELLIOT ZUPNICK

New York, New York
March, 1957

Contents

Tables

Britain's Postwar Dollar Problem

1 Introduction

THE INABILITY to attain and maintain equilibrium on dollar accounts at a viable level of trade was one of the major economic problems faced by Great Britain in the postwar period. On the one hand, the dollar shortage posed the most serious threat to the maintenance of full employment; on the other hand, it precluded attempts to restore sterling convertibility and adherence to the principle of nondiscrimination in trade. In addition, it acted as a strong divisive factor in relations between the United Kingdom and the United States, the United Kingdom and the Western European countries, and the kingdom and the rest of the sterling area.

In this study, an attempt is made to analyze the basic factors responsible. It is hoped that setting the problem in its proper perspective will make a modest contribution toward evolving solutions. At the very least, it will indicate the sources of the difficulties, frequently a prerequisite for a meaningful attack on a problem.

DEFINITION OF THE DOLLAR SHORTAGE

For the purposes of this study a dollar shortage is defined as existing when, at an acceptable level of employment, real income, and import restrictions, the quantity of dollars demanded exceeds the disposable supply of dollars.[1] The basic underlying consideration in this definition is that a dollar shortage entails more than a foreign exchange market phenomenon. The view that in the absence of a foreign exchange market disequilibrium a dollar shortage cannot exist is categorically rejected. If, for example, a dollar-sterling balance is attained or maintained at the expense of an acceptable level of employment and real income or through the imposition of import restrictions above

----

[1] Compare the definition of a dollar shortage given in the text with Professor Nurkse's definition of balance of payments equilibrium in his "Conditions of International Monetary Equilibrium," reprinted in American Economic Association, *Theory of International Trade*, pp. 4 ff.

the level dictated by *non*balance of payments considerations, a dollar shortage is asserted to exist as surely as when, with an acceptable level of real income, employment, and import restrictions dictated by non-balance of payments considerations alone, the quantity of dollars demanded exceeds the disposable supply.

It is recognized, of course, that the concept of an acceptable level of real income is troublesome and not amenable to precise measurement. It must be emphasized at once that there is no implication that so long as the level of Britain's real income, for example, is below that of the United States, the United Kingdom must suffer a dollar shortage. The concept of an acceptable level of real income, as used in this context, is intimately related to the traditional standard of living of the country under discussion. More specifically, the term is meant to suggest a level below which real incomes may not be driven without generating tensions that threaten the stability of the social and political equilibria. It is evident that this level cannot be determined a priori and that it varies from country to country and from time to time even within the same country. But knowledge of a country's history, customs, traditions, and institutions should enable the investigator to ascertain in a general way the limit below which the level of real income may not be safely driven.

The definition of the dollar shortage given above differs in important respects from others found in the literature. The conventional way of defining a dollar shortage is to treat it solely as a foreign exchange market phenomenon. Harris defined a dollar shortage as "an excess of dollars used over dollars supplied, the difference being made up by borrowing on short term account from the United States and shipping gold to the United States." [2] Kindleberger defined it as

a persistent departure or a persistent tendency to depart from equilibrium in the balance of payments of the United States in the direction of a surplus in excess of net long term capital outflows. Viewed from abroad the dollar shortage is the tendency of current accounts of foreign balances of payments to show larger deficits in dollars than are covered by long term borrowing.[3]

Finally, Ellis defined the dollar shortage simply as a condition where at the "going rate of exchange, demand exceeds supply." [4]

    [2] Harris, "Dollar Scarcity," *Economic Journal*, June, 1947, p. 165.
    [3] Kindleberger, *Dollar Shortage*, p. 170.
    [4] Ellis, "The Dollar Shortage in Theory and Fact," *Canadian Journal of Economics and Political Science*, August, 1948, p. 360.

Though the futility of definitional disputes is well known and the desire to avoid them commendable, I believe the tendency to define the dollar shortage exclusively as a foreign exchange market phenomenon has contributed to both mistaken analysis and to ill-conceived policy proposals. Indeed, if the dollar shortage is regarded as nothing more than a foreign exchange market phenomenon, the very possibility of its posing a serious problem can be denied. This logical conclusion was drawn by Harrod who indignantly wrote that "the allegation of a 'world dollar shortage' is surely one of the most brazen pieces of collective effrontery that has ever been uttered. In fact, it is no more than the young man going forward and living beyond his means without leave." [5]

The problem posed by the dollar shortage is not comprised of a lack of technical knowledge concerning the manner in which a foreign exchange disequilibrium can be corrected. Rather, the problem is one of restoring equilibrium without inducing an intolerable decline in the levels of real income and employment. This distinction has not always been perceived.

The views of Graham and Harrod are illuminating in this context. Harrod argued that,

The external deficit in any period of time is necessarily equal to the excess of capital outlay over domestic savings. Consequently, if we plan to have a capital outlay in excess of anything likely to be yielded by domestic savings we are in effect planning to have an external deficit. That I suggest is what we are now doing. We are deliberately planning not to avoid an external deficit but to incur one. There are only two ways out—one to increase savings . . . by the amount required, the other to curtail capital outlays.[6]

In a similar vein Graham argued that

we need never look to anything more recondite than an inappropriate relationship between the internal and external value of the currency of any country, rich or poor, to have a *complete explanation* for the lack of balance in its international accounts. With a few notable exceptions . . . the degree of internal inflation of the dollar has at most times been less (or as the case might be the degree of deflation has been greater) ever since World War I. . . . Combined with a predilection for the attainment and maintenance of fixed exchange rates, this has meant that there has been a tendency for the sale of dollars on the exchange market at prices, in other currencies, below the figure which the respective purchasing power of the dollar and other currencies

[5] Harrod, *Hardships Necessary?* p. 43.
[6] Harrod, Letter to the Editor, *The Economist,* May 24, 1947, p. 796.

would warrant. . . . The upshot has been a chronic excess of American commercial exports over imports (italics added).[7]

On a formal level, these arguments are irrefutable. It is commonplace that, measured ex post, the sum of expenditures on capital formation and the government deficit equals the sum of savings and the import surplus. The existence of an international deficit is thus prima facie evidence that the country is, in some sense, living beyond its means. Likewise, there is little disagreement that some exchange rate exists that will equilibrate the demand for dollars with the supply of dollars. Regarded as a foreign exchange market phenomenon, a dollar shortage cannot exist unless rigidities are present with respect either to the exchange rate or to the wage rate.[8]

Graham's and Harrod's arguments are vitiated by two considerations, however. First, there is an implied belief that the dollar shortage can be "completely explained" by reference to relative inflation. This does not constitute an explanation; it is possible to subsume everything under this portmanteau. Second, and more important, their arguments fail to consider the probable effects of the application of their "solutions" on the levels of income and employment. It cannot be emphasized enough that the difficulties associated with the dollar problem are due not to lack of knowledge of techniques which could eliminate a foreign exchange disequilibrium, but rather to the probability that application of these techniques would lead to a dangerous decline of employment and real income.

EXTENT OF THE DOLLAR PROBLEM

The definition of the dollar shortage advanced above precludes the possibility of accurately measuring the severity of the dollar shortage by reference to balance of payments data alone. These data reveal the transactions that have taken place but do not show those that were frustrated by the necessity of imposing restrictions because of the existence of a dollar shortage. It is known, however, that import restrictions on dollar goods were important in restraining the expansion of dollar imports in the postwar period. Furthermore, the transactions that actually occurred were influenced, in part, by the extension of extraordinary American aid which, in turn, was induced by the severe dollar shortage. Were it not for this aid, the volume of dollar imports into the United Kingdom,

---

[7] Graham, *Causes and Cures of a Dollar Shortage*, p. 5.
[8] See Lutz, *The Marshall Plan*, p. 9.

for example, would undoubtedly have been even more severely reduced than was actually the case.

Despite these important limitations, it is necessary to use the balance of payments data to measure the severity of the dollar shortage; there simply is no available substitute. If the inadequacies of the data are realized, however, the dangers resulting from this procedure can be minimized.

Before the evidence pertaining to Britain's postwar dollar problem is examined, however, it is necessary to introduce a complication. It is not possible to analyze that problem by limiting the discussion to the United Kingdom's direct current and capital accounts with the dollar area.[9] There are two reasons for this: first, Britain was the custodian of the hard currency reserves of the whole sterling area and was thus responsible for the dollar payments on associated members' accounts; second, the general dollar shortage in the postwar period resulted in Britain's (and in the rest of the sterling area's) having to make dollar payments to non-dollar countries for essential imports derived from these countries. The drain of dollars to these "third countries" was a substantial component of the postwar dollar deficit.

There were, therefore, three distinct components in Britain's dollar problem: the United Kingdom's direct dollar accounts; the rest of the sterling area's direct dollar accounts, including, however, any gold sales made to the United Kingdom; and the dollar transactions of the whole sterling area with non-dollar countries. Table 1 shows the relative importance of each of these components in the postwar period.

Examination of the table reveals that between 1946 and the first half of 1955, 96 percent of the sterling area's total dollar deficit was accounted for by Britain's direct dollar deficit on current and capital accounts. During this period the rest of the sterling area contributed 1,809 million dollars to the central pool,[10] and dollar payments made on the whole sterling area account to third countries provided for 27 percent of the total deficit.

[9] The dollar area consisted of countries which had American account status in the postwar period. For a listing of the American account countries in the preconvertibility and postconvertibility periods see page 165.

[10] Since we are concerned with the effects of the rest of the sterling area's external transactions on the dollar pool, it is appropriate to lump together its direct dollar deficits (surpluses) and its gold sales to the United Kingdom. A gold sale from the rest of the sterling area to the United Kingdom increases the gold reserves as well as Britain's sterling liabilities.

Two things are obscured by the figure showing the net contribution of the rest of the sterling area to the central pool between 1946 and the first half of 1955. The first is that in particular years the drain of dollars attributable to the rest of the sterling area's deficit with the dollar area was an important component of the total dollar drain. This was particularly true, as reference to Table 1 shows, for the "crisis" year 1947,

TABLE 1

STERLING AREA DOLLAR ACCOUNTS, 1946–55

(*In millions of U.S. dollars*)

Year	U.K. Current Account Balance with Dollar Area	U.K. Capital Account Balance with Dollar Area	Rest of Sterling Area Dollar Balance	Dollar Payments to Third Countries	Total Dollar Balance
1946	– 1211	83	41	183	– 904
1947	– 2059	– 178	– 890	– 1004	– 4131
1948	– 1016	– 267	– 41	– 317	– 1642
1949	– 1093	– 4	– 25	– 293	– 1416
1950	– 224	346	754	– 14	862
1951	– 1192	– 286	506	– 167	– 1140
1952	– 484	96	305	– 405	– 489
1953	– 36	63	462	183	672
1954	– 263	184	463	– 140	244
Jan.-June, 1955	– 214	31	234	– 133	– 82
Total	– 7792	+ 68	+ 1809	– 2107	– 8026

Sources: 1946–51 data derived from *United Kingdom Balance of Payments 1946–1953,* Cmd. 8976; 1952–55 data derived from *United Kingdom Balance of Payments, 1946–1955,* Cmd. 9585.

when the drain attributable to the rest of the sterling area accounted for rather more than 20 percent of the total. The rather large drain accounted for by the rest of the sterling area between 1947 and 1949 stands in sharp contrast with the situation that existed in the interwar period when Britain succeeded in earning sufficient gold and dollars from the rest of the sterling area to offset her own direct dollar deficits.

The second thing obscured by the net figure showing the contribution made by the overseas sterling area to the dollar pool in the postwar period is the fact that the overseas *independent* members of the sterling area were heavy drawers on the resources of the central pool. The significance of this development is discussed in detail below.

Attention should also be focused on the dollar payments made on whole sterling area account to third countries.[11] These payments were

[11] The absence of information precludes the allocation of these payments between the United Kingdom and the rest of the sterling area.

particularly large in the "crisis" years 1947, 1949, and 1951; in the first year these payments accounted for 24 percent of the total dollar deficit, while in the last two they accounted for 21 percent and 17 percent respectively. It is argued below that these payments reflected the general dollar shortage and measure the extent to which third countries succeeded in shifting the burden of this shortage to the sterling area.

FINANCING THE DEFICIT

The 8,026 million dollar deficit incurred by the sterling area between 1946 and the first half of 1955 was financed by the loans and grants the United Kingdom received in the postwar period. In view of the fact that the value of these loans and grants exceeded the total dollar deficit, the sterling area's gold and dollar reserves increased by 204 million dollars during this period. Table 2 shows the manner in which the sterling area's

TABLE 2

FINANCING OF DOLLAR DEFICITS, 1946–52

(In millions of dollars)

	1946	1947	1948	1949	1950	1951	1952	Total
U.S. line of credit	600	2850	300					3750
Canadian line of credit	523	423	52	116	45			1159
IMF drawings		240	60					300
South African gold loan			325					325
ERP loans and grants			682	1132	705	175		2694
Drawings on or additions to (−) gold and dollar reserves	− 220	617	223	168	− 1612	965	489	632
Total financing	− 904	− 4131	− 1642	− 1416	862	− 1140	− 489	8859

Source: Derived from *United Kingdom Balance of Payments, 1946–1953*, Cmd. 8976, Table 22.

dollar deficits were financed between 1946 and 1952. In 1953 and 1954, the sterling area earned dollar surplus and thus enjoyed an increase in its reserves.

The importance of extraordinary finance in the form of American and Canadian loans and grants in financing the postwar dollar deficits is apparent. The fact that the reserves increased in the postwar period is attributable to the availability of these loans and grants. It should not be overlooked, however, that the reserves were subject to strains which, given their low level,[12] were particularly severe and necessitated drastic action at times. Moreover, with the growing scarcity of other forms of compensatory finance, the brunt of future dollar deficits will probably fall more heavily on the reserves. Even during the period 1946–52 an increasingly heavier burden was placed on the reserves.[13]

SCOPE OF THE STUDY

It is necessary, at the outset, to sound a note of caution about the scope of the study. An examination of the factors responsible for an international disequilibrium inevitably leads the investigator into many peripheral areas which, though extremely important and interesting in themselves, must be treated rather less intensively than would be the case were they in the major focus. Thus, though it is necessary to examine the course and control of inflation in Britain, the evolution of Britain's postwar payments machinery with non-dollar countries, the historical development of the sterling area, the American extraordinary aid program, the consequences of the 1949 sterling devaluation (to cite only a few such items) it is not possible to do full justice to any of these topics (that would require a study devoted to each). An attempt has been made to treat

[12] The following table shows the quarterly movements in the sterling area's gold and dollar reserves in the postwar period:

(*In millions of U. S. dollars*)

Quarters	1945	1946	1947	1948	1949	1950	1951	1952	1953	1954	1955
March 31		2384	2380	2241	1912	1984	3758	1700	2166	2685	2677
June 30		2301	2410	1920	1651	2422	3867	1685	2367	3017	2680
September 18					1340						
September 30		2682	2383	1777	1425	2756	3269	1685	2486	2901	
December 31	2476	2696	2079	1856	1688	3300	2335	1846	2518	2762	

[13] For our purposes the three great postwar crises can be limited as follows: January 1, 1947–September 30, 1947; April 1, 1949–September 30, 1949; and July 1, 1951–June 30, 1952.

The following table shows the manner in which these crises were "financed."

	Jan. 1, 1947– Sept. 30, 1947	April 1, 1949– Sept. 30, 1949	July 1, 1951– June 30, 1952
Drawing on U.S. credit	2750		
Drawing on Canadian credit	353	59	
ERP aid		624	46
IMF loans	60		
Drawing on reserves	314	1161	1524
Total compensatory finance	3477	1844	1570

Despite the fact that each postwar crisis was less severe than the one preceding, the drain on the reserves became increasingly larger.

these and other related issues which arose in the course of the analysis of Britain's dollar shortage only to the extent necessary to show their relationship to the major problem.

The plan of the study is as follows. Chapters II and III are devoted to setting up the problem. In Chapter IV the thesis that the dollar shortage can be ascribed to Britain's failure to pursue sufficiently dis-inflationary policies in the postwar period is examined in detail. This examination was motivated by the persistence with which this thesis has been advanced in the literature and by the belief that it is responsible for a large part of the obscurity which shrouds the dollar problem. In Chapters V, VI, and VII an attempt is made to assess the relative impor-tance of the various factors responsible for the emergence and severity of the dollar shortage between 1946 and 1951. Chapter VIII is concerned with developments subsequent to 1951; Chapter IX, with trade principles best adapted to mitigate a dollar shortage. Chapter X is devoted to a critical examination of some frequently proposed solutions for a dollar shortage, while Chapter XI states the more important conclusions that emerge from this study.

II *Setting the Problem*

BRITAIN'S postwar payments problem was the result of the impact of a concatenation of forces that profoundly affected the structure of world production, trade, and payments and fundamentally altered Britain's position in the world economy. Some of these forces were induced by the war; others date as far back as the last third of the nineteenth century. In this chapter are examined the basic factors which impaired Britain's competitive position in the world's markets and which were responsible, directly or indirectly, for the emergence of the postwar disequilibrium.

THE DETERIORATION OF BRITAIN'S COMPETITIVE POSITION IN WORLD MARKETS

Britain's industrial supremacy in the nineteenth century was predicated on the competitive advantage she enjoyed in the staple industries. With these industries as a base—coal, iron and steel, textiles, and engineering —the United Kingdom succeeded in becoming the world's leading manufacturer and exporter. Their export proceeds [1] more than sufficed to enable Britain to pay for her primary product imports. Indeed, between 1815 and 1875 the United Kingdom exported no less than 500 million pounds of capital to the rest of the world.[2]

The year 1875 is a milestone in Britain's economic history. Prior to this Britain's dependence on foreign sources of supply was moderate, as the expansion of Britain's manufacturing industry was not marked by a serious decline in agricultural production. In 1868, for example, Britain produced 80 percent of the grain, meat, dairy products, and wool consumed in her domestic market. Only with respect to a few commodities, like cotton, was Britain highly dependent on foreign sources. "The 'great commerce' was still of the nature of adventure, the fruit of superabundant energy of Great Britain more than the essential root of her economic

---

[1] Foreign receipts derived from the international services which grew *pari passu* with Britain's export trade were also extremely significant.

[2] Jenks, *Migration of British Capital*, p. 333.

existence." [3]   Ten years later the picture was radically altered.   In 1878 domestic production of grain, meat, dairy products, and wool could meet only 50 percent of the total demand; the remainder had to be obtained from abroad.   Britain's prosperity was henceforth linked to her competitive position in world markets.

Unfortunately for Britain, her increased dependence on imports for survival coincided with a marked deterioration of her competitive position in world markets.   While many factors were responsible for this development, the more significant were: the displacement of the old technology on which Britain's prosperity was based by a new one in which her chief rivals, the United States and Germany, excelled; the dramatic growth of the general productive power of the United States; the development of the older staple industries within many of Britain's former markets; and, most important, the shift of international demand away from products in the production of which the United Kingdom had a comparative advantage to those which could be produced more efficiently in other centers.[4]

These developments resulted in a shift of the hub of manufacturing and exporting from the United Kingdom to the United States and Germany. The extent of this change is reflected in the relative shares of manufacturing capacity accounted for by the United Kingdom, the United States, and Germany in 1870 and 1913.   Whereas in the earlier year the United Kingdom had accounted for 32 percent of the world's manufacturing capacity, the United States for 23 percent, and Germany for 13 percent, by 1913 Britain's share had fallen to 14 percent while the shares of the United States and Germany had increased to 36 percent and 16 percent, respectively.[5]

By the end of the First World War Britain's situation was critical. Fundamental adaptations to the new circumstances ushered in by the basic developments in the world economy were required.   These adaptations could have been realized by a bold frontal assault, but Britain's industrial and commercial policies in the interwar period were geared toward the maintenance of as large a share of the older markets as was possible in the circumstances, while her financial policy, at least until 1931, failed to recognize the real changes that had occurred in the world economy

---

[3] *Ibid.*, p. 329.

[4] For a good description of the basic forces operating to effect a deterioration of Britain's competitive position, see Kahn, *Great Britain in the World Economy*, chaps. 4–6.

[5] League of Nations, *Industrialization and Foreign Trade*, p. 13.

that so altered her international position. The consequences of Britain's nearly catastrophic financial policies in the interwar period have been well chronicled,[6] and the details need not be repeated. In view of the effects of Britain's industrial policies on her postwar economy, however, it is necessary to review them briefly.

The two cornerstones of Britain's industrial policy in the interwar period were protection of her home market and participation in cartel and other restrictive arrangements to preserve her share of the older markets. The execution of the reorganization schemes was left under the aegis of the various industries concerned as Britain plunged headlong into the industrial government experiment.[7] In lieu of effecting the necessary adaptations and reorganizations, the industries sponsored associations designed to regulate production, trade, and prices. The underlying philosophy of these associations was "that competition is incapable of performing its traditional functions," therefore new methods "were necessary to repair the ravages wrought by the intense competition." [8]

Effective reorganization of weak industries is, of necessity, a painful and costly process. At best, it entails complete disregard for the existing equities of the least efficient members of the industry. Because the struggle to maintain equities is likely to be relentless, the necessary adaptations can be made only if they are imposed upon the industry by blasts of competition or by the government; they can rarely succeed when entrusted to the interested parties under cover of protective devices of one sort or another. The history of the industrial government experiment in interwar Britain provides ample illustration of the futility of attempting to effect the needed changes in this manner.

One of the most dismal and, from the point of view of the postwar situation, most disastrous results of the industrial policies pursued in the interwar period was the almost complete failure to modernize Britain's industrial machine. The adaptations that were required to meet the new circumstances were either not effected at all or done on a piecemeal basis with the result that in many areas the economy lagged still further behind Britain's major competitors. It is neither possible nor desirable to render, at this point, an exhaustive account of Britain's industrial history in the

6 For an excellent analysis of Britain's early post-First World War financial policy, see Brown, *The International Gold Standard*, chaps. 9–12.

7 See Davies, *National Capitalism*, for a bitter indictment of Britain's industrial government experiment.

8 Lucas, *Industrial Reconstruction*, p. 46.

interwar period.[9] A few illustrations will suffice to demonstrate the chaotic state into which some of the major British industries fell and the ineffectualness of the industrial policies pursued. The examples are drawn from the coal, steel, and textile industries.

The Coal Industry in the Interwar Period. Few industries are more important to the economic well-being of the United Kingdom than coal, and few, if any, were in a more chaotic state at the end of the Second World War. To a large extent, the severe deterioration of the coal industry occurred during the interwar period. The Reid Committee reported that in the period before the First World War, "output per man shift in Britain compared favorably with that of practically all the major coal-producing countries other than the United States." [10] In the interwar period Britain's coal industry lagged seriously behind the industries of other major coal producers. Inferior geological conditions in the United Kingdom do not explain this phenomenon because many countries with basically similar geological conditions outstripped the United Kingdom. Thus, though the Ruhr, the Netherlands, and the United Kingdom had substantially the same geological conditions, the increase in output per man shift (OMS) between 1925 [11] and 1936 amounted to 81 per cent, 118 per cent, and 14 percent, respectively.[12] The wide differences in the increase in OMS in the Ruhr and the Netherlands on the one hand and the United Kingdom on the other can be explained, in large part, by the different rates of technical advance in the three countries.

Consolidation of mine holdings so that actual mining can be planned as a unit is a prerequisite for the effective operation of a coal industry.[13] The atomistic nature of Britain's coal industry precluded the possibility of a rationally planned exploitation of her coal.

"The ownership of the mineral was . . . [dispersed]. When, therefore, a mine was to be sunk it was often necessary to obtain leases from a number of different owners each wanting his coal to be worked quickly, so that he could draw his royalty. Even where a single landowner held the mineral rights of an area in which an undertaking wished to work, he sometimes pursued a

---

[9] For detailed accounts of Britain's interwar industrial history, see Kahn, *Great Britain in the World Economy;* Lucas, *Industrial Reconstruction;* Davies, *National Capitalism;* and Brady, *Crisis in Britain.*

[10] Reid Committee, *Coal Mining,* Cmd. 6610, p. 29. Henceforth referred to as the Reid Report.

[11] The base year for the United Kingdom is 1927.

[12] *Ibid.*

[13] Reid Report, p. 30.

deliberate policy of granting leases for comparatively small areas with the intention of increasing his royalty receipts by having several undertakings working his coal simultaneously." [14]

This state of industrial organization precluded economies of scale and resulted in an immobilization of valuable coal.[15]

The chaotic situation is attributable, in large part, to the ineffectual policies pursued by the government in the interwar period.   The coal acts passed in the thirties, without exception, made the necessary reorganization of the industry virtually impossible.[16]   The failure to reorganize precluded modernization,[17] which in turn accounted for the relatively poor showing of the coal industry.   The inadequate mechanization of the British mines is reflected in the fact that whereas one haulage worker was required for every 50 tons of coal mined in the United States and for every 20 to 25 tons mined in the Netherlands, the proportion in the United Kingdom was one such worker for every 5 tons mined.[18]   This high proportion of haulage workers to miners working on the face was one of the major factors responsible for the relatively low OMS in the British mines. The Reid Committee estimated that the modernization of Britain's haulage system to bring it to the level achieved in the Netherlands would increase her OMS by 25 percent, that the installation of the most technically advanced equipment in the more backward mines would result in a 100 percent increase in OMS, and, finally, that a reorganization of the industry that entailed nothing more than the transfer of miners from the hopelessly inefficient to the more efficient mines would result in a 25 percent increase in OMS in even the most modern British mines.[19]

Considering the importance of coal to the British economy, inefficient organization of the industry could not but have deleterious effects.   Aside

[14] *Ibid.*   [15] *Ibid.,* p. 122.

[16] The Coal Mines Act of 1930 established the Coal Mines Reorganization Committee to "promote and assist . . . the amalgamations of . . . coal mines when such amalgamations appear to the commission to be in the public interest."   (20 and 21 George V, chap. 24.)   The effectiveness of this act was completely nullified by the proviso that the proposed amalgamations could not be made if they were proved to be injurious to the interests of any of the operators.   A 1936 amendment which would have eliminated this proviso was defeated.   In 1938 a parliamentary bill required the approval of the Select Committee of both Houses before an amalgamation could be made.

[17] The chaotic state of the industry resulted in losses or exceedingly small profits in every year between 1924 and 1938 (Reid Report, Appendix 2).   This state of affairs precluded the possibility of accumulating internal finance or resorting to the capital markets for the necessary finance.

[18] Reid Report, p. 33.   [19] *Ibid.,* p. 120.

from weakening the competitive position of the major coal-using industries, the inefficiency of the British coal industry was in large part responsible for the decline in the relative importance of Britain as a coal exporter in the interwar period [20] and for the necessity to resort to foreign sources for coal in the early postwar period. Had the British coal industry maintained the rate of progress achieved by the other major coal-producing countries in the interwar period, Britain's postwar payments difficulties would have been very much less severe.[21]

The Iron and Steel Industry. In iron and steel, as in many other industries, Britain paid dearly for her head start and for her failure to introduce new and more efficient methods of production.[22] The relative deterioration of Britain's steel industry dates from 1879 when, with the introduction of the Thomas process on the Continent, the competitive advantage shifted from British to Continental producers. Because the British steel industry did not introduce the new methods of production, her ability to maintain a virtual monopoly on iron and steel exports was adversely affected. In the early 1880s, the British accounted for approximately 80 percent of the total world exports of iron and steel; by the outbreak of the First World War the proportion accounted for by the British was reduced to 33 percent. It was not until the interwar period, however, that the situation became critical. The Sankey Committee reported that the "smelting and coke making branches of the industry were wholly antiquated and inadequate; ore mining and steel making less so, but still in need of great expenditure." [23] The average plant size was considerably below the size of the plants found in other leading countries and also considerably below the optimum required to effect economies of scale. The integration of the industry both on the plant level and within the economy was poor. The former precluded the possibility of taking full advantage of by-products and thus added to the total cost of production, while the latter led to the incurrence of additional transportation and reheating costs and resulted in "bottlenecks . . . at every

[20] The proportion of the world coal exports, including bunkers, accounted for by the United Kingdom declined from 50 percent in 1909–13 to 35 percent in 1936. Kahn, *Great Britain in the World Economy*, p. 85.

[21] The coal shortage of 1946–47 alone cost the United Kingdom approximately 200 million pounds of exports. See Dalton's remark in Hansard, V, 441, c. 1656 (All references to Hansard are to *Debates of the House of Commons*.).

[22] For a detailed history of the steel industry, see Burn, *History of Steel Making*.

[23] This report, never officially published, appeared in the *Ironmonger* in summary form on November 29, 1930, pp. 67–8. See Burn, *History of Steel Making*, p. 436.

stage from raw material to finished product." [24]   Brady was so impressed
with the uneconomical locational structure of the industry that he concluded that "until something was done about this general pattern, individual changes, however desirable in themselves, were likely to cancel one
another." [25]

The government's response to these conditions in the 1930s was in
line with its industrial government experiment.   Appeals to the government for help led to the recommendation by the Import Duties Advisory
Committee (IDAC) that a 33 percent ad valorem tariff be imposed against
foreign steel with the proviso that the industry use the breathing space
thus afforded to modernize and reorganize.[26]   In 1934 the ad valorem
duty was raised to 50 percent and the Iron and Steel Federation was or-
ganized to aid in carrying out the reorganization and modernization.

The Iron and Steel Federation's attitudes were inimical to the basic
tasks of modernization and reconstruction that the situation demanded.
As the federation conceived its functions, they were to increase the profits
of the industry and to pursue all policies that resulted in this end, provided existing equities were not threatened.[27]   To accomplish this, the
federation joined the international steel cartel in 1935 to secure for British
producers the home market and a fraction of the foreign market.[28]   In
the secured home market the federation was free to pursue policies of
production controls, and price maintenance, in short, to destroy the last
remaining vestiges of competition.

The federation did succeed in increasing the profits of the steel industry.[29]   This development was not so much the result of reorganization
or modernization, however, as of production control and price fixing.   The
index of Britain's steel prices rose faster than the general wholesale index
and that for all other metals after the formation of the Iron and Steel
Federation,[30] a development which posed a serious threat to Britain's steel-
using industries.

[24] Brady, *Crisis in Britain*, p. 209.

[25] *Ibid.*

[26] See the report of the IDAC, *Iron and Steel Industry*, Cmd. 5507.

[27] Brady characterized the federation as "a supercartel of the type which not
even the Germans succeeded in effecting for any major industry until the rise of the
Nazis in the thirties." *Crisis in Britain*, p. 195.

[28] For a description of the operation of the steel cartel, see E. Haxner, *The
International Steel Cartel* (Chapel Hill, N.C.: University of North Carolina Press,
1943).

[29] See Davies, *National Capitalism*, p. 73.

[30] Cole, *Why Nationalize Steel?* p. 18.

It is not to be inferred, however, that modernization was completely neglected. Actually, between 1934 and 1939 the industry did expend 50 million pounds for this purpose, but a substantial part of this expenditure was devoted to makeshift improvements and accomplished little toward increasing the size of plants, achieving better integration of the various processes within the firm and the industry, or creating a more rational locational structure. Lucas summed up the achievements of the federation with respect to modernization and reorganization of the industry as follows:

The net result of the reorganization movement in the iron and steel industry . . . seems to be little more than an elaborate scheme for the further suppression of competition, including some of the more doubtful implements employed by monopoly to strengthen its position at the expense of the consumer. Technical reorganization is being achieved, it is true, but not as a result of concerted action.[31]

In the interwar period the exports of the United Kingdom's steel industry declined precipitously. Part of the decline may be attributed to the world-wide depression, which affected all the major steel exporters. More serious, however, was the decline in the relative importance of Britain as a steel exporter not only to South America but even to parts of the Commonwealth.[32] Though many factors contributed to this, the inefficiency of the British steel industry must undoubtedly be included as a major one among them.

The failure to modernize in the interwar period was also an important contributory factor to the severity of Britain's postwar payments difficulties. Of all the shortages from which Britain suffered in the postwar period that of steel was one of the most critical, and it, perhaps, more than any other bottleneck prevented a still greater expansion of British exports to the dollar area or to other areas with which Britain had to discharge part of her deficits in gold or dollars. A healthy steel industry in the postwar period would have aided greatly in alleviating the dollar shortage not only of the sterling area but also of Western Europe.

The Textile Industries. The major factors responsible for the cotton industry's difficulties in the interwar period were the growth of cotton manufacturing in areas formerly supplied by the United Kingdom and the emergence of Japan as a major exporter of cheap cotton goods. Britain's cotton industry was a prime victim of the shift of international demand

[31] Lucas, *Industrial Reconstruction*, p. 123.
[32] *The Economist*, March 23, 1946, pp. 461–62.

away from her staple products. Between 1913 and 1937 world consumption of raw cotton increased by some 36 percent, while the volume of international trade in cotton declined by 38 percent.[33] The manner in which Britain was affected by these two developments is amply illustrated by the trend of Indian cotton imports. Between 1909 and 1913, India produced, on an average, 1,141 million square yards of cotton goods and imported, largely from Britain, an average of 2,741 million square yards annually. In 1937, India produced 3,951 million square yards and imported only 688 million square yards. Of these imports only about half came from the United Kingdom, while a large share of the remainder was derived from Japan.[34] This pattern was repeated in other countries. Britain's cotton exports to the United States declined from 163 million square yards in 1924 to 11 million square yards in 1931, largely as a result of the imposition of tariff barriers to protect the American producer.[35] The growth of cotton production in Brazil was primarily responsible for the decline in British cotton exports there from somewhat more than 63 million square yards in 1925-27 to less than 3 million square yards in 1932.[36]

The loss of markets for British cotton exports resulted in a precipitous decline in cotton production, machine activity, and employment in the industry. Cotton yarn production declined from 1,963 million pounds in 1913 to 1,070 million pounds in 1938, while the production of cloth declined from 8,050 million square yards to 1,912 million square yards during the same period. Employment in the cotton industry declined from 621,500 in 1912 to 393,000 in 1938; the number of spindles and looms in operation declined from 61.4 million and 786,000 to 42.1 million and 494,000, respectively, between 1932 and 1938.[37]

The broad picture that emerges from these statistics is that of a very sick industry. The obstacle imposed by a drastic decline in international demand for cotton goods would have been almost insuperable even for a well-organized, closely integrated modern industry, and Britain's cotton industry did not possess this characteristic.

The industry's plant and equipment was inadequate even in the prewar period. A partial inventory of the industry's capital assets in 1930 revealed that 65 to 75 percent of the machinery was twenty years old or more. Since little reequipment occurred after that, it is safe to say that the same proportion of the equipment in the early postwar period

[33] Board of Trade, *Working Party Report, Cotton*, p. 119.
[34] *Ibid.*   [35] *Ibid.*, p. 5.   [36] *Ibid.*   [37] *Ibid.*

was forty-five or more years old. A survey of buildings used in the cotton industries during the war revealed that 67 percent of the buildings in the spinning section and 69 percent of those in the weaving section were constructed before 1900. The Working Party found that "judged by the standards and methods of some other countries, the equipment of the Lancashire industry is (a) old fashioned and (b) extremely extensive in relation to the turnover handled." [38] The spinning section was equipped predominantly with mule spindles, "a type which no other country retains on an appreciable scale and which textile machine makers in general have ceased to manufacture." [39] Only 5 percent of the looms in use were automatic as compared with fully 95 percent automatic in the American cotton industry. In general, the Working Party reported that "a substantial proportion of the machinery now in place is . . . not only old in type but beyond its efficient working life." [40]

Though the need for modernization and organization was certainly apparent in the interwar period, progress was slow. The Cotton Spindles Reconstruction levy did little to remove excess equipment and saddled the more efficient firms with an extra cost of production. In 1939 a bill was passed that empowered the industry to fix prices and production quotas and to effect reorganization schemes. In short, the government ultimately fell back on the industrial government method of getting modernization and reorganization.

The picture painted for the cotton industry was substantially the same for the other textile industries. Machines over eighty years old were in use in the woolen industry at the end of the war. A quarter of the worsted spindles and a higher proportion of the woolen spindles dated back to the nineteenth century. Many of the looms still in use were fifty or more years old.[41] Even granting the extreme durability of this type of machinery, the age of Britain's machinery was undoubtedly a deterrent to more efficient production. The Heavy Clothing Working Party reported that machinery in that industry also, at the end of the war, was wholly inadequate and that a vast re-equipment program was necessary to make the industry competitive.[42]

The New Industries. This survey of Britain's industrial history before the Second World War has dealt, thus far, with the declining staple industries. This is justifiable in view of the importance of these industries to Britain's

---

[38] *Ibid.,* p. 66.   [39] *Ibid.*   [40] *Ibid.*
[41] Board of Trade, *Working Party Report, Wool,* p. 76.
[42] Board of Trade, *Working Party Report, Heavy Clothing,* p. 54.

economy. It is important, however, in order to prevent distortion, to present briefly the progress Britain made in the interwar period in the new industries.

The new industries were the automobile and aircraft industries; the rayon and chemical industries; the aluminum, electrical goods, and electrical supply industries; and the scientific instrument and apparatus industries. These had their origins in the twentieth century and assumed an important position in Britain's economy in the interwar period. In a sense, the growth of these industries measures the degree to which the British economy adapted to the basic forces which adversely affected her competitive position in the world economy.

Though the proportion of net output of the new industries to total output increased from 6 percent in 1907 to 20 percent in 1935, the situation was not entirely satisfactory. There is evidence to suggest that these industries flourished largely because of the protected home market and were, in the main, uncompetitive in foreign markets where they did not enjoy imperial preference. Furthermore, they failed to take up the slack in the export field created by the decline in the exports of staples. Indeed, a large part of the increase in the relative importance of these industries as exporters is ascribable to the severe decline in the exports of the staple industries.

The progress of the new industries, however, precludes drawing facile conclusions concerning the stagnation of the British economy in the interwar period. Rostas estimated that industrial production in the United Kingdom increased by 84 percent between 1907 and 1937.[43] This increase, as G. C. Allen has indicated, was in large part attributable to technological advances initiated in the new industries after 1924.[44]

Though the stagnationists' dismal view of the interwar period is rejected, it remains true that industrial progress in the United Kindom proceeded at a slower rate than in the United States. Between 1907 and 1937 industrial production and productivity in terms of output per man hour in the United Kingdom increased by 84 percent and 64 percent respectively. During the same period American industrial production and productivity increased by 134 percent and 133 percent respectively.[45]

The broad conclusions that emerge from the brief survey of interwar

[43] Rostas, *Comparative Productivity,* p. 49.

[44] Allen, "Economic Progress, Retrospect and Prospect," *Economic Journal,* September, 1950, p. 466.

[45] Rostas, *Comparative Productivity,* p. 49.

industrial history are that Britain's industrial machine was sorely in need of modernization and that the economy failed to make the necessary adaptations to altered circumstances. Security rather than innovation became the *desideratum* of many of Britain's entrepreneurs. A leading efficiency expert, thoroughly familiar with British industry, argued that this quest for security which resulted in cartel arrangements, trade associations, price rings, territorial allocation schemes, and so forth, was "the real, the only tangible handicap of the British economy compared with its American counterpart. . . . The difference [moreover], is becoming greater not less." [46] Though this certainly overstates the case, its partial validity cannot be ignored when seeking the factors responsible for Britain's postwar difficulties.

The significance of these developments to Britain's postwar difficulties is apparent. The failure to make the necessary adaptations to altered circumstances and the antiquated state of British industries resulted in a serious impairment of Britain's competitive position in world markets. The highly progressive American economy, on the other hand, enabled that country to provide the lion's share of the commodities for which demand increased in the postwar period. Had Britain succeeded in adapting her economy in the interwar period to the new pattern of international demand, her postwar difficulties would undoubtedly have been mitigated.

Besides having an adverse effect on Britain's competitive position in world markets, the serious state of disrepair of Britain's industries was an important factor [47] in the need for capital formation in the postwar period, which had to be given a high priority. This need for reequipment competed for resources required to expand exports and imposed additional burdens on an already strained economy.

BRITAIN'S TRADE IN THE INTERWAR PERIOD

The failure to effect the necessary adaptations to changing world conditions was also reflected in the movements of Britain's interwar trade. Between 1913 and 1938, the volume of Britain's exports declined by approximately 30 percent, while her imports expanded in approximately the same proportion. It is true that these developments were not due

---

[46] Ord, *Secrets of Industry*, p. 146.

[47] The state of disrepair into which industries fell in the interwar period was not, of course, the only reason for the need for a large capital formation program. Equally important developments were the deterioration and destruction of capital during the war.

entirely to the relative inefficiency of Britain's industries; in part they reflect the stifling financial policy of the early interwar period, the deterioration of the terms of trade of many of Britain's customers, the world-wide depression after 1929, and the reduction in the volume of capital exports from Britain. The evidence strongly suggests, however, that the weakening of Britain's competitive position in world markets was an important contributory factor; between 1913 and 1929 the volume of British exports declined by 13.4 percent though the volume of world exports increased by 27 percent.[48] It should be pointed out, however, that in the 1930s Britain succeeded in maintaining her relative share of world exports though this latter development was due partly to the intro- duction of Imperial Preference, which discriminated in favor of British exporters.

Despite the worsening of Britain's real trade account, the underlying difficulties were concealed during the interwar period. This was because Britain's commodity terms of trade improved, because the real value of invisible earnings in terms of imports increased,[49] and because the rate of capital exports decreased culminating at the end of the period with a partial liquidation of overseas assets. These factors tended to cushion the economy against the adverse effects discussed above, and rendered less imperative the necessity for corrective measures.[50]

The improvement in Britain's terms of trade in the interwar period was the most important of the three factors above in shielding the British economy from the consequences of failing to adapt to changing world conditions. Colin Clark estimated that Britain's terms of trade improved by 38 percent between 1913 and 1938.[51] Moreover, a substantial part of this improvement occurred in the 1930s when, with the collapse of primary product prices, Britain was able to purchase her food and raw materials imports at bargain prices.[52] This tremendous improvement in the terms

[48] League of Nations, *Network of World Trade*.

[49] This factor may properly be considered but a variant of the improvement in Britain's terms of trade.

[50] The problem of causation is extremely difficult. It may very well be that the tremendous improvement in Britain's terms of trade obviated the necessity for ef- fecting the basic changes. Undoubtedly the problem is one of interaction rather than causality.

[51] Table 3 shows the course of Britain's terms of trade in the interwar period.

[52] The improvement in the terms of trade in the interwar period was no doubt a factor in the decline in the volume of exports. Keynes, who was the first to note that the interwar terms of trade improved, argued that "we are no longer able to sell a growing volume of manufactured goods (or a volume increasing in propor-

TABLE 3

BRITAIN'S TERMS OF TRADE IN THE INTERWAR PERIOD

(*1913 = 100*)

Year	Import Price Index	Export Price Index	Terms of Trade [a]
1919	243	292	120
1920	288	368	128
1921	186	272	146
1922	149	199	134
1923	148	189	128
1924	154	190	123
1925	155	185	129
1926	141	174	123
1927	136	161	118
1928	136	159	117
1929	133	155	116
1930	115	148	129
1931	93	133	143
1932	86	122	142
1933	82	119	145
1934	85	121	142
1935	97	121	139
1936	91	123	135
1937	104	133	128
1938	98	135	138

[a] The terms of trade index is derived by dividing the export price index by the import price index. An increase represents an improvement in the terms of trade.

Source: Clark, *Conditions of Economic Progress,* p. 453.

of trade offset, in large part, the loss of receipts due to the decline in the volume of British exports.

The increase in the real value of invisible earnings in terms of imports, though less significant than the improvement in the commodity terms of trade, was nevertheless important in enabling Britain to finance an increased volume of imports in the face of a decline in the volume of exports. Table 4 shows the proportion of total imports paid for by invisible earnings in selected interwar years.

The increase in the real value of invisible earnings in terms of im-

---

tion to population) at a better real price in terms of food." He concluded that a deterioration in the terms of trade was essential if Britain were to restore full employment in the export industries. See Keynes, "A Reply to Sir William Beveridge," *Economic Journal,* December, 1923, p. 482. Robertson suggested that there were three alternatives available to Britain to solve the problem of unemployment in the export industries: a deterioration of the terms of trade as Keynes suggested, an increase in capital exports, or a diversion of resources from the export to the home-oriented industries. See Robertson, "A Note on the Real Ratio of International Interchange," *Economic Journal,* June, 1924, pp. 286–91.

ports was due to the much smaller decline in the value of invisible earnings than that in the value of imports. This, in turn, resulted from the relative fixity of returns on income account; shipping earnings followed more closely movements in the volume of trade as well as the fluctuations in the world price level.

TABLE 4

NET INVISIBLE EARNINGS AS A PERCENTAGE OF IMPORTS

(*In millions of pounds*)

Year	Net Shipping Earnings	Net Interest, Dividends, and Profits	Other	Total Invisible Earnings	Total Imports	Invisibles as Percentage of Imports
1924	140	220	48	408	1277	32
1929	130	250	57	485	1221	29
1935	70	180	52	302	757	46
1938	100	200	43	343	920	37

Source: Derived from Chang, *Cyclical Movements*, p. 144.

The decreasing rate of capital exports and the eventual liquidation of some foreign assets was the third factor which enabled the United Kingdom to finance a larger volume of imports in the interwar period despite the decline in the volume of exports. In 1913 Britain's foreign exchange earnings exceeded by 30 percent the amount of foreign exchange she needed to discharge her payments on current account. Between 1923 and 1930 the excess (available for foreign investment) was reduced to 7 percent. Thereafter, the surplus of receipts over payments was replaced by a deficit; between 1930 and 1937 Britain's foreign exchange earnings sufficed to pay for only 97 percent of her imports and in 1938 the proportion was reduced to 92 percent. In the last decade of the interwar period Britain relied on a partial liquidation of her foreign assets to cover the difference between her foreign exchange receipts and payments. In view of her vast foreign holdings, this partial liquidation was not sufficient to cause any consternation. Lord Kindersley estimated that Britain's overseas holdings in 1938 amounted to 3.7 thousand million pounds,[53] so a disinvestment of some 50 to 100 million pounds a year was not regarded as serious.

With hindsight, it is manifest that Britain's international accounts in the interwar period represented an "equipoise on a trapdoor." The

[53] Kindersley, "British Overseas Investment," *Economic Journal,* December, 1939, p. 693.

factors discussed [54] hid, by and large, the precarious nature of the balance and seemingly obviated the necessity for making the required adaptations. Wartime developments, however, which included a severe deterioration of the terms of trade, a drastic reduction in the real value of invisible earnings, and a heavy liquidation of overseas assets, precluded the possibility of viewing further liquidation with equanimity and served to expose, with a vengeance, the basic weaknesses of Britain's position.

WARTIME DEVELOPMENTS

Though the origins of Britain's postwar payments problem were rooted in the interwar period, wartime developments brought the problem to a head and gave it crisis proportions. Among the more important wartime developments that contributed to the problem were the war-induced dislocations in Britain's occupational structure, the deterioration and destruction of capital assets, the war-induced inflation, the rise in the price levels of internationally traded goods, the deterioration in the terms of trade, the decline in the real value of invisible earnings in terms of imports, the decline in the real value of international reserves, the liquidation of overseas assets, and the incurrence of overseas liabilities. Some of these developments exerted only a transitory effect on Britain's payment problem; others, however, were quite influential. It is necessary to examine all in some detail.

Dislocations in Britain's Occupational Structure. The advantages of specialization and the international division of labor are more frequently recognized during wartime than during peace. Because of Britain's proximity to the war zone, it was agreed that she could best serve the common cause by concentrating on production of war goods. The shipping of 27 thousand million dollars worth of goods to the United Kingdom under the lend-lease program [55] enabled the British to pursue this course of action. Britain ruthlessly sacrificed her export industries and diverted manpower from civilian to military uses. Commercial exports in 1943 amounted to only 29 percent of the 1938 level and were still only 45 percent of that level as late as 1945.[56] The number of men

---

[54] Another factor which should be mentioned was the high level of unemployment in the United Kingdom in the interwar period.

[55] Dalton in Hansard, V, 445, c. 88 (written reply).

[56] *Statistical Material,* Cmd. 6607, p. 8.

employed in the production of exports was reduced from 1,300,000 in June, 1938, to 400,000 in June, 1945. During the same period the number of men employed in production for the home market declined from 15,200,000 to 11,800,000 and the number of persons in the armed forces increased from 600,000 to 5,200,000.

The cessation of lend-lease immediately after the end of the war was a severe blow to the British, who felt, with justice, that the program should have been continued until they had been able to make a start in reorienting their economy to peacetime pursuits. Britain had to reassume responsibility for the financing of her imports at a time when the structure of her economy reflected more the requirements of the late war than the circumstances of the postwar period. This factor undoubtedly contributed to Britain's early postwar difficulties, although, with the passage of time, it became much less significant.[57]

Deterioration and Destruction of Britain's Capital Assets. The deterioration and destruction of Britain's capital assets during the war represented a more serious liability than the distortions in the occupational structure. In contrast to the interwar period, when capital investment was positive in every year,[58] the United Kingdom consumed capital at the rate of 10-15 percent of the gross national product per annum between 1940 and 1945.[59] Paish estimated that the value of capital disinvestment during the war, measured in 1945-46 prices, amounted to between 2,250 and 2,500 million pounds.[60] In addition to this disinvestment of fixed capital, the United Kingdom drew heavily on the stockpiles of working capital. The ensuing shortage of stocks in the early postwar period was one of the chief impediments to increased production and productivity. Furthermore, the necessity to replenish the stockpiles was an important factor in the large dollar deficit incurred in 1947.

The destruction of capital during the war amounted only to slightly less than the consumption of capital. Paish estimated the value of capital destroyed by enemy action, on sea as well as on land, at 1.5 thousand million pounds.[61] Shipping losses suffered by the United Kingdom ac-

[57] The reallocation of manpower which occurred during the war had some favorable side effects as well. Britain had a larger number of men in heavy industry after the war than before.

[58] Clark, *Conditions of Economic Progress,* p. 397.

[59] *Statistical Materials,* Cmd. 6707, p. 15.

[60] Paish, *Post War Financial Problem,* p. 3.

[61] *Ibid.,* p. 9.

counted for no less than 25 percent of Britain's prewar merchant fleet,[62] and represented a particularly severe blow in view of the importance of shipping earnings in Britain's prewar balance of payments. The importance of this factor tended to diminish, however, with the rebuilding of the British fleet.[63] Of greater importance, in the long run, than the destruction of the merchant fleet was the heavy damage suffered by transportation facilities. This proved to be a major obstacle to production in the early postwar years and necessitated huge capital outlays. Finally, the destruction or damaging of 4 million houses during the war accentuated Britain's already serious housing shortage and required large capital expenditures on what, from the short-run point of view, may be regarded as essentially unproductive projects.

It is not possible to ascertain with any accuracy the effects of this capital deterioration and destruction on Britain's production and productivity, although the evidence leaves little doubt that they were important. Certainly, it can be said that the low levels of production and productivity in the early postwar period were due in large part to inadequate capital equipment. Further, the heavy loss of capital necessitated large outlays in the postwar period, and these capital projects competed for the scarce raw materials required to produce the exports for which a ready market existed in the dollar area in the years immediately after the war.

The War-induced Inflation. Many economists attribute Britain's payments difficulties almost exclusively to the strong inflationary pressures which existed in the postwar period. While this interpretation is rejected,[64] it is recognized that the existence of these pressures did make Britain's position more precarious, and tended to contribute to the heavy deficits in particular postwar years. What was the source of these pressures?

Total war almost invariably necessitates inflationary financing. The primary object of war finance is to enable the government to obtain a larger proportion of the total output. In a less than fully employed economy this can be accomplished without contracting the absolute amount of goods and services devoted to the civilian sectors by drawing upon the unemployed resources and manpower.[65] In a fully employed

---

[62] *Statistical Material,* Cmd. 6707, p. 4.

[63] By 1948 the fleet had been restored to the prewar tonnage.

[64] See below Chap. IV for a fuller treatment of this problem.

[65] In the United States, for example, total real consumption increased during the war despite the tremendous increase in real government expenditure.

economy, however, a significant increase in the proportion of current output devoted to the government is likely to mean a reduction in the absolute quantity as well as in the proportion of total resources devoted to the civilian sectors. Theoretically, the diversion of resources from the civilian to the government sectors can be accomplished either in an inflationary or in a noninflationary manner. When resort is had to inflation, the government bids for the available goods, thereby forcing up the price of goods and resources and compelling the consumers, whose incomes have risen less than prices,[66] to reduce their real expenditures. This is the process of forced savings which has received so much attention in economic literature.[67] Alternatively, the government can achieve the necessary diversion of product and resources by restricting consumer spending through a network of physical controls. The use of this method does not prevent the growth of disposable incomes but does prevent an increase in consumption (and private capital formation), with the result that while an inflationary price spiral is avoided, inflationary pressures are generated. A noninflationary diversion of resources from civilian to military sectors involves the curtailment of civilian expenditure by the same amount that government expenditure is increased without the growth of excess liquidity. This can be accomplished by reducing disposable income by the amount necessary to cause a contraction in consumer expenditure equal to the increase in government expenditure.[68]

Though theoretically possible, an attempt, in actual practice, to divert resources without using inflationary financing would have had severe adverse effects on production incentives.[69] The major belligerents invariably found it necessary to rely on inflationary financing to divert men and resources from the civilian to the military sectors. Again, almost invariably, the resort to inflationary financing was accompanied by the introduction of comprehensive control systems designed to repress the inflationary pressures generated.

During the war the United Kingdom relied heavily on government borrowing to supplement tax receipts. Between 1939 and 1945 government outlays amounted to 32,954 million pounds, government borrow-

[66] Except, of course, for the profit receivers.

[67] See Robertson, *Banking Policy*, chap. 5.

[68] It should be noted that simply balancing the budget might not be sufficient to accomplish this. A surplus would be needed if the propensity to spend was less than unity.

[69] See Chandler, *Inflation in the United States, 1940–1948*, chap. 6.

ing to 17,192 million pounds or rather more than 50 percent of all government expenditures.[70]   Moreover, a substantial portion of these loans resulted in the creation of new money.   The English banking system, like its counterpart in the United States, conceived its wartime function to be to insure the government an ample supply of funds even if this meant adding to the inflationary pressures.   One of the results of this policy was a tremendous expansion in currency in circulation and in bank deposits, despite a decline in private bank advances.[71]

Though the United Kingdom resorted to price control during the war and introduced a comprehensive subsidy scheme, a rise in prices was not prevented.   Wholesale prices, reflecting to a large extent the rise in import prices, rose by 67 percent between 1938 and 1945, while the working-class cost-of-living index rose by 31 percent.   Weekly wage rates rose by some 50 percent between 1939 and 1945.[72]

The rise in the price and wage indices is, however, an inadequate gauge of the inflationary pressures generated by the manner in which the war was financed.   The introduction of a comprehensive control system and the liberal use of cost-of-living subsidies operated to suppress the pressures.   And while it is not possible to measure directly the extent of these repressed inflationary pressures, their existence can be detected indirectly.   Two measures which can be used for this purpose are changes in the relationship between savings and disposable income and changes in the real value of money balances.   An application of these measures shows that gross personal savings rose from 6.5 percent of personal disposable income in 1939 to a high of 23.5 percent in 1943, declining slightly thereafter to 19.8 percent in 1945.[73]   The existence of repressed inflationary pressures is also reflected in the ratio of money balances to the price level, i.e., in the change in the real value of money balances; between 1938 and November, 1945, this index rose by 74 percent.[74]

The increase in the proportion of personal savings during the war was associated with a decline in real consumption.   It is estimated that at the

[70] Derived from *National Income and Expenditure, 1938–1946,* Cmd. 7099.

[71] Average currency in circulation increased by 183 percent between 1938 and 1945, total deposits by rather more than 100 percent, and current deposits by some 50 percent.   Central Statistical Office, *Monthly Digest of Statistics.*

[72] Central Statistical Office, *Annual Abstract of Statistics, 1955.*

[73] Derived from *National Income and Expenditure, 1938–1946,* Cmd. 7099.

[74] For the underlying logic of this measure of repressed inflationary pressures see ECE, *Survey of Economic Situation,* p. 78.

height of the war real consumption was approximately 15 percent lower than the prewar level.[75]

The rise in disposable income, the very much smaller increase in personal consumption in monetary terms, the absolute decline in nonwar capital formation, and the heavy inflationary borrowing by the central government left all sectors of the British economy in a highly liquid state at the war's end.[76] This liquidity, accompanied by the serious privations suffered by nongovernment sectors during the war, resulted in the generation of inflationary pressures in the postwar period. Strong action was required to prevent the breakthrough of these inflationary pressures, to enable the United Kingdom to divert a large portion of her product to the export markets, and to maintain a competitive price level. The degree of success Britain enjoyed in these respects in the postwar period is examined below.

Adverse Price Developments and Britain's Balance of Payments. Adverse price developments during the war were among the more important factors in Britain's payments difficulties. These adverse price changes consisted of a general rise in the price level of internationally traded goods, a deterioration of Britain's terms of trade, a decline in the real value of invisible earnings in terms of imports, a decline in the real value of international reserves, and a decline in the real value of gold earnings.

As Britain is normally a deficit country on trade account, any "general" [77] rise in the price level of internationally traded goods will result in a deterioration of her trade account even if this change is unaccompanied by a deterioration in the terms of trade. Britain suffered from both a general increase in prices and a deterioration of the terms of trade. Between 1938 and 1946 the average unit value of British imports rose by 129 percent while the average unit value of her exports

[75] *National Income and Expenditure, 1938–1946,* Cmd. 7099.

[76] Between 1938 and 1945 undistributed profits and depreciation reserves increased by 4,825 million pounds (*National Income and Expenditure, 1938–1945,* Cmd. 7099). The proportion of liquid to total assets of the banking system increased from 29.4 percent in 1939 to 60.2 percent in September, 1945. *The Economist,* Banking Supplement, October 27, 1945, p. 1.

[77] If *all* prices rose, including the price of the international reserves, the increased deficit would not be significant. Under these circumstances the increase in the deficit would not represent any increase in the real burden of the deficit country. It need hardly be added that a general price rise, in this sense, hardly, if ever, occurs.

rose by 114 percent. Thus, in addition to a drastic increase in the price levels of imports and exports, Britain's terms of trade deteriorated by approximately 11 percent. These two developments alone would have sufficed to increase Britain's trade deficit by about 500 million pounds over the 1938 level had all other things remained equal.

The reduction in the real value of invisible earnings during the war was also significant. It was noted above that in 1938 the earnings on invisible account sufficed to pay for 37 percent of Britain's imports. In 1946, for reasons discussed below, Britain incurred a deficit on invisible account. Despite the fact that this deficit was ultimately replaced by a surplus, the real value of these earnings in terms of imports never assumed the prewar size. In 1950, for example, these earnings covered but 17 percent of the imports. The volume of imports into the United Kingdom in this year, moreover, was severely reduced from the pre-Second World War period.[78] The decline in the real value of invisible earnings in terms of imports in the late postwar period is attributable in large part to the increase in the value of imports induced by the rise in the import price level. Thus, in a sense, part of the decline in the real value of invisible earnings in terms of imports was but a special type of deterioration in the terms of trade; the price level of internationally traded services failed to rise *pari passu* with the price level of internationally traded goods.

The rise in the price level of internationally traded goods while the (dollar) price of gold remained constant also reduced the real value of Britain's international reserves and of the newly earned gold from the rest of the sterling area. Had the dollar price of gold risen *pari passu* with the rise in the price of internationally traded goods, the value of Britain's reserves at the end of 1945 would have amounted to approximately 5,000 million dollars rather than 2,476 million dollars. It is manifest that this increase in the value of the international reserves would have supplied Britain with more leeway in the postwar period and would have enabled her to weather comfortably what later in fact became major crises.

It is difficult to exaggerate the importance of the adverse price changes as contributory factors in Britain's postwar difficulties. Indeed, of all the factors these rank as among the most important in precipitating the severe postwar payments crises.

[78] The volume of imports in 1950 amounted to 82 percent of the 1938 level. *Board of Trade Journal.*

The Deterioration of Britain's International Capital Position. The deterioration of Britain's international capital position during the war is frequently cited as a major cause of the postwar payments crisis. This deterioration was due not only to the liquidation of a substantial portion of Britain's overseas assets, but also to the incurrence of huge overseas liabilities in the form of sterling balances. During the war the United Kingdom liquidated overseas assets worth 1,118 million pounds. Of this amount 428 million pounds was lost on account of the sale of North American securities.[79] Assuming an average rate of return of 6 percent, the liquidation of these securities involved the United Kingdom in a loss of rather more than 65 million pounds per annum and of approximately 25 million pounds of hard currency,[80] measured in 1938 prices.

Most of the heavy debts contracted by the United Kingdom during the war assumed the form of sterling balances which increased by 2,576

TABLE 5

BRITAIN'S INTERNATIONAL FINANCIAL POSITION

(*In millions of pounds*)

	August, 1939	June, 1945
Gold and dollar reserves	605	453
Net liabilities to rest of world	476	3,052
Overseas assets	3,535	2,417
External debt [a]		303

[a] Debt incurred with the United States and Canada.

million pounds.[81] Britain also borrowed approximately 303 million pounds from the United States and Canada. The servicing and repayments of these debts imposed a heavy burden on her balance of payments in the postwar period.[82] Neither the liquidation of overseas assets nor the incurrence of heavy debt, however, prevented a reduction in Britain's gold reserves during the war. Between August, 1939, and

[79] *Statistical Material,* Cmd. 6707, p. 9. Exclusive of the securities pledged for the Reconstruction Finance Corporation loan.

[80] Hard currency is defined here to mean dollars.

[81] See Table 6 for the sterling holdings of Britain's major creditors at the end of the war.

[82] The interest burden of the sterling liabilities was rather small. These balances were held either in the form of bank balances or in the form of short-term government securities. As a result of the low interest burden of the sterling debts, the United Kingdom continued to be a creditor on income account though she emerged from the war as a debtor on capital account.

TABLE 6

OWNERSHIP OF STERLING BALANCES, JUNE 30, 1945

(*In millions of U.S. dollars*)

Dominions		
Australia	473	
New Zealand	254	
South Africa	132	
Total	859	
Other major sterling area countries		
Burma	44	
Egypt and Sudan	1,593	
Eire	718	
Iceland	69	
India	4,464	
Iraq	283	
Total	7,171	
British colonies, mandates, and so forth		
African colonies	839	
Ceylon	245	
Hong Kong	131	
Malaya	340	
Trinidad	78	
Other	507	
Total	2,140	
Total sterling area		10,170
Europe		
Belgium	150	
France	160	
Greece	220	
Netherlands	274	
Norway	363	
Portugal	314	
Other	168	
Total	1,649	
South America		
Argentina	342	
Brazil	147	
Uruguay	57	
Other	17	
Total	563	
Rest of world		
China	91	
Iran	87	
All other countries	79	
Total	257	
Total non-sterling countries		2,469
Total sterling and non-sterling countries		12,639

Source: *Congressional Record,* Vol. 92, Part 3, p. 3838.

June, 1945, Britain's gold reserves declined from 605 million pounds to 453 million pounds.

The adverse effects of the war on Britain's international financial position are summarized in Table 5. An examination of the table reveals succinctly the extent to which Britain's international financial position was impaired during the war period.

The developments discussed in this chapter contributed to the deterioration of Britain's international accounts. Since this study is concerned primarily with Britain's postwar dollar shortage, it is necessary to indicate the manner in which this deterioration came to be concentrated on her dollar accounts. This is the problem on which attention is focused in the next chapter.

III *Emergence of the Problem*

THE KEY to why Britain suffered from a dollar shortage rather than a foreign exchange shortage in the postwar period is to be found in the developments which resulted in the virtual collapse of the multilateral trade and payments structure which characterized the prewar economy. In view of the fact that the major part of this study is concerned in one way or another with these developments, it is necessary to sketch them briefly here.

In 1928 (which for the purposes at hand can be taken as representative of the early interwar period) approximately 70 percent of world trade in merchandise was conducted along bilateral lines, while the remainder was financed by multilateral settlements. These multilateral settlements were made possible by an intricate structure of trade balances, based ultimately on geographical and productional differences, which permitted deficits incurred in some regions to be offset with surpluses earned in others. The United States, for example, incurred deficits with the tropical areas and earned surpluses from the regions of recent settlement, Continental Europe, and non-Continental Europe. The situation for non-Continental Europe, mainly the United Kingdom, was the reverse: deficits were incurred with the United States, the regions of recent settlement, and Continental Europe while surpluses were earned from the tropical regions. Continental Europe incurred deficits with the United States, the regions of recent settlement, and the tropics and earned surpluses from non-Continental Europe. Finally, the regions of recent settlement incurred deficits with the United States and the tropics and earned surpluses from Continental and non-Continental Europe.[1]

The trade deficits which the United States incurred with the tropics provided one of the links which enabled a multilateral settlement of balances. Additional links were supplied by gold newly mined in the tropical regions and by the proceeds of American capital exports. The dollars supplied to the tropical countries in these three ways provided them with

[1] See League of Nations, *Network of World Trade.*

the wherewithal to discharge their balance of payments deficits with the United Kingdom.

Even as early as the 1930s severe strains developed in the multilateral trade and payments structure outlined above. Two factors were primarily responsible for this development: the depression in the United States and the unsettled political conditions abroad. The former resulted in a precipitous decline in American imports and capital outflows, while the latter contributed to a flight of capital to the United States.[2] The dollar shortage produced by the operation of these factors led inevitably to the "development and crystallization of foreign economic systems along national and bilateral lines." [3]

Some semblance of the multilateral structure survived the thirties, however. For example, it is estimated that in 1938

the United Kingdom had a deficit with the Western Hemisphere . . . of about 110 million pounds; and the rest of the present sterling area had a further deficit of about £20 million. Against this could be set about 115 million pounds of newly mined gold, most of which ultimately reached the United States.[4]

Britain's ability to earn a substantial portion of the overseas sterling area's newly mined gold obviated the necessity of drawing heavily on the gold reserves to discharge her direct dollar deficits.

Several developments occurred during the war and postwar periods that tended to destroy the basis for this multilateral trade and payments system, characterizing the interwar economy. It is convenient here to discuss these developments as they affected the positions in the world economy of Britain and the rest of the sterling area.

It was noted above that Britain's gold and dollar earnings from the rest of the sterling area in 1938 enabled her to discharge a substantial portion if not the whole of her deficit with the dollar area. It is evident that any development that resulted in a substantial increase in Britain's dollar requirements, or reduced the overseas sterling area's dollar earnings, or impeded Britain's ability to earn dollars from these countries would adversely affect the multilateral trade and payments structure. What happened during the war and postwar periods brought about all these phenomena: Britain's direct dollar deficits and hence her dollar requirements increased; the rest of the sterling area's gold and dollar surpluses were reduced

[2] See Department of Commerce, *United States in the World Economy,* p. 7.
[3] *Ibid.,* p. 9; also see Gordon, *Barriers to World Trade.*
[4] *Economic Survey for 1948,* Cmd. 7344, p. 18.

sharply; and Britain's ability to earn dollars from the rest of the sterling area was impaired. Since a substantial portion of this study is devoted to a detailed examination of these developments, it is necessary only to outline them briefly here.

The increase in Britain's dollar deficits between the prewar and postwar periods is attributable chiefly to adverse price developments and to the increased importance of petroleum, which required dollars to buy and produce, even when it was derived from non-dollar sources. Except for the years immediately following the cessation of hostilities, Britain did not obtain a larger volume of imports from dollar sources.

TABLE 7
PRIMARY PRODUCTION IN 1951–52
(*1938 = 100*)

	Total Farm Production	Food Production	Population	Per Capita Food Production
North America	141	144	121	119
Latin America	115	116	136	85
Europe [a]	101	100	111	90
Near East	124	123	121	102
Far East	101	100	113	86
Africa	122	118	120	98
Oceania	111	110	124	89
Total	111	111	113	98

[a] Exclusive of the U.S.S.R.

Source: FAO, *The State of Food and Agriculture: Review and Outlook,* October 1952.

The decline in the rest of the sterling area's dollar surpluses in the postwar period, on the other hand, was due in large part to an increase in the volume of dollar imports. This increase in the volume of imports from the dollar area is attributable chiefly to two developments: the failure of primary production in non-dollar sources to expand sufficiently (see Table 7) and the increased tempo of industrialization in many overseas independent sterling area countries. The former meant that greater reliance had to be placed on dollar sources of supply for food and raw materials, while the latter induced a large increase in capital goods imports of the overseas sterling area countries, which could be obtained in the postwar period only from the United States.

The increase in Britain's dollar requirements and the reduction in the rest of the sterling area's dollar earnings coincided with a reduction in

Britain's ability to earn surpluses from the rest of the sterling area. The factors chiefly responsible for this development were: the deterioration of Britain's terms of trade vis-à-vis the primary producing countries of the sterling area; the huge liquidation of assets and the incurrence of debts which reduced Britain's earnings on income account; and Britain's failure to adapt her economy in the interwar period, which rendered her incapable of supplying the outer sterling area countries with the sorts of goods they most desired in sufficient quantities. The last was a major factor in the large increase in the volume of capital goods imports the rest of the sterling area derived from the United States in the postwar period.

The developments discussed thus far would have sufficed to destroy the basis of the interwar multilateral payments structure. In the event, still other factors contributed to the sterling area's difficulties. Among the more important of these were: the reduction in dollar earnings resulting from the failure of the dollar price of gold to rise and the increased reliance the United States placed on synthetic rubber; the tendency for the increase in the value of American imports to be derived from countries in which the competitive position of the United States was stronger than that of Britain; and the tendency for American capital exports to flow to areas which had strong ties with the United States and to assume the form of direct investments.

In the interwar period gold and rubber were two of the major dollar earning exports of the sterling area. The failure of the dollar price of gold to rise while the dollar price of goods in general more than doubled resulted in a drastic deterioration of the terms of trade of the sterling area gold producers vis-à-vis the dollar area. In addition, the adverse price movement discouraged gold production and thus inhibited the expansion of gold exports to the United States, which otherwise would surely have occurred. In like fashion the increased reliance placed by the United States on synthetic rubber inhibited as large an expansion of natural rubber exports to the United States as there would otherwise have been and also tended to prevent the price of natural rubber from rising as much as it would have otherwise. As a result of these developments the dollar loss to the sterling area was undoubtedly significant.

The tendency for American trade to become more bilateral is apparent from an examination of the pattern of American imports in the postwar period. The Economic Commission for Europe noted that rather more than 75 percent of the increase in American foreign expenditure between 1937–38 and 1949–51 was due to an increase in the imports of nine commodity groups: coffee, cocoa, nonferrous metals, petroleum and petroleum products, raw wool, timber, paper and paper products, sugar, and rubber. Of these commodities, wool, cocoa, and rubber came from sources outside the Western Hemisphere, but the greater part of the increase in American imports was derived from Western Hemisphere countries which currently have strong ties with the United States.[5]

As the United States made greater use of Western Hemisphere import sources in the postwar period, similarly American capital exports in the postwar period were directed in large part to the Western Hemisphere and were predominantly direct investments in form. Both of these circumstances made it almost inevitable that the dollars made available as a result of these capital exports would be spent directly in the United States. The contribution these capital exports made toward the reestablishment of a multilateral payments system was, therefore, negligible.

The various developments discussed in this chapter contributed to the breakdown of the old multilateral payments structure and militated against the establishment of a new one. In view of the fact that Britain traditionally depended on indirect dollar earnings to discharge her direct dollar deficits, the reduction in her ability to earn dollars from third sources, together with a substantial increase in the direct dollar deficits, could produce no other effect but a dollar shortage.

---

[5] ECE, *Economic Survey of Europe Since the War,* p. 16. It should be noted that the increase in available dollars due to the rise in the importation of coffee accrued to Central America and Brazil; that due to the increase in the imports of timber and paper, to Canada; that due to the increase in the value of imports of metals, to Canada, Bolivia, and Chile; while that due to the increase in the importation of oil, largely to the Caribbean. All these countries and areas had close ties to the United States.

Among the more important reasons for the heavier reliance the United States placed on Western Hemisphere sources in the postwar period as compared with the prewar period were the disruption of trade during the war which made it necessary to obtain imports from sources less subject to enemy action, and the desire to avoid having to rely on areas from which she might in future wars be cut off. The precipitous decline of imports derived from Far Eastern sources in the postwar period, for example, was undoubtedly due to the second factor cited.

IV Course and Control of Inflation in the Postwar Period

THIS CHAPTER is devoted to an examination of some relevant aspects of Britain's domestic economic developments in the postwar period. Two considerations motivated this examination. First, despite the existence of the numerous and powerful forces which produced the dollar shortage, many students have argued that the disequilibrium was due primarily to the pursuit of inappropriate domestic policies, especially the alleged failure to restrain inflationary pressures. It is submitted that the importance of this factor has been vastly overemphasized, especially for the early postwar period (1946–51). Second, a preoccupation with the dollar problem may result in failure to appreciate the significant achievements of the British economy in the postwar period. It is believed that the dollar problem can be placed in proper perspective only after some of the salient domestic features of this period have been scrutinized.

An examination of the evidence reveals that Britain made impressive progress in the postwar period along several different but related lines. Production and productivity increased significantly, mass unemployment was eliminated, extreme poverty was dramatically reduced, the allocation of resources increasingly reflected the needs at hand, and at least until toward the end of the period the adverse effects of the inflationary pressures were minimized. In terms of this study it is not possible to give an account of all these varied developments; it will, however, suffice to examine Britain's progress in increasing production and productivity, in restraining the inflationary pressures, and in effecting a more "rational" allocation of resources.

PRODUCTION AND PRODUCTIVITY IN THE POSTWAR PERIOD

Britain's production and productivity increased at a satisfactory rate in the postwar period. Between 1946 and 1954 real domestic product increased by 24 percent,[1] industrial production by 48 percent,[2] and agricul-

---

[1] Derived from Central Statistical Office, *National Income and Expenditure, 1955*, Table 12.

[2] Central Statistical Office, *Monthly Digest of Statistics*.

tural production by 42 percent.[3]   These increases in production were due in part to increases in productivity,[4] which, as the following table suggests, were widely distributed and more prevalent in the "newer" industries than in the older staple industries.[5]

Among the more important factors which contributed to these increases in productivity were the improved working stock position after the initial reconversion difficulties were overcome, the postwar capital formation program, the more efficient use of capital equipment, and the "productivity consciousness" of the postwar period.[6]   It is futile to speculate whether more significant increases in production and productivity could have been effected had policies other than those actually adopted been pursued.   The

TABLE 8
INCREASES IN PRODUCTIVITY, 1948–54
(Average yearly percentage increases in output per man year)

	Percentage
Agriculture	5.5
Manufacturing industries	3.0
Mining and quarrying	2.0
Building	2.0
Selected Manufacturing Industries	
Chemicals	8.0
Vehicles	4.5
Engineering and electrical	4.0
Iron and steel	3.5
Textiles	2.0
Clothing	1.0

Source: United Kingdom Treasury, *Bulletin for Industry,* April, 1955.

evidence does not suggest that Britain's postwar economy was stagnant or moribund, or that it was ossified by inflationary pressures.   Rather, the picture that emerges is that of a strong, vigorous economy.

THE POSTWAR INFLATIONARY PROBLEM

The adverse wartime developments discussed in Chapter II necessitated an expansion of exports if international equilibrium were to be attained and maintained at a viable level of trade.   This expansion was contingent

[3] OEEC, *General Statistics,* November, 1955, p. 48.

[4] Productivity measures are inevitably little more than approximations and should be treated with the utmost circumspection.

[5] For the significance of this see p. 69.

[6] Rostas, "Changes in Productivity of British Industry," *Economic Journal,* March, 1952, p. 22.

upon the pursuit of policies designed to increase production and productivity, while limiting the expansion of domestic demand and maintaining a competitive price level on world markets. It is evident that the achievement of these objectives was, in large part, a function of the success Britain enjoyed in restraining the inflationary pressures in the postwar period.

The inflationary problem in postwar Britain is most conveniently discussed under two headings: demand inflation and cost inflation. These two facets of the problem, though sometimes treated together, are different. "The chief danger from excess demand was not that it would cause price inflation [7] but that it would divert output and resources to the home market and create additional balance of payments difficulties." [8] The major danger associated with cost inflation, on the other hand, was that it would lead to an uncompetitive price level and thus frustrate exports. Moreover, policies which may prove efficacious in restraining the one type of inflationary pressure may prove incapable of restraining the other. It is thus necessary to examine the extent to which Britain's postwar payments difficulties can be ascribed to the failure to restrain inflationary pressures acting through demand as well as those acting through costs.

Demand Inflation. It was noted above [9] that the United Kingdom emerged from the war in an excessively liquid state, induced, in large part, by the resort to inflationary financing during the war and the serious privations suffered by the private sectors. This situation alone would have sufficed to bring about a high level of demand in the postwar period. However, several additional factors were operating in the early postwar period to accentuate the dangers of an inflationary breakthrough. Among the more important of these were the determination on the part of the government to maintain full employment at any cost, the inflationary impact of government operations arising from war obligations, the desire to effect a more equitable distribution of income, the necessity of alleviating the severe housing shortage, and the drastic decline in the ratio of private savings to gross national product.

Under the circumstances several, but not alternative, lines of policy were available to restrain the inflationary pressures. The authorities could

[7] "The dangers of price inflation being generated by excess demand were less in an economy where there was quite a wide range of price control, some rationing, a great deal of resale price maintenance and with manufacturers tending to fix prices on a cost plus basis." Ross, "The Food Subsidies and the Budget," *Bulletin of the Oxford University Institute of Statistics,* March, 1952, p. 80.

[8] *Ibid.*   [9] See pp. 29–32.

have: (1) introduced a "monetary reform" to reduce excess liquidity; (2) pursued restrictive monetary policies; (3) followed disinflationary budgetary policies; and (4) maintained the wartime direct controls to repress but not remove the inflationary pressures. The United Kingdom relied on the third and fourth methods in the early postwar period to prevent an inflationary breakthrough. A monetary reform was never seriously considered on an official level although it had been urged by leading economists,[10] and monetary policy between 1946 and 1951 did not serve to restrain the inflationary pressures but instead contributed to them. With the assumption of office by the Conservative party in 1951, the emphasis changed. The emphasis on budgetary policy was drastically reduced, physical controls were relaxed, and a great deal more significance was attached to monetary policy. It is necessary to examine these developments in greater detail.

Postwar Monetary Policy. During the war, in order to reduce the cost of borrowing by the Exchequer, the government pursued policies designed to lower the yields on the whole range of securities. Between 1938 and 1946 the average yield on short-term securities was reduced from 2.73 percent to 2.44 percent, on medium dated securities from 3.27 percent to 2.99 percent, and on consols from 3.38 percent to 2.92 percent.[11] In addition, the Exchequer sought to lessen the cost of government borrowing by relying more heavily on short dated securities. At the war's end, 29 percent of the total internal debt was in the form of floating debt, 37 percent in the form of dated stock, 16 percent in the form of funded debt, and 18 percent in savings certificates, defense bonds, tax reserve certificates, and so forth. This composition of the debt contrasted sharply with that which existed in 1939, when floating debt accounted for only 13 percent of the total while 46 percent was funded.[12]

At the war's end, orthodox monetary policy dictated a funding of a substantial portion of the outstanding floating debt and a conversion of some of the dated securities into obligations payable at the option of the government. In addition, with the huge inflationary potential resulting from the excessively liquid state of the economy and the severe privations suffered by the private sectors during the war, orthodox monetary policy required an upward revision of the whole pattern of yields. In the event,

---

[10] See, for example, Hawtrey, *Balance of Payments,* p. 41.
[11] Central Statistical Office, *Monthly Digest of Statistics.*
[12] Derived from Central Statistical Office, *Annual Abstract of Statistics.*

Hugh Dalton, as Chancellor of the Exchequer, rejected these lines of approach and initiated instead policies designed to reduce still further the average yields on government securities.

Several considerations prompted this course of action, of which some of the more important were: a belief that deflation rather than inflation was the imminent danger; [13] a tendency (encouraged by empirical findings) to deprecate the importance of the rate of interest [14] as a mechanism of control; a desire to reduce both the burden of the debt to the Exchequer and the burden of the accumulated sterling balances; a desire to encourage borrowings by the local authorities; and the usefulness of a cheap money policy in effecting a redistribution of income. The last consideration was especially attractive to Britain's postwar Labor government.[15]

Accordingly, in the autumn of 1945, Dalton lowered the peg on Treasury bills from 1 percent to .5 percent and reduced the rate on Treasury Deposit Receipts from 1⅛ percent to ⅝ percent. The ultimate objective, as announced by Dalton at the time, was to reduce the long term rate to 2.5 percent. This goal was achieved in October, 1946, with the issue, at par, of a new 2.5 percent Treasury stock. The market collapsed shortly thereafter, however, and, despite a slight recovery, remained weak. The heavy drain on the reserves during the summer of 1947 brought the "cheaper money" experiment to an end.[16]

The extreme phase of the cheap money policy was abandoned with the appointment of Sir Stafford Cripps as Chancellor of the Exchequer in the autumn of 1947. Medium and long term rates were allowed to rise, and there was a slight but perceptible tightening of the supply of money. Short term rates continued to decline, however, and this nullified, in part, the disinflationary effects that might otherwise have resulted from the rise in the long and medium dated yields.[17]

---

[13] It is interesting to note that as late as 1947 Dalton invoked the authority of Keynes as justification for the cheap money policy. Cf. Hansard, V, 436, c. 64.

[14] Cf. Oxford Economic Papers, No. 1, reprinted in *Oxford Studies in the Price Mechanism,* Oxford University Press, 1951.

[15] Cf. Dalton's statement in the House of Commons as printed in Hansard, V, 414, c. 1881.

[16] For a detailed discussion of the monetary developments in this period see Kennedy, "Monetary Developments," in Worswick, *British Economy,* pp. 198 ff.

[17] Between 1947 (average) and November, 1951, the average yield on short-term-dated securities was reduced from 2.18 percent to 1.17 percent while the average yields on medium- and long-dated securities rose from 2.67 percent and 2.76 percent respectively to 3.78 percent and 3.95 percent. Central Statistical Office, *Monthly Digest of Statistics.*

More significant, for the purposes at hand, than a detailed description of monetary developments in this period is a discussion of the effects of a cheap money policy on the postwar inflationary problem and hence on Britain's payments difficulties. Though it is not possible to come to definitive conclusions concerning the role played by the cheap money policy, it would appear from the large increase in advances and deposits during this period that it was not insignificant (see Table 9).

TABLE 9

ADVANCES AND DEPOSITS OF THE LONDON CLEARING BANKS, 1946–51

(*In millions of pounds*)

Year	Advances	Deposits
1946		5097
1947	1129	5650
1948	1354	5913
1959	1495	5974
1950	1684	6014
1951	1921	6162

Source: Central Statistical Office, *Annual Abstract of Statistics, 1955.*

A cheap money policy can accentuate inflation by causing or enabling capital formation, government expenditures, and personal consumption expenditures to increase. In so far as private fixed capital formation is concerned, it is doubtful whether the pursuit of a cheap money policy between 1946 and 1951 had seriously deleterious effects; direct controls on capital issues and building materials constituted the most important restraints on private fixed capital formation during this period.[18] It is not probable that a harder money policy would have eventuated in a smaller amount of fixed capital formation than actually occurred, although it would undoubtedly have enabled the government to relax some of the direct controls which were in force.

If the cheap money policy had little effect on the level of private fixed capital formation, there can be little doubt that it had an appreciable effect on investment in working capital. The ease with which bank loans could be obtained as well as their relative inexpensiveness led many businesses to build up their stockpiles and contributed to that state of affairs which Hicks called the empty economy.[19] Had bank advances been less readily available and if the cost of borrowing had been higher, the demand for

[18] See p. 55.
[19] Hicks, "The Empty Economy," *Lloyds Bank Review,* July, 1947.

working capital would have been reduced and the available stocks better allocated.

The cheap money policy probably also stimulated government and personal consumption expenditures. It was noted above that one of the major reasons advanced by Dalton for the pursuit of a cheap money policy in the postwar period was that it would encourage local governments to borrow. It undoubtedly had just this effect. It is not unreasonable to assume that the cheap money policy was at least partially responsible for the large proportion of investment resources devoted to nonindustrial, non-commercial, and nonagricultural construction in the early postwar period. It is necessary, however, to temper this conclusion with the reminder that the decision to construct residential homes was, in large part, a political one and that a high level of residential construction *might* have been under-taken by the local authorities even if money rates had been allowed to rise, provided this was not accompanied by too drastic a tightening in the supply of money.

While the effect of the cheap money policy on personal consumption expenditures cannot be determined precisely, it was probably not insignifi-cant. A harder monetary policy might have had some effect in inhibiting the rise in consumer debt and might have reduced the expenditures of those who enjoyed capital gains as a result of the decline in interest rates.

Taking into account the probable deleterious effects of the cheap money policy on the expenditures of local authorities, businesses, and con-sumers, it can scarcely be doubted that the cheap money policy had adverse effects on Britain's balance of payments in the early postwar period. Furthermore, these effects were not limited to those that resulted from the encouragement of domestic expenditure. The cheap money policy had an even more direct effect on Britain's balance of payments by encouraging speculation against sterling by enabling traders to build up stocks during crisis periods in anticipation of more intensified restrictions against im-ports. (It is noted below that the fluctuations in investment in working capital were an important factor responsible for the biennial crises which characterized the British economy between 1946 and 1951.)

It was a recognition of these harmful effects of the cheap money policy, in conjunction with ideological considerations, that prompted the Con-servative government to return to orthodox monetary policies upon its assumption of office in the autumn of 1951. One of the basic tenets of the Conservative philosophy entailed the removal of controls and the restora-tion of a "free" economy. It was recognized, however, that this objective could not be achieved so long as the economy was subject to inflationary pressures. The government believed, moreover, that the huge expansion in bank advances was a major factor responsible for these pressures and that a policy designed to check the growth of bank advances was necessary if the economy were to be freed without injuring imports and exports. Since the expansion of advances in the postwar period was due to the extremely large holdings by the banks of short-term, low-yielding assets and the previous government's policy of pegging Treasury bills at .5 percent, a policy designed to check the growth of bank advances had to concentrate on these two features of the financial picture.

The Conservative government's program to restrain monetary expansion was outlined by the Chancellor of the Exchequer in his Financial Address of November, 1951. It consisted of the return to orthodox measures of central bank control, which entailed flexible bank rates and open market operations, the retirement of a substantial portion of the floating debt, and an intensified use of qualitative credit controls.

The first step in the direction of monetary orthodoxy involved raising the bank rate from 2 percent to 2.5 percent. By itself, this rise was not designed to be an effective bar against borrowers wishing bank accommodations. It was hoped, however, that the increase in the bank rate would discourage the banks from extending as many advances as in the immediate past. By March, 1952, the government had evidently decided to take another step toward a hard money policy, and raised the bank rate to 4 percent. It remained at this level until September, 1953, when it was reduced to 3.5 percent. A further reduction to 3 percent was effected in May, 1954. With the deterioration of the balance of payments toward the end of 1954 and the beginning of 1955, the rate was raised to 4.5 percent, the highest level it had attained since the late 1920s.

The increase in the bank rate was associated with increases in the whole yield structure at least until 1953. In 1954 the yields on government securities declined, and the structure was not substantially different from that existing in 1951. The accompanying table shows the course of yields on government securities between 1951 and 1954.

The second feature of the government's move toward monetary orthodoxy involved restoring open market operations to their traditional importance. It was noted that the policy in the early postwar period dictated that the Bank of England purchase all Treasury bills offered at a fixed discount. This policy prevented the bank from employing open market operations to check the expansion of bank advances. One of the first

TABLE 10

SECURITY YIELDS, 1951–54

(*In percentages*)

Security	1951	1952	1953	1954
Short-dated	1.85	2.98	3.03	2.61
Medium-dated	3.59	4.25	3.95	3.55
3½ percent war loans	3.98	4.55	4.30	3.99
2½ percent consols	3.78	4.23	4.08	3.75

Source: Central Statistical Office, *Monthly Digest of Statistics.*

measures introduced by the Conservative government removed the peg on Treasury bills. The Bank of England was no longer required to purchase all Treasury bills at a fixed discount, but could charge whatever rate it deemed desirable in the light of economic and financial developments. It should be noted, however, that this policy was put into effect gradually; the Bank of England, like its counterpart in the United States after the famous accord of March, 1951, felt obliged to ease the transition to a free market by continuing its purchase operations at a rate that was still below that which would have eventuated from the free interplay of market forces.

The restoration of open market operations to their traditional role was facilitated by the government's policy of reducing the outstanding volume of floating debt. This was accomplished by the offer of 1,000 million pounds of Treasury Fund Stocks bearing interest at 1.75 percent which could be purchased only with British Treasury bills with not more than sixty days to run to maturity. The effect of this operation was to reduce the bank holdings of Treasury bills by some 500 million pounds, and resulted in reducing the clearing banks' liquidity ratio to 30 percent, the conventional norm of the interwar period. This was probably the most important restraining effect of all as it tended to increase the banks' reluctance to dispose of their remaining liquid assets and thus impaired their ability to extend loans.

These quantitative controls were reinforced by the strengthening of qualitative controls and by renewed resort to moral suasion. The banks were advised by the Chancellor of the Exchequer to be less liberal in extending advances. The Capital Issues Committee received new instructions to apply more rigid tests before approving applications for loans that normally require the committee's approval, and not to allow the automatic flotation of issues to repay bank advances. Finally, a Board of Trade order in February, 1952, introduced a Regulation W type of control to restrain bank advances for purposes of consumption.

The evidence since 1951 suggests that the return to orthodox monetary policies gave the government an additional weapon against inflation. Between 1951 and 1954 bank advances declined slightly for the first time in the postwar period, and the ratio of total money supply to gross national product declined from 37 percent in 1951 to 33 percent in 1953. The restraining influence of the harder money policies on investment in stocks was, perhaps, of even greater significance. It is noted below that the biennial payments crises from which Britain suffered between 1946 and 1951 were due, in part, to the easy money policy operating on investment in working capital. It is significant that this pattern was broken after the introduction of the orthodox monetary policies.

Postwar Budgetary Policies. The decision to pursue an easy money policy in the early postwar period necessitated the use of budgetary policy and direct controls to restrain the inflationary pressures. The success Britain enjoyed in restraining the inflationary pressures must be attributed, in large part, to these policies. It is convenient in discussing this to subdivide the postwar period into two parts: the period between 1946 and 1951 when budgetary policy was extremely important in checking the inflationary pressures, and the period subsequent to 1951 when it was decidedly less so.

Budgetary Policies, 1946–51. It has become fashionable, in discussing Britain's postwar fiscal policies, to make a sharp distinction between the Daltonian inflationary policies and the Crippsian disinflationary policies. Though there is some evidence to suggest that in the pre-Cripps period there was a less than full appreciation of the interdependence between domestic policies and the outcome on international accounts,[20] it is believed that this has been widely exaggerated. This is not to deny, of course, that during a large part of Dalton's tenure in office [21] budgetary policy not only failed to restrain the inflationary pressures but actually added to them; a casual examination of the evidence precludes such denial. Nevertheless, it is submitted that, given the conditions prevailing in the early postwar period, Dalton went as far as he reasonably could in reducing the inflationary impact of government operations. With hindsight, it is easy to criticize Dalton for not having gone further. It is necessary to bear in mind, how-

[20] Cf. Dalton's financial statements in the early postwar years as reported in Hansard.

[21] It should be noted, however, that the first "disinflationary" postwar budget was introduced by Dalton in the autumn of 1947. The budgets introduced by Cripps in subsequent years were, in a sense, modeled after this emergency budget.

TABLE 11

GOVERNMENT SAVINGS AS A PERCENTAGE OF GROSS NATIONAL
PRODUCT AND GROSS CAPITAL FORMATION

(*In millions of pounds*)

Year	Government Savings [a]	Gross National Product	Government Savings as a Percentage of Gross National Product	Gross Capital Formation	Government Savings as a Percentage of Gross Capital Formation
1946	− 454	8,783	− 5	851	
1947	124	9,364	1	1482	9
1948	520	10,379	5	1581	30
1949	581	11,099	5	1617	36
1950	662	11,666	6	1468	44
1951	590	12,785	5	2426	24

[a] Government savings equal government surplus minus taxes on capital plus capital transfers.

Source: Central Statistical Office, *National Income and Expenditure, 1955* (computed from Table 4).

ever, that budgetary policy must be conceived in the light of existing circumstances and within the framework imposed by what, in the short run at least, must be regarded as fixed obligations.

Table 11, which shows the proportion government savings bore to gross national product between 1946 and 1951, as well as the proportion to the domestic gross capital formation program "financed" by government savings, indicates the important disinflationary role assumed by budgetary policy during this period.[22]

[22] The item "government savings" in the table is substantially different from the government surpluses and deficits given in the Exchequer's Financial Statements. These surpluses and deficits do not give an accurate picture of the impact of government operations on the economy, as they are the resultants of all government receipts and all government outlays including receipts from capital accounts and outlays to capital accounts. The following table shows the outcome on government account for the postwar fiscal years as shown in the Financial Statements of the Exchequer (in millions of pounds).

Year	Ordinary Revenue	Ordinary Expenditure	Above the Line Balance	Below the Line Balance	Over-all Balance
1946–47	3341	3910	− 569	− 560	− 1109
1947–48	3847	3210	635	− 650	− 15
1948–49	4007	3176	831	− 489	352
1949–50	3924	3375	549	− 478	62
1950–51	3978	3257	721	− 473	248
1951–52	4433	4054	379	− 529	− 150

Source: Financial Statements of the Exchequer as reported in Hansard.

Ordinary revenues and expenditures comprise current items and are placed "above the line" in Britain's budget. The "below the line" items consist of capital

An examination of the table reveals that government dissavings in 1946 were replaced by net government savings in 1947 and by large and increasing net savings between 1948 and 1950. Between 1948 and 1950 the proportion of the domestic gross capital formation program "financed" by government savings increased from 30 percent to 44 percent. The increased defense expenditures in 1951 occasioned by the outbreak of the Korean War, however, reduced the size of government savings as well as the proportion of the gross capital formation program financed by these savings.

It is necessary to indicate, however, that the disinflationary impact of government savings was probably less than is suggested by the table. There can be little doubt that the extremely low ratio of personal savings to gross national product was induced, in part, by the high tax rates which made the large government savings possible.[23] The true antiinflationary impact of the government savings is equal to the total government savings minus the decline in private savings induced by the high rates of taxation. It is, unfortunately, not possible to estimate precisely the disinflationary impact of government savings regarded in this way.

The disinflationary impact of government savings might also have been lessened by the deleterious effects the high marginal rates of taxation exercised on production incentives. Again, it is not possible to do more than suggest that this factor might have been operating; there is currently no way in which the negative effect of high marginal rates of taxation can be

transactions. The over-all account is the resultant of current and capital items. This over-all account is a somewhat better measure of the impact of government activities on the economy than the "above the line" balance or the "below the line" balance but is a less reliable guide than the item "government savings" shown in Table 11. For a discussion of the significance of these different balances see Cripps's financial statement in Hansard, V, 449, c. 37.

The course of Britain's budgetary policies in the postwar period can be followed by examining the over-all balance during that period. In 1946–47 the over-all balance amounted to – 1109 million pounds, which was substantially less than the deficit incurred in the fiscal year 1945–46. In the fiscal year 1947–48 the over-all account was brought into substantial balance. A large part of the credit for this must go to the disinflationary policies introduced by Dalton in the emergency budget of the autumn of 1947. These disinflationary policies were pursued with a varying degree of intensity. In 1951, however, the (at times) substantial over-all surpluses were replaced by an over-all deficit as a result of the increased government expenditures occasioned by the rearmament effort following the outbreak of the Korean War.

[23] In 1951 personal savings amounted to but 2 percent of the gross national product and it was even lower in the earlier postwar years.

measured. In view of the satisfactory rate of increase in industrial production and productivity in the postwar period, it is probably unwise to place much emphasis on this factor.

The conclusions that emerge from an examination of Britain's budgetary policies in the period between 1946 and 1951 are clear. Except for the first two postwar years, budgetary policies were effective weapons against inflation. Beginning with the emergency budget of 1947, the United Kingdom relied heavily on disinflationary budgets to restrain the inflationary pressures. It is suggested below that this policy was in large part successful.

Budgetary Policies, 1951–54. The outbreak of the Korean War resulted in an expanded rearmament program. The immediate effect of this was to reduce the importance of the budget as a disinflationary force. Indeed, between 1951 and 1954, monetary policy was more significant than budgetary policy. The declining importance of budgetary policy is reflected in the accompanying table, which shows the proportion govern-

TABLE 12

GOVERNMENT SAVINGS AS A PROPORTION OF GROSS NATIONAL
PRODUCT AND OF GROSS DOMESTIC CAPITAL
FORMATION, 1951–54

	As a Proportion of Gross National Product	As a Proportion of Gross Domestic Capital Formation
1951	5	24
1952	2	17
1953	1	6
1954	1	9

Source: Central Statistical Office, *National Income and Expenditure, 1955.*

ment savings bore to gross national product and to gross domestic capital formation between 1951 and 1954.

It should be noted, however, that the decline in the level of government savings was associated with an increase in personal savings. Indeed, this development was one of the most encouraging features of this period and is to be attributed, at least in part, to the tax revisions introduced by the Conservative government as well, perhaps, as to the return to orthodox monetary policies. In any event, as Table 13 shows, the increase in personal savings more than offset the decline in government savings during this period.

The return to orthodox monetary policies, the reduced importance of budgetary policy, and the increase in personal savings reflect the Conservative government's efforts to restore a free economy. These efforts are also made apparent by an examination of the physical controls employed in Britain in the postwar period.

Direct Controls in the Postwar Period. The resort to inflationary financing during the war made it necessary to rely heavily on direct controls to prevent the breakthrough of inflationary pressures generated by this financing. At the end of the war, most authorities were agreed that maintenance of these controls was necessary, at least until the more blatant dislocations caused by the war were corrected. In the event, direct controls played a rather important role between 1946 and 1951 in supplementing budgetary policy to repress, if not to remove, the inflationary pressures and to effect a more "rational" allocation of resources.[24] This section is de-

TABLE 13

PERSONAL SAVINGS AS A PROPORTION OF GROSS NATIONAL PRODUCT AND OF GROSS DOMESTIC CAPITAL FORMATION, 1951–54

	Personal Savings (*In millions of pounds*)	*As a Proportion of Gross National Product*	*As a Proportion of Gross Domestic Capital Formation*
1951	284	2	12
1952	785	6	37
1953	902	6	38
1954	863	5	32

Source: Derived from Central Statistical Office, *National Income and Expenditure, 1955.*

voted to a brief examination of the more important controls employed during this period to minimize the adverse effects of demand inflation.[25]

Aside from the rationing schemes, the most important controls in the postwar period were those limiting imports, those regulating the level of capital formation, and those governing the allocation of scarce raw materials. The direct control over imports exercised by the government in the postwar period was especially important in view of the fact that Britain's exchange control system was never employed for the purpose of limiting imports. This is to say that provided a license was issued by the authorities authorizing the importation of a specific good, the finance necessary to make payment for it was automatically forthcoming. The government's control over imports was not limited to its power of granting licenses to

[24] See p. 58 for a discussion of the phrase "a rational allocation of resources."
[25] Physical controls to combat cost inflation are discussed below.

import. With the closing of the commodity markets during the war, the government assumed direct responsibility for the purchase of many of the staple imports.[26]

The level of capital formation was controlled by the government through the regulation of capital issues, the requirement of licenses for building, and the planning of capital development in the nationalized industries (which were completely under government control) in the light of balance of payments developments. Of these controls, the last two were the most important: the high degree of liquidity in postwar Britain and the ease with which bank advances could be obtained, at least until 1951, precluded the possibility of effectively controlling capital formation through financial devices alone. The control the government exercised over the capital formation program through the license requirement and the planning of investment in the nationalized industries was sufficiently comprehensive, however, to contain the fixed capital formation program within the limits the government decided upon in the light of the developing balance of payments situation. This effective control over the capital formation program was an important element in Britain's postwar antiinflationary program and played a significant role in enabling the United Kingdom to expand exports and reduce the volume of imports. It should not be overlooked, however, that the fact that investment expenditures were more readily controlled than other forms of private expenditures had some deleterious effects. It meant, in practice, that whenever the balance of payments situation required a cut in domestic expenditure, the brunt of the reduction fell on investment.

The controls governing the distribution of raw materials were also important in effecting a more rational allocation of resources. It is not necessary for the purposes at hand to give a comprehensive account of these controls.[27] Their intent was to insure the allocation of scarce resources in a manner designed to improve, immediately or ultimately, Britain's balance of payments position. Accordingly, a priority system was introduced to allocate scarce materials. Highest priority was given to those

[26] The commodity markets were gradually reopened in the postwar period with the result that trading reverted back to private traders. The dates of the reopening of the major commodity markets are: rubber, November, 1946; coffee, July, 1947; tin, November, 1949; cocoa, January, 1951; lead, October, 1952; raw sugar, November, 1952; zinc, January, 1953; wool futures, April, 1953; grain, June, 1953; copper, August, 1953; and cotton, May, 1954.

[27] See Chester, ed., *Lessons in British War Economy,* and Worswick, *British Economy,* chap. 13.

firms engaged in the export trade with the dollar area, a somewhat lower priority was assigned to those firms engaged in the general export trade, while firms producing predominantly for the home market received the lowest priority. This method of allocating scarce materials was effective in limiting the expansion of home demand and thus in encouraging an expansion of exports.

Finally, the rationing schemes, while initially introduced to insure fair shares for all, played a major role in the early postwar period in restraining the expansion of home demand. These schemes, in conjunction with price controls, were thus also important in encouraging an expansion of exports. Without rationing, the danger that the home market would absorb the total increase in production would have been greater than it actually was.

These direct controls did not eliminate the inflationary pressures, but by suppressing them enabled the United Kingdom to expand the volume of exports and reduce the volume of imports. The expansion in the volume of exports did not, in the main, necessitate directing production into export markets. Indeed, aside from some "informal restrictions on sales of exportable products on the home market as in the case of British motor vehicles," [28] Britain relied on the controls on investment and raw materials and the rationing schemes to insure that increases in home demand did not inhibit the expansion of exports. In conjunction with the disinflationary budgetary policy these controls succeeded between 1946 and 1951 in effecting a significant diversion of resources from domestic to export markets.

In line with the Conservative party's objective to free the economy, direct controls were virtually abandoned following its victory at the polls. Price control and rationing were gradually eliminated, restrictions on building and capital formation were reduced, the local authorities were freed to borrow on the open market and were no longer limited to borrowing from the Public Work Loan Board, as had been the case up to 1951, and the major commodity markets were reopened with the result that trade reverted to private hands. By 1954 Britain had already made a significant "dash for freedom."

Allocation of Resources in Postwar Britain. It was noted above that the major problem arising from excess demand was that it would preclude the diversion of product and resources from the home market to the export market and that it would encourage an expansion of imports. To assess the efficacy of the policies employed to restrain demand inflation, it is thus

---

[28] ECE, *Economic Survey of Europe Since the War,* p. 68.

necessary to examine the pattern of resource allocation in the postwar period.

The absence of objective criteria that can be employed to assess the correctness of the pattern of resource allocation obviously creates a difficulty in an investigation of this nature, and it is this difficulty which more than anything else has prevented agreement as to whether or not Britain succeeded in her attempts to restrain demand inflation in the postwar period. Unfortunately, there is no way to eliminate this difficulty. The only procedure open to the analyst is to state explicitly the desiderata which he has chosen and then to measure the performance of the economy against them. The choice of goals cannot, of course, be arbitrary. But, at the same time, it would be illusory to believe that any one set of goals would be, or could be, universally acceptable.

The two overwhelming requirements of the British economy in the postwar period were the needs to expand exports and to expand production. The "correctness" of the pattern of resource allocation can be gauged in the light of these requirements. Specifically, a pattern of resource allocation which assigned a high priority to exports and productive capital formation would be regarded as "correct," whereas one that assigned low priorities to exports and capital formation would be regarded as "inappropriate."

Table 14 shows the annual changes in available product between 1946 and 1954 expressed in 1948 pounds, as well as the manner in which the increase in available resources was utilized. Perhaps the most striking feature of the table is the success it shows Britain enjoyed in diverting to exports a substantial portion of the increment to available resources. Between 1946 and 1954, available resources, expressed in 1948 prices, increased by 3,740 million pounds. The increase in exports absorbed 34 percent of this total, the increase in private consumption 33 percent, and the increase in fixed gross capital formation 21 percent.

On the basis of the evidence, it would appear that Britain made important strides in the postwar period toward achieving an appropriate pattern of resource allocation. The over-all figures tend to obscure certain details, however, which are significant. It should be noted, for example, that between 1952 and 1954 the increase in private consumption accounted for approximately 56 percent of the total increment to resources, while the increase in exports absorbed but 11 percent of the increase. It is noted below that during this period the accentuation of inflationary pressures in Britain was undoubtedly one of the most important factors responsible for the payments difficulties.

In view of the fact that a large part of the literature dealing with the postwar payments problem makes frequent allusion to the pattern of resource allocation, it is necessary to examine it in greater detail. In the following analysis, attention is focused in turn on Britain's postwar consumption expenditures, the capital formation program, government expenditures, and the course of imports and exports.

TABLE 14

UTILIZATION OF INCREMENTS TO AVAILABLE RESOURCES, 1946-54

(*In millions of pounds, 1948 prices*)

	1946– 47	1947– 48	1948– 49	1949– 50	1950– 51	1951– 52	1952– 53	1953– 54
Change in output	61	376	397	264	446	– 38	443	534
Change in imports	144	– 28	177	36	386	– 302	164	180
Change in available resources	205	348	574	300	832	– 340	607	714
Change in consumption	283	– 29	188	199	– 65	– 89	332	397
Change in government expenditures	– 816	– 12	154	– 20	152	222	62	– 31
Change in gross fixed capital formation	240	134	107	57	– 25	1	195	85
Change in inventories	405	– 161	113	– 247	638	– 416	58	75
Change in exports	93	416	238	311	132	– 58	– 40	188

Source: Central Statistical Office, *National Income and Expenditure, 1955.*

Postwar Personal Consumption Expenditures. Despite the fact that total personal consumption expenditures, in real terms, were severely reduced during the war,[29] the postwar increase in private consumption was moderate. In 1946, total real consumption was some 4 percent below the 1938 level. Between 1946 and 1954, total private real consumption increased by 15 percent,[30] although in view of the approximately 3 percent increase in population,[31] the per capita increase was but approximately 11 percent. The increase in real per capita consumption between 1938 and 1954 was even more moderate, amounting to only 9 percent. This is to be compared with a 46 percent increase in real per capita consumption in the United States between 1938 and 1954.[32]

The increase in total real consumption between 1946 and 1954 was not spread evenly over the entire period. Indeed, the greater part of the

[29] At the height of the war, real consumption was 15 percent below the prewar level.

[30] Derived from Central Statistical Office, *National Income and Expenditure, 1955.*

[31] Central Statistical Office, *Annual Abstract of Statistics, 1955.*

[32] OEEC, *General Statistics,* April, 1956, p. 102.

increase occurred between 1946 and 1947 and between 1952 and 1954. The rather large increase in real consumption between 1946 and 1947 was undoubtedly an important factor contributing to the 1947 payments crisis. After the introduction of the disinflationary policies in the autumn of 1947, however, real consumption increased modestly—by approximately 4 percent between 1947 and 1950—while between 1950 and 1951 it declined slightly. The 8 percent increase in private real consumption between 1952 and 1954 reflected the dismantling of controls by the Conservative government and the subsequent "dash for freedom."

The moderate increase in real consumption between 1947 and 1952— that part of the postwar period characterized by the severe dollar shortage—attests to the success of the disinflationary policies pursued during this period in restraining home demand. Between 1947 and 1952, when the dollar shortage was most intense, per capita real consumption failed to increase. It was only after 1952 when greater reliance was placed on the market mechanism that consumption increased substantially. It is difficult, in the light of the evidence, to attribute the early postwar payments crisis to immoderate increases in consumption. It is noted below, however, that the drain on reserves in 1954 was due in part to the large increase in consumption.

Britain's Postwar Capital Formation Program. A heated debate has centered around Britain's postwar capital formation program. On the one hand, it has been argued that the high level of capital formation undertaken in the postwar period was a major contributory factor to the balance of payments disequilibrium,[33] while on the other hand, responsible observers deplored the fact that Britain was making insufficient provision for the future.[34] In light of the circumstances, it is believed that the second view is the more valid one.

The deterioration of Britain's industrial machine in the interwar period and the capital destruction and consumption which occurred during the war made a large capital formation program imperative if the United Kingdom were to succeed in increasing her production and productivity.[35] It is true,

[33] See, for example, Harrod, *Hardships,* passim. Harrod, however, has since modified his views on the dollar problem considerably. For his more considered views, see "Imbalance of International Payments," *International Monetary Fund Staff Papers,* April, 1953. Also see Harrod, *The Dollar.*

[34] Cf. Schumpeter, "English Economists and the State-Managed Economy," *Journal of Political Economy,* October, 1949.

[35] This is not to deny that an increase in production and productivity can be effected by other means than by capital formation. Even considering these other

as many have contended,[36] that the dollar deficits could have been reduced considerably in the early postwar years had Britain devoted the resources used for capital formation to produce exports for which a ready market existed in the dollar area. Had Britain pursued this course of action, however, she would have sacrificed the possibility of future solvency for temporary gains. Her urgent need in the postwar period was to increase production and productivity as rapidly as possible, and it is doubtful, in view of the state of disrepair of British industry at the war's end, whether significant permanent progress could have been achieved along these lines without rather large outlays for capital formation. The critics who objected to the capital formation program appear to have overlooked the possibility that under some circumstances the only way in which a permanent solution to an international disequilibrium can be effected is by pursuing policies that may result in temporarily larger deficits.[37]

An examination of the magnitude of Britain's capital formation program certainly does not lend support to the view that this program was excessive. Paish estimated that an amount of *net* capital formation equal to approximately 4,500 million pounds (in 1945 prices) was required to repair the capital destruction and replace the capital consumption that occurred during the war.[38] This estimate failed to take into account the need for new capital due to the growth of population in order to restore the prewar capital ratio. E. A. G. Robinson, making this adjustment, estimated that an amount of net capital formation equal to 7,300 million pounds was necessary to restore the prewar capital ratio. Robinson further estimated that between 1946 and 1950 net capital formation actually undertaken barely sufficed to repair the damage and the capital consumption of the war period, and contributed nothing toward restoring the prewar capital ratio.[39] Balogh, in an independent study, reached substantially the same conclusion.[40]

The absence of reliable information concerning depreciation makes it

---

methods of effecting increases in production and productivity it is believed that the conclusion reached in the text is valid.

[36] See, for example, the remarks of Clement Davies as reported in Hansard, V, 443, c. 394.

[37] Cf. Kindleberger, *Dollar Shortage*, p. 154.

[38] Paish, *Post-War Financial Problem*, p. 9.

[39] Robinson, "Britain's Economic Policy," *London and Cambridge Economic Service*, May, 1950, p. 42 .

[40] Balogh, "Investment in Britain and the United States," *Bulletin of the Oxford University Institute of Statistics*, June, 1952.

extremely difficult to estimate net capital formation in the postwar period. Mr. Philip Redfern's estimates which are generally regarded as the most reliable are reproduced in Table 15.

Redfern's estimates of net fixed capital formation confirm the conclusion reached by Robinson and Balogh that it was not until 1950 that Britain's prewar stock of fixed capital was restored.[41] The estimates, however, are still more illuminating in that they suggest that it was not until 1953 that annual net investment in fixed capital approximated the level achieved in 1938. In every year between 1946 and 1952, net investment in fixed capital was substantially below the 1938 level. It is difficult in the light of this evidence, tentative as it is, to argue that Britain's postwar capital formation program was excessive.

TABLE 15
NET INVESTMENT IN FIXED CAPITAL AT CONSTANT PRICES
(*In millions of pounds, 1948 prices*)

	Manufacturing and Distribution	*Agriculture*	*Public Services, Transportation, Fuel and Power*	*Housing*	*Total*
1938	191	3	149	333	676
1948	186	26	74	173	459
1949	225	16	134	155	530
1950	267	11	145	140	563
1951	249	8	122	140	519
1952	193	0	116	207	516
1953	191	− 5	165	316	667

Source: P. Redfern, "Net Investment in Fixed Assets in the United Kingdom, 1938–1953," *Journal of the Royal Statistical Society,* Vol. 118, part 2 (1955).

Some critics of the postwar capital formation program have focused their attention not on the magnitude of the level of investment but rather on its composition. Two criticisms in particular have gained wide currency in the postwar period. The first is that too high a priority was given to the reconstruction of basic industries—projects which, in the nature of the case, have a long gestation period—while the short gestation projects, which, in view of the balance of payments difficulties ought to have been encouraged, were assigned too low a priority. The second criticism centered around the fact that a large proportion of the available investment resources was devoted to "nonproductive" projects. The high level of residential construction in the postwar period was particularly deplored.

In an ideal situation, the choice of projects with different gestation

[41] Also see A. Cairncross, "Savings and Investment Since the War," *Westminster Bank Review,* February, 1955.

periods should be made solely on the basis of their respective yields, due consideration given to the discount rate. In postwar Britain these decisions could not be made, however, without some consideration to the state of the reserves. It would have been absurd, for example, to decide in favor of a project with a long gestation period on the basis of its superior yield if the project could not be brought to fruition because of the depletion of reserves, precluding the possibility of obtaining the requisite imported materials. It is evident that the time element cannot be ignored in these circumstances. It does not follow, however, that all projects with long gestation periods must inevitably give way to projects with short gestation periods. If a long gestation project is necessary, in the sense that effecting any significant increase in production and productivity is contingent upon its being undertaken, it may very well be wise to sacrifice many short gestation projects for it. The reconstruction of the basic industries in postwar Britain is a case in point. The history of the postwar period offers many dramatic instances where the inability of the basic industries to supply the requisite raw materials was a major impediment to production. The coal crisis of 1946–47 was but one instance, albeit an important one, of this tendency. Equally important, though much less dramatic, were the recurring shortages of transportation, steel producing capacity, and electricity generating capacity—shortages which in the postwar period resulted in a loss of production and exports.[42]

It was considerations of this nature that prompted the Labor government to assign equal priority to the reconstruction of the basic industries and to the export drive.[43] The government was not oblivious of the dangers involved and was interested, as the following quotation from the official economic survey shows, in minimizing them.

Apart from the big programmes for re-equipment of the basic industries and services, the most important projects on the industrial side are those which yield a quick return in terms of increased output per man year, especially in the undermanned industries. Long term projects must inevitably take second place to projects which will quickly help to solve the special difficulties which are limiting the expansion of total national production and are distorting its balance.[44]

The criticism centering around the composition of Britain's postwar capital formation program is not without justification. Reference to Redfern's estimates of net investment in fixed capital at constant 1948 prices reproduced in Table 15 reveals that net investment in housing between

[42] See *Economic Survey for 1948*, Cmd. 7344, p. 24.
[43] *Economic Survey for 1947*, Cmd. 7046, p. 20.
[44] *Ibid.*, p. 24.

1948 and 1953 accounted for 1,311 million pounds or for approximately 32 percent of the total. Even granting the extreme need for housing in the postwar period and the fact that a substantial portion of the housing program was linked with attempts to achieve a more desirable allocation of manpower, it is difficult to condone the extremely large proportion of investment resources devoted to this sector. Given the need for industrial expansion and modernization to increase production and productivity, a concerted effort should have been made to expand industrial plant and equipment as rapidly as possible.

This criticism should not obscure the fact, however, that net capital formation in manufacturing, distribution, and public utilities between 1948 and 1953 expressed in constant 1948 prices amounted to 2,117 million pounds and accounted for 66 percent of the total and the further fact that as large as the housing program was, in no year between 1948 and 1953 did net capital formation in this sector approximate the level reached in 1938 when the housing shortage was very much less severe. The effects of investment in the "productive" sectors, moreover, are not far to seek.[45] The relatively high level of capital formation in the steel industry, for example, enabled an increase in steel output from 12.9 million metric tons in 1946 to 18.8 million metric tons in 1954 and the current target is to expand output still further to 22 million tons by 1957–58. The effects of the capital formation program in the petroleum industry are, perhaps, even more impressive. The huge capital formation program undertaken in this sector has created a virtually new industry, which has contributed significantly to British exports while at the same time it has allowed a reduction in her imports. In 1946, for example, Britain's refineries produced only 2,453,000 long tons. By 1954, output of Britain's refineries amounted to 26,859,000 long tons. Exports of refined petroleum, which were negligible in the prewar period, ranked as the ninth most important British export in 1954 and was just below the export of cotton goods as a foreign exchange earner. In addition to this dramatic achievement, notable gains were also made in the postwar period in agriculture,[46] shipping, and the generation of electricity.[47]

[45] For a breakdown of Britain's postwar capital formation program see Central Statistical Office, *National Income and Expenditure, 1955,* Table 48.

[46] In 1953 Britain produced approximately 50 percent of the total caloric content of her food consumption as compared with 30 percent in the prewar period.

[47] The merchant fleet was substantially larger in 1953 than in the prewar period. Electric power production increased from 43 billion KWH in 1946 to 74 billion KWH in 1954.

Two general conclusions emerge from an examination of Britain's postwar fixed capital formation program. The first is that unless the view is adopted that any level of capital formation that is not consistent with the maintenance of international equilibrium is unjustified, the postwar capital investment program was not excessive. Indeed, a strong case can be made for the argument that it was not sufficiently large. Second, though the evidence suggests that a disproportionately large share of the available investment resources was devoted to housing and other "nonproductive" projects, industrial investment was substantial and made a significant contribution toward expanding production and exports.

Investment in Working Capital in the Postwar Period. The influence of the cheap money policy Britain pursued between 1946 and 1951 is perhaps nowhere more apparent than in the movement of stocks during this period. The ready availability of funds enabled firms to hold larger amounts of working capital than would otherwise have been advisable. The increase in stocks, however, exerted pressure on the balance of payments and necessitated the intensification of import restrictions. Anticipation of this intensification, moreover, lent impetus to investment in working capital. It is not surprising, therefore, to find an inverse relationship between working capital and monetary reserves; in the years when stocks were increasing the monetary reserves declined, while in years when the stockpiles were depleted monetary reserves increased. This relationship is apparent from an examination of Table 16.

TABLE 16
NET CHANGE IN BRITAIN'S STOCKS AND MONETARY
RESERVES, 1947–51

	Change in Stocks (In millions of pounds)	Change in Reserves (In millions of U.S. dollars)
1947	309	– 617
1948	175	– 223
1949	65	– 168
1950	– 210	1612
1951	575	– 965

Sources: Central Statistical Office, *National Income and Expenditure, 1955,* and *United Kingdom Balance of Payments, 1946–1953,* Cmd. 8976.

The inverse relationship that existed between the movement of stocks and the change in monetary reserves can be looked at in a somewhat different way. The years when investment in working capital was high were generally crisis years, while the years when investment in working capital was moderate or negative were generally characterized by a favorable outcome on the balance of payments. In 1946, for example, investment in working capital was negative and the deficit on balance of payments was modest. The disinvestment in 1946 necessitated, however, a heavy investment in working capital to repair the stockpiles in 1947, and this was an important factor responsible for the severe deterioration in current accounts in that year. In 1948 and 1949 investment in working capital was substantially lower than in 1947 as were the current account deficits. The severe drain on the gold and dollar reserves in the latter half of the year necessitated the intensification of import restrictions and resulted in a heavy depletion of stocks in 1950. Again this factor was extremely important in the favorable outcome on current account in that year. In 1951, largely as a result of the need to repair the stockpiles which had been depleted in 1950, but also as a result of the need to increase the stocks of strategic goods occasioned by the outbreak of the Korean War, investment in working capital was rather high. This increase in the stockpiles was once again an important factor responsible for the deterioration of Britain's current account in that year.

The alternate depletion and repairing of the stockpiles was undoubtedly a major factor responsible for the biennial balance of payments crises which characterized the British economy between 1946 and 1951. The influence of the cheap money policy on this pattern is suggested by the fact that with the abandonment of this policy the two year balance of payments cycle disappeared.

Government Expenditure on Goods and Services in the Postwar Period. As in other countries, the relative importance of the government as a purchaser of goods and services increased significantly in postwar Britain. Government expenditures, which accounted for 14 percent of the total national expenditure in 1938, amounted to 26 percent in 1946, 17 percent in 1948, 19 percent in 1951, and 20 percent in 1953. Some critics have emphasized the importance of this absolute and relative increase in government expenditures as contributing to the postwar payments difficulties.

Two items of expenditure, defense and social services, were largely responsible for the increase in the proportion of total resources absorbed by the government between the prewar and postwar periods. Of the two, defense expenditures were by far the more important. As the accompanying table shows, defense expenditures accounted for 65 percent of total central government expenditure between 1946 and 1954, and the proportion was considerably higher in the early postwar years. The burden of the defense program on Britain's economy in the postwar period is indicated by the fact that it accounted for approximately 10 percent of the total gross national expenditures between 1946 and 1954.

Social service expenditures, though less important than defense expenditures, were significant. Central government expenditures on the health services alone rose from 182 million pounds in 1948 to 460 million pounds in 1954. Furthermore, extending the age for compulsory education necessitated a larger expenditure. Between 1948 and 1954 the net expenditure of all public authorities on health, education, and child care accounted for approximately 5 percent of the total gross national product at market prices.

Though it is difficult to come to any conclusion concerning the optimum size of social service expenditures, it would appear, on balance, that the introduction of so ambitious a social service program during a period of financial stringency was unwise. These expenditures raised the proportion of the available resources devoted to consumption, a luxury that Britain was ill able to afford. It is necessary to temper this judgment with two considerations, however. The introduction of the social service program undoubtedly had beneficial effects on production and productivity. It is almost certain, for example, that the National Health Service aided greater productivity by improving the health of the workers. Second, a large part of the expenditures on the social services did not have a directly adverse effect on Britain's balance of payments. The fees paid to physi-

TABLE 17

EXPENDITURES FOR DEFENSE IN THE POSTWAR PERIOD

(*In millions of pounds*)

Year	Total Central Government Expenditures	Expenditures for Defense	Defense Expenditures as a Percentage of Total Government Expenditures
1946	1823	1560	86
1947	1220	930	76
1948	1233	740	60
1949	1437	770	53
1950	1507	820	54
1951	1814	1090	60
1952	2206	1445	65
1953	2350	1570	67
1954	2312	1520	66

Source: Central Statistical Office, *National Income and Expenditure, 1955,* Table 37, p. 35.

cians and hospitals under the National Health Plan, for example, were in sense a form of transfer payment.[48] Nor can it be argued that the operation of the National Health Plan had an appreciable effect on Britain's occupational structure. British doctors were unlikely to enter the mines were they deprived of the fees they derived from the National Health Service.

These considerations merely suggest that the damage inflicted by these social service expenditures might have been less than that averred by the critics. The problem still remains, however, whether, under the circumstances, alternative lines of expenditure might not have been more desirable.

Britain's Balance of International Payments on Current Account. A country's current account balance is determined by the volume of goods imported and exported, the prices of these imports and exports, and the value of services imported and exported. In discussing Britain's current account in the postwar period, it is convenient to treat these determinants separately.

The expansion in the volume of exports by some 68 percent over the 1938 level by 1954 (using postwar weights) was the most impressive achievement of the British economy in the postwar period. This huge increase in the quantum of exports, more than any other single item, stands as a tribute to the success of the postwar disinflationary policies, and serves to refute the frequently expressed view that the pressures of excess demand in the early postwar period prevented the diversion of product from domestic to export markets. While it is true that the expansion of exports was aided by the deterioration of Britain's terms of trade, by the liberal release of sterling balances and other capital outflows to the sterling area, by the virtual disappearance of Germany and Japan as exporters in the early postwar years, and by the generally inflated economies in the soft currency countries, the fact remains that Britain did succeed in diverting a large portion of the increment to product from the home to the export markets.[49]

---

[48] It is true, however, that these fees increased disposable incomes and thus contributed somewhat to the difficulties that were felt in restraining the inflationary pressures. I would regard this effect as of relatively minor importance.

[49] Britain's success in expanding the volume of exports in the postwar period contrasts sharply with the pessimistic outlook in the early postwar years. The prevalent attitude in that period is summed up in a letter to the editor of *The Economist* by a manufacturer who wrote that as long as a buoyant demand existed in the home market there was no reason for him to undertake the "trouble, inconvenience and risk" of attempting to export. See *The Economist*, November 17, 1945, p. 720.

The expansion in the volume of exports was accompanied by a change in the composition of exports which may be of even greater significance in the long run. It was noted above that the decline of the relative importance of Britain as an exporter was due, in large part, to the shift in international demand away from the older staple products in the production of which she excelled. Britain was unable to retain her position as an exporter because she failed to adapt her economy in a way which would have enabled her to compete successfully with the United States in the export of those commodities for which international demand was increasing. It is, therefore, salutary to note that between 1938 and 1953 the absolute as well as relative importance of the exports of the newer industries increased while that of the older staple industries declined. This tendency is apparent from an examination of the ranking of Britain's most important exports in the prewar and postwar periods (see Table 18).

TABLE 18
BRITAIN'S NINE LEADING EXPORTS IN 1938 AND 1953
(*In order of importance*)

1938	1953
Nonelectrical machinery	Nonelectrical machinery
Cotton yarn and fabrics	Road vehicles and aircraft
Coal and coke	Chemicals
Iron and steel manufactures	Electrical machinery
Chemicals	Manufactures of metals
Manufactures of metals	Iron and steel manufactures
Road vehicles and aircraft	Cotton yarns and fabrics
Electrical machinery	Woolen and worsted yarns
Woolen and worsted yarns	Petroleum and petroleum products

Source: *Board of Trade Journal.*

The increase in the relative importance of exports of the newer industries is also apparent from the accompanying table which shows the value of exports of some selected "newer" industries in the pre- and postwar periods and the proportion these exports bore to total exports of manufactures.

This increase is a measure of the success Britain enjoyed in adapting her economy to the requirements of the mid-twentieth century world. As a result of this adaptation Britain was more prepared to engage in international competition in 1953 than she was either in the interwar period or in the years immediately following the end of the war.

The huge expansion in the volume of exports was not associated with an increase in the volume of imports. Indeed, in 1954 the quantum of

TABLE 19

VALUE OF EXPORTS OF SELECTED INDUSTRIES

(*In millions of pounds*)

Industry	1938	1953
Electrical machinery	21.6	172.3
Nonelectrical machinery	50.9	397.0
Road vehicles and aircrafts	23.4	290.4
Scientific instruments	2.9	27.3
Synthetic fibers and fabrics	3.5	39.4
Total exports listed	102.3	926.4
Total exports of manufactures	354.3	2098.4
Percentage of selected industries	29	44

imports was still some 10 percent less than in 1938 (using postwar weights). The low volume of imports in the postwar period is attributable to two major factors: the stringent import restrictions which Britain maintained throughout the postwar period, and the shift to the production of commodities in which imported materials played a much smaller role and domestic value added a much larger one.[50] The use of import restrictions undoubtedly interfered with the operation of market forces and thus resulted in a less than "ideal" composition of imports. The degree of disinflation that would have enabled the United Kingdom to dispense with these import restrictions, however, would likely have resulted in a substantial volume of unemployment. In the circumstances, the loss of real income attributable to the imposition of import restrictions was probably considerably less than that which would have resulted from the introduction of a disinflationary program stringent enough to limit the volume of imports to the level actually attained through the application of import restrictions.

Though over-all, Britain's performance with regard to the volume of imports and exports in the postwar period was more than satisfactory, developments since 1950 give some cause for concern. Between 1950 and 1954 the volume of imports increased by 14 percent while the volume of exports increased by 4 percent. Should this development presage a period of increased difficulties in the export markets—a possibility which is extremely great in view of the return of Germany as an exporter—Britain's payments difficulties are likely to become even more acute with the passage

---

[50] One example of this tendency may be noted. In 1950 imports valued at 38 pounds were necessary to produce 100 pounds worth of output in the textile, leather, and clothing industries whereas only 12 pounds of imports were required to produce 100 pounds worth of output in the metals, engineering and vehicles industries. Central Statistical Office, *National Income and Expenditure, 1955,* Table 18.

of time. The decline in the rate of increase of Britain's exports in the last few years assumes an even more ominous note in view of the fact that this decline was associated with a significant reduction in Britain's share of world exports and an increase in West Germany's share. The relevant data is shown in the accompanying table.

TABLE 20

PROPORTION OF WORLD[a] EXPORTS OF LEADING COUNTRIES

	1938	1948	1950	1952	1954
United States	15	24	18	20	20
United Kingdom	12	12	11	10	10
Federal Republic of Germany			4	5	7
Japan	4	[b]	1	2	2

[a] Excluding the exports of China, the U.S.S.R., and nonreporting eastern European countries.

[b] Less than 1 percent.

Source: Computed from International Monetary Fund, *International Financial Statistics*, January, 1956, p. 28.

The huge increase in the volume of exports along with the reduction in the volume of imports did not appreciably improve Britain's merchandise account. In 1938 she incurred a deficit on merchandise account equal to 243 million pounds. In 1954 her merchandise deficit amounted to 191 million pounds.[51] The reason the merchandise account failed to improve by more than it did is not far to seek. Between 1938 and 1951 Britain's terms of trade deteriorated by approximately 30 percent, and while they improved subsequently, in 1954 they were still some 18 percent less favorable than in the prewar period. Unfavorable price developments in the postwar period thus deprived Britain of a great deal of the improvement that would otherwise have taken place as a result of the huge relative expansion in the volume of exports. It should not be overlooked, however, that this expansion in the volume of exports was made possible in part by the deterioration in the terms of trade.

Unfavorable price movements were not the only development operating to adversely affect Britain's current account in the postwar period as compared with the prewar period. The deterioration of her invisible account was of some importance in the early postwar period. In 1946 and 1947 Britain's traditional surplus on invisible account was transformed into rather sizable deficits, and it was not until 1950 that invisible earnings began to approximate the role they played in Britain's prewar balance of

[51] The improvement in real terms was, of course, significant.

payments. Among the more important factors responsible for the decline in invisible earnings between the prewar and early postwar periods were the large increase in government overseas expenditure, the severe decline in earnings on income account, and the sharp but apparently temporary decline in shipping earnings.

Despite these adverse developments, Britain's balance of payments showed a slight improvement in the late postwar period when compared with the prewar period. Indeed, between 1949 and 1954 the United Kingdom earned a surplus in every year except 1951, while the average deficit on current account between 1946 and 1954 amounted to but 22 million pounds. While this cannot be regarded as a good outcome, it must not be overlooked that the factors responsible for it were beyond Britain's control. The villains were the unfavorable price developments of the war and postwar periods, which did much to offset the large expansion in the volume of exports, and the heavy costs of financing the war, which, together with the increase in government overseas obligations in the postwar period resulted in a substantial increase in Britain's invisible debits.

Britain's balance on dollar accounts in the postwar period is treated at length in the following chapters. At this point, it is unnecessary to say more than that the same factors that were operating to preclude a substantial improvement on over-all accounts were operating to effect a deterioration on dollar accounts. Thus, despite the fact that the volume of dollar exports increased significantly between the pre- and postwar periods while the volume of dollar imports was reduced, Britain's dollar current account suffered a severe deterioration. Unfavorable price movements between the pre- and postwar periods, as well as a deterioration on invisible dollar accounts, were mainly responsible for this.

Summary and Conclusions. The fact that Britain incurred a deficit on international accounts in the postwar period indicates that she was, in some manner of speaking, living beyond her means. If this is what is meant by those proponents who hold that Britain's basic postwar difficulties arose from excessive demand, there can be no disagreement. A reduction in the level of claims on Britain's resources would have eliminated the current account deficits and, had the policy of restraint been carried sufficiently far, would also have eliminated the dollar deficits.

A more significant approach to the problem, however, must consider both the reasons for the excessive demand on Britain's resources and the manner in which the available resources were allocated among the various claimants. The reasons for the problem of excess demand are easily found.

The more important include: the low levels of consumption during the war which made necessary an increase in consumption in the postwar period; the state of disrepair of British industry resulting from neglect during the interwar period as well as from capital destruction and consumption during the war, which necessitated a rather high level of capital formation to increase production and productivity; the heavy postwar defense program; the need to expand exports if the current account deficits were not to increase as a result of the deterioration of the terms of trade and the increase in invisible debits.

Given the huge demand on Britain's resources, it was necessary to pursue policies of restraint designed to ensure that the available resources would not be dissipated. In the early postwar period, Britain relied for the most part on budgetary policy and physical controls to accomplish this objective. Monetary policy was not used as a restraining influence until the Conservative party assumed office in the autumn of 1951. On the whole these policies succeeded in restraining domestic demand and thus contributed toward the achievement of an "appropriate" allocation of resources. The increase in real consumption in the early postwar period when the dollar problem was most acute was moderate, while a substantial portion of the increment to resources was devoted to capital formation and exports. There were undoubtedly mistakes. The composition of Britain's postwar capital formation program left something to be desired, and the relatively large expenditure on the social service program during a period of financial stringency can be criticized. Despite these shortcomings, the evidence strongly suggests that the factors responsible for the severe disequilibrium, especially in the early postwar period, must be sought elsewhere than in immoderate increases in home demand.

Cost Inflation. The dangers of cost inflation in postwar Britain were primarily due to the rising price of imports and the maintenance of full employment. Considering the importance of imports to British manufactures, any significant rise in the price of imports, unless offset by government action, is likely to be translated into a rise in the price of British goods. Furthermore, the existence of a strong labor movement at a time of full employment posed the threat that any rise in the cost of living, whether originating from a rise in the price of imports or in the price of domestically produced goods, would result in a demand for higher wages, which, in turn, would induce a further rise in costs, prices, cost of living, and so forth. It is evident that an effective program designed to prevent a cost-price spiral would have to embrace measures that would mitigate the rise in the price of imports, moderate the decline in the workers' standard of living, and induce the labor unions to practice restraint. Britain's postwar antiinflationary program was designed to achieve these objectives.

Little could be done to restrain the rise in import prices. Bulk buying and long-term contracts can postpone the impact of a rise in prices of internationally traded goods but cannot avoid them, unless the price increases are caused by transitory factors. For a while, these devices did succeed in moderating the increase in the cost of imports to Britain, but when the contracts came up for renegotiation, the agreed prices always reflected the higher market prices.[52]

If the government had no effective control over the prices paid for imports, it could control the extent to which the increase in the import price level was translated into higher domestic prices. It accomplished this in two distinct yet related ways: by controlling the prices at which goods sold on the home market and by subsidizing domestic consumption.[53] Though the cost of living subsidies were widely criticized,[54] they proved effective weapons in the early postwar period in moderating labor's demand for higher wages. These subsidies, together with the utility schemes, succeeded in restraining the rise in the retail price index in the face of the continued increase in the price level of imports. It is noted below that the decision to set a ceiling on the food subsidies at a time when the price of food imports continued to rise was an important factor responsible for the abandonment of restraints by the labor movement.

The use of subsidies and price controls were but two ways in which the United Kingdom attempted to avoid a cost inflation in the early postwar period. Other methods resorted to included the heavy taxation of profits [55] and exhortation to the workers to moderate their demands for higher wages. The latter took the form of a *White Paper on Personal Incomes* in which the government's policy with respect to wage increases was spelled out. The principle enunciated in this document was that "there should be

---

[52] Between 1945 and 1951 the United Kingdom bought a substantial part of her food imports at prices lower than those prevailing on the market. When world prices declined in the middle of 1951 the impact of these declines was felt less by the United Kingdom than by countries which did not engage in long-term bulk buying.

[53] It should be noted that the maintenance of price controls was another effective way to expand exports by making the export market relatively more profitable than the domestic market.

[54] Cf. *The Economist,* December 31, 1947.

[55] The heavy taxation of profits was necessary to make wage restraint more palatable.

no further general increase in the level of personal incomes without at least a corresponding increase in the volume of production." [56]   The government was prepared to view with favor wage increases that were associated with increases in productivity and those necessary to encourage "the movement of labor to those industries where it was most needed" but not wage increases designed to maintain traditional differentials.

Adherence to the principles enunciated in the *White Paper on Personal Incomes* was completely voluntary.[57] Nevertheless, the government warned that if the principles therein enunciated were ignored "there can be no presumption . . . that the resulting costs will be taken into account in settling the controlled prices, charges or margins or other financial matters requiring government action." [58]   In short, the government placed part of the responsibility for restraining labor's demands for higher wages on the employers who were admonished that they would have to absorb the increased costs resulting from "unwarranted" wage increases.

The Trade Unions Congress acquiesced to the government's request to practice wage restraint, provided effective measures were taken to prevent too rapid a rise in the cost of living.[59]   Between 1948 and 1950 the cost of living subsidies succeeded in tempering the rise in the retail price index with the result that the increase in weekly wage rates was moderate.   The failure to increase the subsidies sufficiently between 1950 and 1951 to offset the tremendous rise in import prices, however, resulted in the abandonment of the policy of restraint; weekly wage rates rose by 8 percent, although as a result of a 9.6 percent increase in the retail price index, real wages continued to decline slightly.   The Conservative government's decision to severely reduce the subsidies after 1951 contributed to a further rise in wages.   The decline in import prices during this period, however, tended to moderate the increase both in retail prices and in wage rates.   Table 21 shows the course of the index of weekly wages and of retail prices between 1947 and 1954.

The reduction in the cost of living subsidies contributing to the

[56] *White Paper on Personal Incomes,* Cmd. 7321, p. 2.
[57] Even during the war the government refused to interfere with wage bargaining.
[58] *White Paper on Personal Incomes,* Cmd. 7321, p. 4.
[59] Even after the devaluation, the Trade Union Conference adopted a report calling on the unions to refrain from seeking wage increases until January, 1951, and to waive the provisions of the sliding scale wage agreements.   The wage standstill was to be abandoned, however, if retail prices rose by more than 6 percent.   *The Economist,* November 26, 1949, p. 1169.

TABLE 21

INDEX OF WEEKLY WAGES AND RETAIL PRICES, 1947–54

	Index of Weekly Wages (June 30, 1947 = 100)	Retail Price Index (June 17, 1947 = 100)	Real Wages (June, 1947 = 100)
1948	106	108	98
1949	109	111	98
1950	111	114	97
1951	120	125	96
1952	130	136	96
1953	136	140	97
1954	142	143	99

Source: Central Statistical Office, *Monthly Digest of Statistics.*

abandonment of restraint by the labor unions must be regarded as a key factor responsible for the cost-wage spiral in the late postwar period. Between 1948 and 1950, when subsidies were liberally employed, the rise in wage rates was approximately matched by the increase in productivity.[60] Between 1950 and 1954, however, the index of weekly wage rates rose by approximately 28 percent, although productivity in manufacturing industries is computed to have risen by less than 20 percent. It should also be noted that during this period the index of weekly wages was rising more rapidly than the retail price index with the result that real wages increased. It should not be overlooked, however, that real wages in 1954 were still some 1 percent lower than in 1947.

The extent to which the postwar increase in prices and costs has contributed to Britain's balance of payments difficulties cannot be readily ascertained. It would appear that between 1946–48 the inability to produce rather than an uneconomic price level was the major factor inhibiting a greater expansion of exports than had actually occurred. With the reappearance of a buyers' market, however, in the early part of 1949, it is probable that the cost-price structure was somewhat out of line.[61] The sterling devaluation of 1949 tended to correct the imbalance temporarily, although the rapid increase in wages and prices since 1950 did much to offset its effects. The recent decline in Britain's share in world exports, was undoubtedly due to the rise in the British price level while Germany's price level was actually declining. These developments bring to the fore

[60] The rise in the weekly wage index is here compared with the rise in productivity in manufacturing industries.

[61] This has been disputed by Harrod (among others), who argued that the British cost and price structures were not out of line in 1949. See Harrod, *Pound Sterling,* p. 27.

the necessity for Britain to restrain the increase in her costs and prices. With the return of Germany as an exporter and the imminent return of Japan, a failure to moderate the increase in the cost and price levels would inevitably weaken Britain's competitive position on world markets and would add to the difficulties of attaining a balance on international accounts at viable levels of trade, income, and employment.

Several conclusions emerge from an examination of the cost-inflation problem in postwar Britain. First, in this area Britain was fighting an uphill battle. The precipitous rise in import prices, which was only partially offset by the long term bulk-purchase agreements, was potentially explosive in a society with a strong labor movement. In the event, Britain succeeded in restraining labor's demand for higher wages by subsidizing consumption and by placing heavy reliance on price controls and utility schemes. The decision to limit and then reduce the cost of living subsidies in conjunction with a continued rise in import prices made wage restraint virtually impossible, and wages and prices rose. Second, though it is difficult to come to any definitive conclusions concerning the inhibitory effects of Britain's cost and price structure on the level of exports, it is certain that, should her cost and price structure rise more rapidly in the future than those of her competitors, British exports will suffer. It is imperative that all means be exerted to maintain a competitive price level. Third, given the commitment to maintain a high level of employment, it is difficult to see how it is possible to avoid cost inflation in a period of rising import costs without resorting to direct controls and subsidies. At least part of the responsibility for the rather substantial increases in the cost and price levels after 1951 must be attributed to the Conservative government's "dash for freedom" policy.

CONCLUSIONS

In this chapter we were primarily concerned with examining the achievements of the British economy in the postwar period. The conclusions that emerge from this examination are both salutary and disquieting. Taking the period as a whole, production and productivity increased significantly and the battle against inflation was sufficiently successful to effect a more rational allocation of resources. On the basis of the evidence, I would submit that the major factors responsible for the postwar disequilibrium must be sought elsewhere than in domestic developments. If attention is focused on the developments since 1950, however, many "danger spots" become immediately apparent.　Among the more important of these are the substantial increase in domestic consumption, the upsurge of investment, the increase in the cost and price levels, the leveling off of the volume of exports, and the rather rapid increase in the volume of imports.[62] Should these adverse tendencies continue, they will undoubtedly increase Britain's difficulties.　Thus, though viewed as a whole, domestic economic developments were not unsatisfactory, they do not justify complacency.

[62] See Chap. VIII for a fuller analysis of developments during this period.

V Britain's Dollar Accounts, 1946-51

IN THIS and the succeeding chapters the factors responsible for the sterling area's dollar problem in the period between 1946 and 1951 are examined. Beginning in mid-1952, the sterling area's dollar accounts improved and a huge dollar deficit was temporarily transformed into a substantial dollar surplus, but the factors responsible for this development will be examined in Chapter VIII.

The deterioration of Britain's direct dollar current account between the pre- and postwar periods was one of the more important reasons for the emergence and the severity of the dollar problem.[1]

Table 22 compares Britain's dollar current accounts during this period, revealing that the increase in the value of merchandise imports derived from the dollar area was the most important single development responsible for the deterioration of her dollar current account. The deterioration of the invisible account, though somewhat less important than the increase in the value of imports, was another extremely significant factor. Indeed, this development accounted for no less than 30 percent of the total deteri-

TABLE 22

BRITAIN'S DOLLAR CURRENT ACCOUNTS, 1938 AND 1946–51

(*In millions of U.S. dollars*)

	1938	1946	1947	1948	1949	1950	1951
Imports (f.o.b.)	949	1571	2283	1634	1606	1206	2055
Exports and re-exports (f.o.b.)	249	404	523	792	711	907	1102
Trade balance	− 700	− 1167	− 1760	− 842	− 895	− 299	− 953
Balance on invisible account	170	− 44	− 299	− 174	− 198	75	− 250
Defense aid							+ 11
Balance on current account	− 530	− 1211	− 2059	− 1016	− 1093	− 224	− 1192

Sources: 1938 data from ECE, *Economic Bulletin for Europe*, Second Quarter, 1949. Postwar data derived from *United Kingdom Balance of Payments, 1946–1953*, Cmd. 8976, Table 20.

[1] See Introduction, p. 8.

oration between 1938 and 1947. It is apparent that an isolation of the factors responsible for (a) the increase in the value of dollar imports and (b) the deterioration of the invisible accounts will go far toward explaining the emergence and the severity of the dollar shortage. In addition, many economists place particular emphasis, when analyzing the dollar problem, on factors that allegedly impeded the expansion of British exports to the dollar area. It is necessary, in the account that follows, to examine carefully the more important of these factors as well, and to assess their relative importance.

BRITAIN'S DOLLAR IMPORTS

Though the dollar area consisted of countries other than the United States and Canada, Britain's trade with these two countries was decisive, as far as the outturn on dollar accounts was concerned. In the following analysis of Britain's dollar imports, the discussion is limited to those imports derived from North America. Furthermore, in view of the fact that the detailed trade statistics that are required for the following analysis are to be found only in the annual and monthly trade accounts published by the Bureau of Customs and Excises and the Board of Trade, it was necessary to utilize these data although they differ in important respects from those shown in the balance of payments statements. The most important difference concerns the manner in which imports are valued; the monthly and annual trade accounts employ a c.i.f. valuation while the balance of payments statements value imports f.o.b.[2] Another rather important difference between the data recorded in the annual and monthly trade accounts and those shown in the balance of payments statements involves the timing of the transactions. The former record transactions as of the time the imports arrive in the United Kingdom, while the latter record transactions "when a change in the ownership of goods takes place"[3] though this may occur, as is frequently the case, in the country of origin.

Table 23 shows the value of imports the United Kingdom derived from North America in the pre- and postwar periods as derived from the monthly and annual statements of trade.[4]

---

[2] C.i.f. valuations can be transformed into f.o.b. valuations by subtracting from the former approximately 10 percent.

[3] *United Kingdom Balance of Payments, 1946–1950*, Cmd. 8065, p. 30.

[4] It should be noted that part of the increase in the sterling value is due to changes in the exchange rate. Even allowing for these changes the increase in the value of dollar imports was significant.

The precipitous increase in the value of imports could have been due to an expansion in the volume of dollar imports, a rise in the price level of American exports, a combination of the two, or a decline in the volume of imports associated with a more than offsetting rise in the price level of American exports. It is extremely important for an understanding of the factors responsible for the postwar dollar shortage to determine the reasons for the large increase in the value of dollar imports. The remainder of this section is devoted to that problem. Attention is focused, in turn, on the factors operating on the value of dollar imports between 1935–38 and 1947, 1947 and 1950, and 1950 and 1951.

TABLE 23

BRITISH IMPORTS FROM NORTH AMERICA

(*In millions of pounds*)

Year	From the U.S.	From Canada	Total
1935–38	104	75	179
1946	230	201	431
1947	297	239	536
1948	183	223	406
1949	222	225	447
1950	211	180	392
1951	380	261	641

Source: Derived from the *Annual Statements of Trade of the United Kingdom with British and Foreign Countries.*

Britain's Imports from North America, 1935–38 to 1947. The steep rise in the value of imports from North America between 1935–38 and 1947 is attributable both to an increase in the volume of imports derived from this source and to a drastic rise in the American export price level. It is necessary to examine the relative importance of these two factors.

Contrary to widespread belief, the expansion in the volume of imports the United Kingdom derived from North American sources between the prewar period and 1947 was rather moderate; the volume of imports derived from the United States increased by only 8 percent and from Canada by only 20 percent.[5] This increase was due almost wholly to the inability to obtain supplies from traditional sources. Among the more important factors responsible for this development were the low levels of production in the non-dollar world, the almost complete collapse of trade and payments machinery in the early postwar period, the virtual disappearance of Germany as an exporter, and the increased tempo of industrialization in many

[5] ECA, *Sterling Area,* p. 66.

TABLE 24

PROPORTION OF BRITISH IMPORTS FROM NORTH AMERICA, 1935–38, 1946, AND 1947

	UNITED STATES			CANADA			TOTAL FROM NORTH AMERICA		
	1935–38	1946	1947	1935–38	1946	1947	1935–38	1946	1947
Food, drink, and tobacco (category 1)									
Grain and flour	7	15	14	30	64	63	37	79	77
Meat	4	10	5	7	6	18	11	16	23
Dairy imports		37	33	4	12	12	4	49	45
Tobacco	80	85	66				80	85	66
Total	9	22	16	9	18	17	18	40	33
Raw materials									
Wood and timber	8	7	16	14	49	36	22	56	52
Raw cotton	40	18	30	5			45	18	30
Total raw materials	11	6	10	5	11	10	16	17	20
Manufactures									
Iron and steel	10	45	33	7	21	27	17	66	60
Nonferrous metals	6	5	17	32	40	28	38	45	45
Machinery	46	73	72	6	8	5	52	81	77
Chemicals	17	25	34	4	8	5	21	33	39
Oils, fats, resins	23	34	35				23	34	35
Vehicles	4	40	36	14	25	23	18	65	59
Total manufactures	16	24	28	10	14	11	26	38	39

Source: Derived from Bureau of Customs and Excises, Annual Statements of Trade of the United Kingdom with British
and Foreign Countries and Trade and Navigation Accounts of
the United Kingdom.

primary producing countries.[6] That the inability to obtain supplies from traditional sources was an important factor contributing to Britain's postwar dollar problem is apparent from a comparison of her import trade in 1935–38 and in 1947.

During this period the value of imports Britain derived from North America increased by 357 million pounds.[7] This increase was largely seen in the value of a selected group of imports. Thus, the increase in the value of grain and flour, meat, and dairy imports accounted for 162.4 million pounds, or for 87 percent of the total increase in the value of food, drink, and tobacco imports. Likewise, the increase in the value of wood and timber imports amounted to 48 million pounds, or to 70 percent of the total increase in the value of raw material imports derived from North America. Finally, the increase in the value of manufactured oils, fats and resins, nonferrous metals and manufactures, machinery, chemicals, and iron and steel manufactures accounted for 72 million pounds, or 77 percent of the total increase in the value of manufactured imports derived from North America between 1935–38 and 1947.

The fact that the increase in the value of these imports from North America was associated with an increase in the importance of this source as a supplier of these commodities is significant. Since the total volume of these imports into the United Kingdom in the early postwar period was considerably below the prewar level, the increase in the relative importance of North America as a supplier suggests that the inability to obtain supplies from the traditional sources was responsible for the heavier reliance the United Kingdom placed on the dollar area. Table 24 shows the proportion of selected imports the United Kingdom derived from North America in the pre- and early postwar periods.

In practically every case listed in the table where the proportion of British imports derived from North America increased, it was due to the inability to obtain supplies from the traditional sources. With respect to some imports—mainly in category 1—the inability to obtain imports from the traditional sources was accompanied by an increase in the volume of

[6] The increased tempo of industrialization in primary producing countries reduced their exportable surpluses in two ways. First, it resulted in a decline in the production of primary products. Second, the rise in incomes associated with the development schemes induced an increase in domestic consumption and thus reduced still further the exportable surplus.

[7] Food, drink, and tobacco imports increased by 186 million pounds; the value of raw material imports increased by 68 million pounds; and the value of manufactured imports increased by 93 million pounds.

imports from North America. In other cases, however, the increase in the relative importance of North America as a source of supply resulted from a smaller reduction in the volume of North American imports than in the volume of total imports.

The severe reduction in the volume of category 1 imports derived from non-dollar sources necessitated an increase in the volume of these imports from North America. The increase in the importance of North America as a supplier of grain and flour, for example, is attributable, in part, to the expansion in the volume of these imports derived from North America as a result of the severe reduction in the volume of grain and flour imports from Argentina, Australia, the U.S.S.R., and other sources mainly in Eastern and Western Europe. In the prewar period Argentina, Australia, the Soviet Union, and the miscellaneous sources provided the United Kingdom with 23 percent, 15 percent, 4 percent, and 22 percent respectively of her grain and flour imports. By 1947 the proportion of grain and flour imports derived from these sources was severely reduced. Argentina's share fell to 4 percent, Australia's to 3 percent, the miscellaneous sources' to 16 percent, and imports from the Soviet Union all but ceased. Likewise, North America's share in Britain's meat imports increased largely as a result of the severe decline in meat imports obtained from nondollar sources, mainly in Europe. The reduction in the share of meat imports supplied by Denmark was the most spectacular: in the prewar period Denmark provided the United Kingdom with 20 percent of her meat imports, by 1947 the proportion from this source was reduced to 5 percent. Finally, the increase in the proportion of dairy imports derived from North America in the early postwar period is attributable in large part to the need to increase the volume of imports from this source following the rather drastic decline in imports derived from Denmark, the Netherlands, and other non-dollar sources. In the prewar period Denmark provided the United Kingdom with 22 percent of her dairy imports, the Netherlands with 10 percent, and the miscellaneous sources with 22 percent. By 1947 the proportion of dairy imports supplied by these sources declined to 11 percent, 2 percent, and 5 percent respectively.

The increase in the *volume* of category 1 imports derived from North America did not suffice to offset the decline in the volume of imports obtained from nondollar sources. The total volume of category 1 imports in 1947 amounted to but 73 percent of the 1938 level while the volume of grain and flour, dairy, and meat imports was 64 percent, 81 percent, and 66 percent of the 1938 level respectively.[8]

[8] *Board of Trade Journal.*

It was noted above that the increase in the value of wood and timber imports from North America between 1935–38 and 1947 accounted for approximately 70 percent of the total increase of raw material imports from this source. As in the case of the category 1 imports discussed above, the increase in the value of these imports from North America was due, in part, to the increase in the volume of imports made necessary by the decline in imports derived from the traditional sources. In the prewar period the United Kingdom obtained somewhat more than 30 percent of her wood and timber imports from Sweden and Finland and 23 percent from the Soviet Union and Poland. By 1947, however, the proportion from Sweden and Finland was reduced to 25 percent while wood and timber imports from the Soviet Union and Poland all but ceased. Replacing in part the imports which in the prewar period were obtained from European sources led to an increase in the volume of imports from North America. This increase in the volume of wood and timber imports from North America, however, did not succeed in offsetting the decline in the volume of imports from non-dollar sources; the volume of wood and timber imports derived from all sources in 1947 amounted to but 79 percent of the 1938 level.

The increase in the relative importance of North America as a supplier of manufactures to the United Kingdom in the early postwar period was likewise due to the severe reduction in the volume of imports the United Kingdom derived from prewar sources of supply. The virtual disappearance of Germany as an exporter in the early postwar period was mainly responsible for this development, although the low levels of production in other European countries and some non-European sources must share part of the responsibility. In the prewar period (1935–38) Western Europe provided the United Kingdom with 32 percent of her manufactured imports, with Germany alone supplying approximately 13 percent. By 1947, however, the proportion of manufactured imports supplied by Western Europe declined to 18 percent and Germany's share to 1 percent. This severe reduction in the volume of imports from Western Europe in general and Germany in particular was largely responsible for the increase in the importance of North America as a supplier of iron and steel manufactures, machinery, and chemicals. The decline in petroleum imports derived from Iran and Rumania as a result of the disruption of production in these countries as well as the East-West rift in the postwar period led to an increase in the volume of dollar oil imports and to the increase in the importance of North America as a supplier of petroleum to the British market. The share of Britain's petroleum imports supplied by Iran and Rumania declined from 32 percent in the prewar period to less than 12 percent in 1947.

Though the necessity of placing heavier reliance on North America as a source of supply in the early postwar period contributed to the steep increase in the value of dollar imports between the prewar period and 1947, this factor was overshadowed in importance by the drastic rise in the price level of American exports. There can be no doubt that this development was the most important single factor responsible for the deterioration of Britain's dollar accounts between the prewar and postwar periods. Its importance is apparent from Table 25 which shows the index of unit values of selected American exports.

TABLE 25

UNIT VALUES OF SELECTED AMERICAN EXPORTS

(1938 = 100)

	1938	1946	1947
Wheat	100	232	284
Tobacco	100	166	167
Meat (beef)	100	197	286
Cheese	100	157	181
Cotton	100	260	310
Soft wood	100	191	242
Hard wood	100	225	254
Crude petroleum	100	120	150
Motor fuel	100	110	145
Iron and steel	100	144	220
Refined copper	100	126	193
Motor trucks	100	216	259
Passenger cars	100	168	202

Source: Derived from Department of Commerce, *Statistical Abstract of the United States*, 1953, p. 318.

The table reveals that the large increase in the value of imports the United Kingdom derived from North America between the prewar and early postwar periods was due, in large part, to the precipitous rise in the American export price level. The operation of this factor alone would have sufficed to effect a dollar shortage in the postwar period. By comparison, the moderate increase in the quantum of imports the United Kingdom derived from dollar sources between 1935–38 and 1947 was a rather unimportant factor.

This conclusion has an important bearing on an argument frequently advanced by critics of the American trade philosophy that forced adherence to the principle of nondiscrimination in the early postwar period [9] was a

[9] Under the terms of the Anglo-American Financial Agreement, the United Kingdom pledged to adhere to the nondiscriminatory principle. For an analysis of this agreement, see below, Chapter IX.

factor responsible for the severity of the dollar shortage. The preceding analysis indicates that this argument is deficient on two counts. First, the increase in the value of imports from the dollar area between the prewar period and 1947 was largely the result of the drastic rise in the price level of American exports. Adherence to the principle of nondiscrimination had little effect on this development. Second, and more significant, the moderate increase in the quantum of imports the United Kingdom derived from dollar sources between the prewar and early postwar periods is mainly attributable to the inability to obtain supplies from other sources. The ability to discriminate implies, at the minimum, a choice of sources. The fact is that the United Kingdom did not have alternative sources of supplies in the early postwar period. Her only choice was to obtain imports from dollar sources or to forego them completely. Attlee stated the case succinctly: "With respect to non-discrimination the provision of the loan agreement has hardly any operation at all. It is because of the low levels of production in other countries that we have been driven to buy so largely from the Western Hemisphere." [10] In the one case where adherence to the principle of nondiscrimination might have impeded Britain's progress, permission was requested and obtained to discriminate: trade with the colonies was specifically exempt from the nondiscrimination clause of the Anglo-American Financial Agreement, despite the American government's insistence at the time that the imperial preference system be abandoned.

Britain's Imports from North America, 1948–50. Even before the suspension of convertibility in August, 1947, the government was conscious of the need to reduce imports from dollar sources in order to stay the drain on Britain's reserves. As early as April, 1947, Dalton announced an increase of 50 percent in the tobacco duty in order to curtail tobacco consumption by an estimated 25 percent. Dalton conceived this measure as the "first stage . . . in bringing our dollar expenditures, which have become too large, more in relation to our reserves and also the first step in bringing about a more balanced situation as between exports and imports." [11] The second step to reduce dollar expenditures was taken in June, 1947, with the announcement of slight import cuts aimed at dollar goods.[12] The object behind these cuts was to curtail the importation of less essential goods; the importation of petroleum products, tobacco, newsprint, and consumer goods other than food was particularly affected. With

[10] Hansard, V, 441, c. 1506–7.

[11] Hansard, V, 436, c. 864.

[12] Eden estimated that the cuts would result in a saving of but between 25 million and 30 million pounds. Hansard, V, 439, c. 2153.

the deterioration of the dollar accounts in August, 1947, the government announced still more drastic import restrictions. On August 6 the government announced the reduction of food imports from the dollar area by 144 million pounds per annum and on August 27, 1947, after the suspension of convertibility, further import cuts designed to save an additional 31 million pounds of hard currency were announced.[13] Finally, in June, 1949, just preceding the devaluation of the pound, the United Kingdom restricted dollar imports to 75 percent of the July, 1948–June, 1949, level.[14]

The suspension of convertibility and the imposition of severe import restrictions against dollar goods ushered in a new import policy. It was clear that the ability to restrict imports from the Western Hemisphere was contingent upon the replacing of these imports from nondollar sources. To ensure this result, the government announced its intention not to be bound by the nondiscrimination clause of the Anglo-American Financial Agreement since adherence to this principle would impede Britain's progress toward achieving a better dollar-pound balance. In addition the government sought to enter into bilateral agreements with nondollar countries to replace the imports formerly derived from the hard currency areas.

Though the government was "well satisfied that . . . the provision of section 9 of the loan agreement [did not] operate to prevent the United Kingdom from importing any goods, including foodstuffs, which we are anxious to take and which we can afford to buy," it was recognized that with the revival of production by many of Britain's traditional suppliers, continued adherence to the principle of nondiscrimination might militate against recovery. The attempt to replace hard currency imports with soft currency imports, even if the latter should be more expensive, was, however, a violation of the nondiscrimination clause. Yet this replacement was necessary if imports from the hard currency areas were to be reduced. To prevent the emergence of difficulties, Attlee declared his intention to explore the "situation with the United States Government to see what steps may be taken to enable Britain to obtain supplies from the soft currency areas." [15] In August, 1947, the Eady Mission arrived in Washington to discuss revision of the nondiscrimination obligation. The discussions,

[13] These cuts were based on programed imports rather than on actual imports of the preceding period.

[14] The import restrictions levied in November, 1951, and in January and March, 1952, were not directed against dollar goods as such. In 1951 the United Kingdom was suffering from an over-all disequilibrium and the import restrictions were thus of a general nature.

[15] Hansard, V, 441, c. 1507.

which were continued in London after the suspension of convertibility, resulted in the issuance of a communiqué in which the United States tacitly approved the use of discrimination by Britain so long as she suffered from balance of payments difficulties. The relevant section of the communiqué stated:

The framers of the Anglo-American Financial Agreement specifically recognized the existence of unusual aspects of the United Kingdom's position requiring certain deviations from an inflexible rule of non-discrimination. It is basic to an understanding of section 9 of the agreement to appreciate that this was never intended to constitute a straitjacket on Britain's trade.[16]

The way cleared, the British negotiated a series of bilateral agreements with her major trading partners to ensure the continuance of supplies and to reduce her dependence on dollar sources. The resort to bilateralism was regarded by the government as a pragmatic undertaking rather than a repudiation of the obligations Britain undertook under the terms of the Anglo-American Financial Agreement. Harold Wilson, President of the Board of Trade, stated the government's position clearly.

We do not regard the bilateral agreements in any way inconsistent with the obligations we have assumed. . . . During a period of world shortages when it is necessary to build up the productive powers of the old world, anything which could be done by bilateral agreements or other means of economic cooperation to increase the flow of goods . . . is a real benefit to the economic well being of the world and a real contribution to the restoration of world trade.[17]

The government tirelessly argued that with the return of more propitious conditions the United Kingdom would again adhere to the principles of trade embodied in the Anglo-American Financial Agreement.[18]

The judicious use of discrimination, the revival of production in non-dollar countries, the Intra-European Payments Schemes, and the bilateral agreements [19] enabled the United Kingdom to reduce her dependence on

[16] Hansard, V, 443, c. 55 (written reply).

[17] Board of Trade Journal, January 24, 1948, p. 176.

[18] For the provisions of the Anglo-American Financial Areement, see below, Chap. IX.

[19] A brief description of the more important bilateral agreements may be in order. The most spectacular agreement, negotiated in 1948, provided for the purchase by the United Kingdom of Argentinian food and feeding stuff valued at 110 million pounds during 1948. Payment for these imports was effected by the sale of Britain's interests in the Argentine railroads. Thus, in effect the United Kingdom agreed to barter away important capital assets for one year's supply of meat.

Most of the bilateral agreements into which the United Kingdom entered provided

dollar sources of supply. Between 1947 and 1950 the value of total imports into the United Kingdom increased by 812 million pounds, while the value of imports derived from North American sources was reduced by 144 million pounds. This reduction in the value of imports derived from North American sources was achieved in the face of a continued rise in the dollar

---

for the expansion of mutual trade, however. The agreement with Brazil (Cmd. 7438) reached in May, 1948, for example, provided for the exchange of Brazilian foodstuffs and raw materials valued at 31.5 million pounds for British coal, tinplate, cement, petroleum and petroleum products, alkalis, tin, and other less essential commodities. The Anglo-Danish agreement of February, 1948, provided for the expansion of butter and bacon exports to the United Kingdom; Denmark agreed to supply the United Kingdom with not less than two thirds of her exportable surplus of butter and guaranteed at least 40,000 tons, 80 percent of her exportable surplus of bacon in 1948 and 90 percent of her exportable surplus of bacon in 1948–49. In addition the United Kingdom contracted to purchase Danish eggs, cheese, meat, fish, and condensed milk. The United Kingdom agreed to supply Denmark with 870,000 tons of coal per annum and 50,000 tons of iron and steel per annum, and petroleum products were to be purchased from British controlled sources.

The United Kingdom also contracted agreements with Sweden, the Netherlands, and Ireland whereby the United Kingdom agreed to make available specified amounts of steel and coal, among other manufactures, for basic raw material and food imports. Bilateral agreements were also entered into with Eastern European countries. The Anglo-Soviet agreement of December, 1947, provided for the supply by the Soviet Union of a substantial volume of barley, oats, and maize in return for British vehicles, locomotives, other machinery, and narrow gauge rails. A five-year agreement with Poland provided for the supply to the United Kingdom of an increased volume of eggs, bacon, and other agricultural and raw material products in return for manufactured and industrial capital goods. Similarly an agreement with Yugoslavia provided for the shipment to the United Kingdom of timber, wood products, and foodstuffs in return for textile raw material, crude oils, chemicals, and machinery.

Commercial agreements were also contracted with Finland and Hungary. The Anglo-Finnish agreement provided for the export to the United Kingdom of wood and timber in return for which the United Kingdom was to supply coal, coke, and steel. The Anglo-Hungarian agreement provided for the expansion of Hungarian egg, bacon, poultry, and raw material exports to the United Kingdom in return for steel, coal, and machinery.

The agreements cited above are only a few of the many agreements into which the United Kingdom entered following the suspension of convertibility. The object of all these agreements, and this is amply brought out by those cited, was to reduce the dependence of the United Kingdom on dollar sources by providing for an increase in the volume of essential food and raw material imports from non-dollar sources. The agreements were, for the most part, expansionary in that they invariably provided for an increase in the volume of trade.

Critics of the bilateral agreements argued that since the United Kingdom frequently had to acquiesce to the delivery of steel and other commodities which could have found a ready market in the hard currency areas, the bilateral agreements tended to accentuate the dollar shortage by causing a reduction of exports (or inhibiting an expansion of exports) to the dollar area. This argument overlooks the

export price level,[20] thus reflecting a reduction in the quantum of these imports. Indeed, between 1947 and 1950 the *volume* of imports the United Kingdom derived from the dollar area was reduced by 40 percent while the volume of total imports increased by 12 percent.[21]

The success the United Kingdom enjoyed in substituting soft currency sources for the dollar area is reflected in the accompanying table which shows the proportion of imports Britain derived from the major areas between 1946 and 1950.

TABLE 26

PERCENTAGE OF IMPORTS FROM MAJOR AREAS, 1946–50

	1946	1947	1948	1949	1950
Dollar area	36	36	22	22	18
Other western hemisphere	9	10	10	5	7
OEEC and dependencies	14	15	18	23	24
Other nonsterling	6	6	13	11	11
Rest of sterling area	35	32	36	39	40

Source: Bureau of Customs and Excises, *Annual Statement of the Trade of the United Kingdom with British and Foreign Sources.*

The decline in the proportion of imports the United Kingdom derived from the dollar area between 1947 and 1950 was accompanied by an increase in the proportion of imports derived from the OEEC,[22] the rest of the sterling area, and other nonsterling countries. The evidence attests to Britain's success in replacing the dollar sources by soft currency sources of supply. It is of some interest to examine in greater detail the manner in which this replacement was effected.

For the reasons given above, it is convenient to concentrate attention on Britain's trade with North America in analyzing the manner in which

---

important fact that the steel and other potential dollar earning exports the United Kingdom consented to supply to the soft currency countries represented but a small proportion of the total exports these countries agreed to take. Without her steel and other potential dollar earning exports, the United Kingdom could not have successfully concluded the agreements. The inclusion of a relatively small portion of steel and other potential dollar exports, in effect, enabled the less essential exports to earn food and raw materials which, were it not for the bilateral agreements, would have had to be derived from hard currency sources. For the government's defense of the bilateral agreements see *Board of Trade Journal*, February 19, 1949.

[20] The price level of American exports to the United Kingdom rose by 33 percent between 1947 and 1950. *Board of Trade Journal*, August 1, 1953, p. 220.

[21] *Ibid.*, p. 220.

[22] The increase in imports from the OEEC is attributable to an increase in production in Western Europe as well as to a steady liberalization of imports. In December, 1950, 86 percent of Britain's private trade with the OEEC countries was free of import restrictions.

she succeeded in replacing the dollar area with soft currency areas as a source of supply. Table 27 shows the imports from North America between 1947 and 1950, the reduction in the value of which was most important in reducing the total value of imports derived from this source.

The decline in the value of category 1 imports accounted for 67 percent of the total reduction in the value of imports derived from North America between 1947 and 1950. Moreover, the heavy reduction in the value of meat, dairy, and other food imports from North America was mainly responsible for this decline. The reduction in the value of raw material and manufactured imports derived from North America between 1947 and 1950 was decidedly less important than the decline in the value of category 1 imports. Considering the fact that the total value of raw material and manufactured imports increased by 595 million pounds during this period, however, even a reduction of 42 million pounds was rather remarkable. The reduction in the value of wood and timber, cotton yarn and manufactures, and manufactured oils, fats, and resin imports was chiefly responsible for the decline in the value of raw material and manufactured imports derived from North America between 1947 and 1950.

TABLE 27

SELECTED IMPORTS FROM NORTH AMERICA, 1947–50

(*In millions of pounds, c.i.f.*)

	1947	1950	Change between 1947–50	Change in Total Imports 1947–50
Food, drink, and tobacco (category 1)				
Total	262	168	– 94	226
Grain and flour	108	105	– 3	18
Meat	28	9	– 19	49
Dairy	56	9	– 47	31
Fresh fruits and vegetables	8		– 8	15
Other food	27	4	– 23	37
Raw materials (category 2)				
Total	109	90	– 19	431
Wood and timber	60	14	– 46	– 15
Manufactures (category 3)				
Total	149	129	– 23	164
Cotton yarn and manufactures	6		– 6	11
Oils, fats, resins	33	16	– 17	36
Total imports	530	391	– 139	812

Source: Derived from Bureau of Customs and Excises, *Annual Statement of the Trade of the United Kingdom with British and Foreign Countries* and *Trade and Navigation Accounts of the United Kingdom.*

The increase in the value of total imports in the face of a reduction in the value of imports derived from North America is only partially attributable to an increase in the volume of imports derived from non-dollar sources. In part the large increase in the value of British imports between 1947 and 1950 reflects the familiar fact that imports from non-dollar sources were, in the main, more costly (in pounds) than dollar imports in the postwar period. Thus, though the total value of imports of grain and flour and meat in 1950 exceeded the 1947 level, the volume of imports of these commodities in 1950 amounted to but 97 percent and 96 percent of the 1947 level respectively.[23] In other cases, however, the increase in the value of imports from non-dollar sources was accompanied by an increase in the volume of imports as well: the volume of total imports in 1950 exceeded the 1947 level by 12 percent while the volume of category 1 imports, raw material imports, and manufactured imports surpassed the 1947 levels by 7 percent, 20 percent, and 21 percent, respectively.[24]

It is of some interest to examine in detail the manner in which Britain found other sources of supply than North America for particular commodity groups. The groups chosen for analysis are grain and flour, meat, dairy products, wood and timber, raw cotton, iron and steel, chemicals, oils, fats and resins, and machinery. The value of these imports from all sources increased by 271 million pounds between 1947 and 1950, while their value from North America was reduced by 124 million pounds. The accompanying table shows the proportion of these imports the United Kingdom derived from North America in 1947 and 1950.

In each of the commodity classes listed, the proportion of imports the United Kingdom derived from North America declined between 1947 and

[23] *Board of Trade Journal.*

[24] The following table shows the volume of selected imports in 1950 relative to 1947 (100).

Grain and flour	97
Meat	96
Fresh fruits and vegetables	117
Other food	115
Tobacco	102
Wood and timber	79
Raw cotton and waste	139
Wool	113
Seeds and nuts for oil	147
Nonferrous metals and manufactures	151
Oils, fats, and resins	114

Source: *Board of Trade Journal.*

TABLE 28

PROPORTION OF SELECTED IMPORTS FROM NORTH AMERICA,
1947 AND 1950

Import	1947	1950
Grain and flour	77	70
Meat	23	4
Dairy	45	7
Wood and timber	52	22
Raw cotton	30	26
Iron and steel and manufactures	60	26
Chemicals	39	29
Oils, fats, and resins	35	12
Machinery	77	55

Source: Derived from *Annual Statement of the Trade of the United Kingdom with British and Foreign Countries* and *Trade and Navigation Accounts of the United Kingdom.*

1950, albeit, in some cases, slightly. Furthermore, the decline in the proportion of imports supplied by North America was due to an increase in the value of total imports, accompanied by a reduction in the value of imports derived from North America in all the cases listed with the exception of wood and timber, raw cotton, chemical, and machinery imports. With respect to wood and timber imports, the decline in the relative importance of North America as a supplier is attributable to a greater decline in the value of imports from North American than in the total value of imports. The decline in the relative importance of North America as a supplier of chemicals and machinery was due to an increase in the value of total imports while the value of imports from North America remained substantially constant. Finally, the decline in the relative importance of North America as a supplier of raw cotton resulted from the proportionately smaller expansion in the volume of North American imports than in the expansion of total raw cotton imports.

Thus in every case listed, including that of wood and timber imports, the decline in the relative importance of North America as a supplier of imports was associated with an expansion in the value (and generally in the volume) of imports from non-dollar sources. Indeed, it was this expansion which enabled the United Kingdom to reduce her imports from dollar sources. Thus the increase in the value of grain and flour imports from Australia and the U.S.S.R. and of meat imports from Denmark, New Zealand, France, the Netherlands, and Poland, prevented as large a reduction in the volume of these imports as would otherwise have occurred following the intensified import restrictions levied against the dollar area.[25] The increase in dairy imports from Denmark, New Zealand, and Australia was particularly important in enabling the United Kingdom to enjoy an increase in the total volume of dairy imports despite a drastic decline in the value (and volume) of these imports derived from North America.

The increase in production and exports in Western Europe in general, and in Germany in particular, enabled the United Kingdom to reduce her dependence on North America as a source of supply for manufactures. The expansion in the value of machinery imports derived from Western Europe increased the proportion supplied by this source from 4 percent in 1947 to rather more than 11 percent in 1950, and enabled an expansion in the total volume of these imports despite the relative constancy of machine imports from North America. Likewise, the increase in the value (and volume) of chemical imports from Western Europe, particularly Germany, enabled the United Kingdom to increase the total volume of these imports, despite a constant value (and a slightly reduced volume) of imports from North America. Finally, the expansion in the value of imports of iron and steel manufactures from Western Europe [26] increased the proportion supplied by this area from 30 percent in 1947 to 64 percent in 1950 and allowed for an increase in the total volume of these imports, despite the reduction in value and volume of imports from North America.

The decline in the relative importance of North America as a supplier of raw cotton and wood and timber imports is attributable, in the former case, to a less than proportionate increase in the value of cotton imports from the United States, and, in the latter case, to a greater decline in the value of imports from North America than in total wood and timber imports. The expansion in the value (and volume) of wood and timber imports from non-dollar sources, notably the U.S.S.R., Yugoslavia, France, Poland, and British countries exclusive of Canada, while not sufficient to completely offset the reduction in the volume of imports from North America consequent to the intensification of import restrictions against dol-

[25] The proportion of grain and flour imports provided by Australia increased from 3 percent in 1947 to 8 percent in 1950 while the proportion supplied by the U.S.S.R. increased from nothing in 1947 to 8 percent in 1950. Denmark's share in Britain's meat imports increased from 6 percent in 1947 to 20 percent in 1950. New Zealand's share remained substantially constant while the shares of Poland, France, and the Netherlands each increased from nil in 1947 to 6 percent in 1950.

[26] Western Europe, in this context, includes Germany, Belgium, France, Luxemburg, Sweden, and Norway.

lar goods, succeeded in mitigating the effects of this reduction. The increase in the value (and volume) of cotton imports from Egypt, Peru, Brazil, and the Anglo-Egyptian Sudan was greater than the increase in the value of cotton imports from the United States and resulted in a decline in the relative importance of North America as a supplier of raw cotton imports.

Finally, the increase in the value of manufactured oils, fats, and resin imports from non-dollar sources, while the value (and volume) of these imports from North America was reduced, resulted in a decline in the importance of North America as a supplier of these imports; between 1947 and 1950 the proportion of Britain's oils, fats, and resins supplied by the United States declined from 35 percent to 12 percent. Particularly important in effecting this result was the increase in the value (and volume) of oil, fat, and resin imports from Iran, British countries exclusive of Canada, France, the Netherland Antilles, and the Netherlands. The increase in the value (and volume) of imports from non-dollar countries more than offset the reduction in the value (and volume) of imports from the dollar area; in 1950 the volume of oil, fat, and resin imports amounted to 114 percent of the 1947 level.[27]

The review of Britain's import trade between 1947 and 1950 indicates a high degree of success in reducing the dependence of the United Kingdom on dollar sources. While many factors were responsible for this development, the most important appear to be the intensification of restrictions against dollar goods [28] following the suspension of convertibility, the revival of production in the nondollar world, the bilateral agreements into which the United Kingdom entered to ensure the continuance of supplies after the decision to discriminate against dollar goods was made, and the Intra-European Payments Schemes which facilitated trade between non-dollar countries. It is futile to speculate which of these factors were most important; in the last analysis all were necessary for success.

Despite the drastic reduction in the *volume* of imports from North America,[29] the *value* of imports from this source in 1950 was still considerably greater than it had been before the war. This highlights the

[27] *Board of Trade Journal.*

[28] See below, p. 98, however, for a discussion of the manner in which the degree of intensification of import restrictions against dollar goods varied in the postwar period and the effects of this on Britain's dollar problem.

[29] The volume of imports derived from North America declined by 40 percent between 1947 and 1950.

important fact emphasized above that the major factor responsible for the rise in the value of dollar imports into Britain between the pre- and post-war periods was the precipitous rise in the American export price level.

British Imports from North America, 1950–51. The 1951 payments crisis was induced, in large part, by the drastic rise in the value of imports not only from the dollar area but from other areas as well. Several factors were responsible for this. First, the depletion of stocks in 1950 necessitated their rebuilding in 1951 and resulted in a larger volume of dollar as well as nondollar imports. Second, the outbreak of the Korean War was accompanied by a scramble for primary products which caused a precipitous rise in the prices of imports. Third, the accelerated defense program induced by the Korean War necessitated a larger volume of imports.

The expansion in the volume of imports from dollar sources between 1950 and 1951 appears to have been a more important factor responsible for the increase in the value of dollar imports than the rise in the American export price level. Between 1950 and 1951 the volume of imports the United Kingdom derived from the dollar area increased by 30 percent. During the same period the price of dollar exports to Britain increased by 24 percent.[30] The order of importance of these two factors was reversed with respect to total imports; the volume of total imports into the United Kingdom increased by 12 percent between 1950 and 1951, while the price of imports rose by 33 percent.[31]

Despite the large increase in the volume of imports the United Kingdom derived from the dollar area between 1950 and 1951, the *quantum* of imports derived from this source in the latter year was still substantially below that of the prewar period. The increase in the value of dollar imports into the United Kingdom between 1938 and 1951 was due to the rise in the American export price level rather than to the necessity of placing heavier reliance on the dollar area as a source of supply in the post-war period. This conclusion has far reaching effects: it emphasizes the superficiality of the view that regards the dollar problem as being caused by transitory developments or by fatuous policies allegedly pursued by the United Kingdom; it also casts grave doubts on the practicability of pro-

[30] *Board of Trade Journal,* August 1, 1953, p. 220.

[31] *Ibid.,* p. 220. The expansion in the value of imports from nondollar sources between 1950–51 was almost as significant in inducing the 1951 crisis as was the increase in the value of dollar imports. Indeed, Chancellor of the Exchequer Butler contended that the 1951 crisis was a "balance of payments crisis and not, as in 1949, a problem predominantly of trade between the sterling area and the dollar area. . . . All foreign currencies are now hard." Hansard, V, 493, c. 195.

posals that the United Kingdom can escape from the dilemma of the dollar problem by still further reducing her dependence on dollar sources of supply. Certainly this last proposal would have a greater significance were it demonstrated that the postwar dollar shortage was due to an increase in the importance of the dollar area as a supplier to the United Kingdom. Actually, it is debatable whether the United Kingdom can succeed in reducing her dependence on the dollar area in the foreseeable future by much more than had already been achieved in the postwar period.

FLUCTUATIONS IN THE VALUE OF DOLLAR IMPORTS, 1946–51

The analysis of Britain's dollar imports to this point has been concerned with the factors responsible for the increase in their value between the pre- and postwar periods. It is necessary, at this stage, to focus attention on the factors responsible for the fluctuations in the value of dollar imports in the postwar period.

Examination of Table 23 reveals that the value of dollar imports increased between the prewar period and 1947, was reduced between 1947 and 1948, increased slightly between 1948 and 1949, declined between 1949 and 1950, and rose sharply between 1950 and 1951. These fluctuations in the value of dollar imports were intimately related to the outcome on dollar current accounts. The years in which the value of dollar imports was reduced were, on the whole, favorable from the point of view of the outcome on the dollar accounts; those years in which the value of dollar imports rose were "crisis" years.

Two interrelated factors were primarily responsible for these fluctuations: the alternate depletion and investment in working capital and the varying degree of stringency with which import restrictions were imposed in the postwar period. In every year between 1946 and 1951, with the exception of 1949, the change in the value of dollar imports was positively correlated with the change in investment in working capital, while in four of the six years (1946, 1947, 1950, and 1951) changes in investment in working capital were particularly important in influencing the result on dollar accounts by affecting the value of dollar imports. In 1946 and 1950 the depletion of stocks was largely responsible for the relatively low level of dollar imports and hence for the relatively favorable outturn on dollar accounts; in 1947 and 1951 the necessity of replenishing the stockpiles contributed to the increase in the value of dollar imports.

The varying degree of stringency with which the import restrictions were applied in the postwar period was the second factor responsible for the fluctuations in the value of imports the United Kingdom derived from the dollar area and influenced, in part, the alternate depletion of and investment in working capital. In general, the degree of stringency was a function of the state of the reserves. An increase acted as a signal for a relaxation of the import restrictions; a decline, for an intensification. This explains in large part the two-year cyclical pattern displayed by British dollar imports in the postwar period; the relatively favorable outcome on dollar accounts in 1946, 1948, and 1950 was followed by a relaxation of import restrictions and by an increase in the value of imports in 1947, 1949, and 1951.[32]

Britain's postwar experience underlines the difficulties involved in attempting to increase reserves to workable levels through the use of import restrictions. Political and social factors combine to make it extremely difficult for a government to maintain the same degree of stringency in applying import restrictions when the reserves are rising as when they are declining; the use of import restrictions is more effective in staying the drain on the reserves than in aiding to bring them to a workable level.[33]

BRITAIN'S DOLLAR EXPORTS, 1946–51

In this section those factors that contributed to Britain's difficulties by inhibiting the expansion of exports to the dollar area are examined. Though these factors were, individually and collectively, less important than those affecting the value of imports, a number of them are subject to control and thus offer some means of mitigating the problem. Before these factors are analyzed, however, it is advisable to review briefly the course of Britain's exports to North America in the postwar period.

Between 1935–38 and 1947 the value of British exports to North America increased by 50 million pounds.[34] This increase was due wholly

[32] Cf. Fleming, "Regional Organization of Trade and Payments," *American Economic Review, Papers and Proceedings,* May, 1952, p. 350.

[33] United States aid policies also militated against the use of import restrictions to repair the reserves as distinct from staying a drain. The United States did not view with favor the use of American aid to build up the reserves of the recipient countries. The dramatic improvement in Britain's reserves in 1950, for example, was the most important consideration leading to the cessation of Marshall aid to the United Kingdom.

[34] The following table shows the value of British exports to North America (in millions of pounds).

to the rise in the British export price level; in 1947 the volume of British exports to the United States amounted to but 80 percent of the prewar level while the quantum of exports to Canada amounted to but 70 percent of the prewar level.[35]   The decline in the volume of exports to North America is partially attributable to the low level of production in the United Kingdom and partially to the fact that the goods for which a ready market existed in the dollar area in the early postwar period were precisely those whose production required resources needed for domestic reconstruction.   The high priority assigned to capital formation in the early postwar period undoubtedly impeded the expansion of exports to the dollar area. It is not to be inferred, however, that this policy was misguided.   It was indicated [36] that in the circumstances prevailing in the postwar period, the decision to devote scarce resources to capital formation even at the temporary sacrifice of exports to the dollar area was warranted.   In addition to the two factors cited, the heavy sterling releases and other capital outflows to the sterling area in the early postwar period impeded the expansion of exports to the dollar area.[37]   The importance of this factor is discussed in greater detail below.

Though the increase in the price level of British exports more than sufficed to offset the decline in the volume of exports to the dollar area, it is necessary to note that the British dollar export prices rose less than British dollar import prices; Britain's terms of trade vis-à-vis the dollar area deteriorated between the prewar and the early postwar periods.[38]   It should also be noted, that even had the British export price level risen *pari passu* with the American export price level, all other things equal, Britain's dollar trade account would have deteriorated.   A general increase in the import and export price levels of a deficit country always increases

Year	To the United States	To Canada	To North America
1935–38	20	23	43
1946	35	34	69
1947	48	45	93
1948	66	73	139
1949	57	80	137
1950	113	126	239
1951	136	137	273

Source: Board of Trade, *Annual Statement of Trade of the United Kingdom with British and Foreign Countries.*

[35] ECA, *Sterling Area,* p. 66.

[36] See above, p. 60 ff.   [37] See below, p. 108 ff.

[38] The ECA estimated that Britain's terms of trade vis-à-vis the dollar area deteriorated by 10 percent between the prewar period and 1947. *Sterling Area,* p. 68.

the size of that deficit.   In the event, Britain's dollar trade account deteriorated as a result of a "general" rise in prices as well as from a deterioration of the terms of trade.

The revival of production in the United Kingdom and the intensification of the export drive resulted in an expansion in the value and volume of British exports to the dollar area between 1947 and 1948; between these years the volume of exports to the dollar area increased by 43 percent.[39] This expansion was interrupted by the inventory recession in the United States in late 1948 and early 1949 as well as by the anticipation of a sterling devaluation.[40]   The recovery of industrial production in the United States, the devaluation of the pound, and the outbreak of the Korean War, however, resulted in a dramatic expansion in the volume and value of Britain's dollar exports; between 1949 and 1951 the volume of exports to the dollar area increased by 50 percent.[41]

The expansion in the volume of exports to the dollar area was associated with a slight increase in the importance of the dollar area as a market for British goods.   The accompanying table shows the proportionate distribution of British exports to the different areas in the pre- and early postwar periods.

FACTORS INFLUENCING BRITISH EXPORTS TO THE DOLLAR AREA

Among the more important factors influencing the value of British exports to the dollar area in the postwar period were the sterling-dollar exchange rate, the rate of release of sterling balances and other capital exports from the United Kingdom to the soft currency areas, the level of industrial activity in the United States, American tariffs and other impediments to manufactured imports, and the apparently greater degree of self-sufficiency attained by the United States with respect to manufactures since 1938.   It is necessary to examine the manner in which the operation of these factors influenced the value of British exports to the dollar area and the extent to which inappropriate policies adopted either by the United Kingdom or the dollar countries were responsible for the large direct dollar deficits the United Kingdom incurred in the postwar period.

[39] *Board of Trade Journal,* August 1, 1953, p. 220.

[40] The volume of exports to the dollar area declined by approximately 7 percent between 1948 and 1949. *Ibid.*

[41] *Ibid.*   Though the British dollar export price level rose throughout the entire postwar period the rise was considerably less than that in the British dollar import price level.   Between 1947 and 1951 Britain's terms of trade vis-à-vis the dollar area deteriorated by approximately 15 percent.

TABLE 29

PROPORTIONATE DISTRIBUTION OF BRITAIN'S EXPORTS

	1938	1946	1947	1948	1949	1950	1951
North America	10.0	7.5	8.1	8.7	7.6	11.0	10.6
Other American account countries	1.6	1.4	1.8	2.1	1.7	2.0	2.0
Rest of sterling area	45.0	45.1	48.7	49.7	52.0	48.0	50.7
OEEC countries	25.0	28.3	23.3	23.4	22.3	25.0	24.2
Rest of world	19.4	17.7	18.1	16.1	16.4	14.0	12.5

Source: Derived from Bureau of Customs and Excises, *Annual Statement of Trade of the United Kingdom with British and Foreign Countries* and *Trade and Navigation Accounts of the United Kingdom.*

Exchange Rate Policy.[42] At the end of the war the United Kingdom decided to continue the rate of exchange which prevailed in September, 1939, one pound equaling $4.03.[43] This rate was maintained until September, 1949, when the pound was devalued by 30.5 percent, one pound equaling $2.80. Both policies were criticized. Some argued that the pound was overvalued in the early postwar period and should thus have been devalued sooner; [44] others denied that a devaluation could possibly contribute to the rectification of the dollar-pound imbalance. It is thus necessary to examine briefly the manner in which a currency devaluation can correct a dollar shortage and whether the prevailing circumstances in the postwar period were propitious for the use of this mechanism of adjustment.

A currency devaluation can contribute toward the correction of a dollar shortage by affecting exports to the dollar area in two distinct ways.[45] It can induce an increase in the value of exports measured in foreign currencies, including the dollar value of exports to the dollar area, and it can effect a redistribution of exports from the soft to the hard currency areas. For the first method to be effective, it is necessary that the foreign, including the dollar area's, elasticity of demand for British exports be greater

[42] For the theory of exchange rates see Robinson, "The Foreign Exchanges," in *Essays in the Theory of Employment;* Machlup, "The Theory of Foreign Exchanges," reprinted in *Readings in the Theory of International Trade;* Lerner, *The Economics of Control,* chap. 28. The postwar literature on the theory of exchange rates is extensive. Most of the articles develop and refine the ideas of the aforementioned works.

[43] Dalton announced at the time that "no evidence has been adduced which would justify a change in this rate at the present time." Hansard, V, 418, c. 16.

[44] It should be stated, however, that this view was rare. It was fairly commonly agreed that little advantage would result from a devaluation of the pound at the time. See below, pp. 103–104.

[45] We are not concerned here with the effect of a devaluation on imports.

than unity, and that the British elasticity of supply of exports be positive. The success of the second method is contingent upon the devaluation making the dollar area relatively more profitable than soft currency areas, and the ability to transfer goods heretofore sold to the soft currency areas to the dollar area.[46] This second condition is a function of, among other things, the type of goods exported to the soft currency and the dollar areas respectively, and the dollar area's elasticity of demand for the type of goods, which, prior to the devaluation, were sold in the soft currency areas, or for the types of goods which could be produced with the resources used to produce the soft currency exports.

It is not possible with the currently available information to arrive at definitive conclusions concerning the dollar area's price elasticity of demand for British exports. Much of the pessimism generated by the earlier studies [47] concerned with the measurement of the American price elasticity of demand for imports in the interwar period has been dissipated, however, in the light of new findings,[48] as well as in the light of weighty criticisms of the methods employed to get the low elasticities. It is probable that a sterling devaluation will result in an increase in the dollar value of exports, at least after a certain length of time has been allowed to elapse.[49]

Accepting the view that the American price elasticity of demand for British exports is likely to be greater than unity does not necessitate the conclusion that Britain should have devalued the pound in the early postwar period. Against this conclusion, the most important point is that at the time the ability to produce rather than to sell inhibited the expansion of exports. A devaluation of the pound in the early postwar period would probably have caused a further deterioration of the terms of trade without resulting in an expansion in the volume of exports.

[46] Or, to be more general, the ability to transfer the resources used in the production of "soft currency exports" to the production of "hard currency" exports.

[47] Cf. Adler, "United States Import Demand During the Interwar Period," *American Economic Review,* June, 1945, and Chang, *Cyclical Movements,* p. 42. For a criticism of the findings of Chang and Adler see Orcutt, "Measurement of Price Elasticities in International Trade," *Review of Economics and Statistics,* May, 1950, and Haberler, "Some Factors Affecting the Future of International Trade and International Economic Policy" in Harris, *Essays in Economic Reconstruction.*

[48] Adler, *Pattern of United States Import Trade.*

[49] *Ibid.,* p. 49. The authors found that the interwar American price elasticity of demand for British manufactures amounted to between 5.2 percent and 6.6 percent depending on the method of computation. Though they caution that no precise significance should be attached to these estimates, the estimates are too high to leave much doubt that a devaluation would result in an expansion of the value of exports to the United States.

It is true that a devaluation of the pound vis-à-vis the dollar but not vis-à-vis other currencies would have increased the relative profitability of exporting to the dollar area and thus might have led to the diversion of some exports from the soft currency to the hard currency areas. But it is debatable whether this was important enough to warrant a devaluation considering the circumstances that prevailed in the postwar period. Since there is evidence that in 1947 the British export price level was below the equilibrium level, the profitability of British exports to the dollar area could have been increased by the simple expedient of raising prices. This would have resulted in an improvement in the terms of trade rather than the deterioration that would have probably been induced by a devaluation. Moreover, with the widespread dislocations in many of the soft currency countries at the war's end, it might have been unwise to divert exports from them to the dollar area, even if this would have led to a temporary improvement in the direct dollar accounts. An attempt to divert exports from the soft currency areas to the dollar area would undoubtedly have resulted in an increase in the value of dollar imports into the soft currency areas and ultimately to an accentuation of the drain of Britain's gold and dollar reserves to these areas.[50] Finally, as is noted below, Britain could have diverted exports to hard currency areas by modifying her policy with respect to sterling releases. These releases in the early postwar period provided the recipients with the wherewithal to purchase British exports.

The 1949 devaluation was severely criticized on the grounds that Britain's costs were not out of line with American costs [51] and that the major impediment to increased exports at the time was not an uneconomic price level but rather the inability to meet reasonable delivery dates, a situation that could not be corrected by a currency devaluation.[52] Indeed, it was argued that, under the circumstances, a currency devaluation could only lead to a deterioration in the terms of trade without any of the attending benefits.

The fact, if indeed it is a fact, that Britain's costs did not rise relatively to American costs (based on prewar years) is not particularly relevant in considering the need for a currency devaluation in the circumstances which prevailed in postwar Britain. Given the severe deterioration of the terms

---

[50] Britain was subject to a loss of gold and dollars to third countries through the operation of the sterling area dollar pool and through the implementation of the monetary agreements.

[51] Cf. Harrod, *Pound Sterling,* p. 27.

[52] Hawtrey, *Balance of Payments,* p. 101.

of trade, the loss of foreign investment income, the reduction in the real value of the gold reserves, and the other factors which impaired Britain's postwar international position, the purchasing power parity doctrine is a wholly inadequate guide to the need for a currency devaluation. The equilibrium rate of exchange must be defined with reference to the balance of payments, rather than with reference to cost-price relationships. More specifically, an equilibrium rate of exchange is defined as one which maintains over-all equilibrium on the balance of payments without aid from the compensatory account,[53] induced unemployment, or import restrictions levied for balance of payments purposes. By the same token, overvalued and undervalued exchange rates are defined as rates that do not succeed in maintaining over-all balance without inducing the changes discussed above. In the light of these definitions, it is manifest that even if the cost-price relationships were relatively favorable the pound was overvalued in 1949.[54]

It requires more than proof that the pound was overvalued, however, to justify the 1949 devaluation. It was noted above that though sterling was overvalued in 1947, it is improbable that a devaluation at that time would have improved Britain's dollar balance. Hawtrey has argued that this conclusion is true for 1949 as well. The evidence, however, does not appear to substantiate this argument. In 1949 the inflationary pressures were receding and the seller's market was being replaced by a buyer's market. Moreover, the appearance of "frustrated exports" on the British domestic market suggests that the elasticity of supply of exports was positive and that price considerations were once again important determinants of the level of exports. The huge expansion in the volume of exports to the United States following the devaluation [55] is a substantial refutation of the view that the British economy was unable to expand the volume of

[53] For convenience's sake the balance of payments can be subdivided into three accounts: the trade account, the capital account, and the compensatory or equilibrating account. The movements on the compensatory account (gold movements and *induced* short-term capital movements) result from a disequilibrium on the trade and capital accounts.

[54] The relatively favorable outcome on current account in 1948 (– 80 million pounds) and in 1949 (– 6 million pounds) was achieved only because of heavy import restrictions. Moreover, when currencies are inconvertible an equilibrium rate of exchange would presumably have to result in not only an over-all balance but an equilibrium vis-à-vis each of the major currency areas.

[55] The volume of exports to the United States expanded by 62 percent between 1949 and 1950 and by 39 percent between 1948 and 1950. Adler, *Pattern of United States Import Trade,* p. 136.

exports.[56]   It should not be inferred, however, that this expansion was
due wholly or even predominantly to the devaluation.[57]

The 1949 devaluation was justifiable on other grounds as well.   The
inflation for the overseas members of the sterling area, fed in large part
by ambitious investment schemes and aided and abetted by huge capital
outflows from the United Kingdom,[58] resulted in an absorption by these
countries of an increasing proportion of British exports.   Between 1946
and 1949 the share of British exports sold to the rest of the sterling area
increased from 45 to 52 percent.   The relative profitability of selling to
the rest of the sterling area undoubtedly contributed to this development.[59]
A pound devaluation vis-à-vis the dollar, but not vis-à-vis the currencies
of other sterling area countries, would thus have increased the relative
profitability of the dollar area and facilitated the transfer of exports from
the rest of the sterling area to it.   It must be emphasized, however, that it
would be erroneous to exaggerate this effect.   It is noted below that there
is reason to believe that a large portion of the British exports to the less
developed parts of the sterling area could not have been sold in the dollar
market.   Nor could the resources used in the production of these exports
be transferred on short notice to industries producing for the dollar market.
Nevertheless, the devaluation would have set the stage for a process which
ultimately had to be effected.

The existence of strong speculative pressures against the pound in
1949 was still another factor which made the devaluation imperative.   It
does not matter whether these pressures were a reflection of "real" factors
or are to be attributed, to quote Harrod, "to some low browed international
banker, swirling the brandy around his glass [uttering] his profound thought
that he did not believe the pound is worth four dollars. . . ." [60]   The in-
controvertible [61] fact is that these pressures existed, were strong, and necessitated drastic action.   Under the circumstances it is believed that devaluation, bitter as it was, was the best alternative.

[56] The volume of total exports increased by 28 percent between 1948 and 1950
and by 15 percent between 1949 and 1950. *Board of Trade Journal.*

[57] See below, p. 107.   [58] See below, p. 108.

[59] The president of the Board of Trade was quoted as having said three months
after the devaluation that some sellers "permitted dollar buyers . . . to return without
placing orders, with no more excuse than that our order books were full, and that
it was easy to sell in other markets." *The Times,* London, December 9, 1949.

[60] Harrod, *Pound Sterling,* p. 28.

[61] The existence of speculative pressures against the pound is evidenced by the
large capital outflows, and by the existence of cheap sterling which resulted in shunting operations and a withholding of orders for sterling area exports.   See S. Katz,
"Leads and Lags in Sterling Payments," *Journal of Political Economy,* February, 1953.

Finally, the sterling devaluation could have alleviated Britain's difficulties by improving her competitive position in third countries to which Britain made substantial dollar payments in 1948 and 1949.[62]   Many observers believed that this was the most promising form of relief offered by the devaluation.   The Economic Commission for Europe, for example, felt that "in general . . . the opportunities for reducing the dollar deficits through the expansion of exports . . . are rather better, at least in the short run, in third countries than they are directly in the United States." [63] The empirical evidence, based on the interwar period, suggests a rather high elasticity of substitution of British for American exports.   Mac-Dougall found that, in the interwar period, a 1 percent decline in the British export price level relative to the American was associated with a 3 percent increase in the volume of British exports to third countries.[64]

The importance of the devaluation on Britain's exports is difficult to gauge.   Though the volume of exports to North America increased by 80 percent between 1949 and 1950 and by 50 percent between 1948 and 1950,[65] many other factors were operating to effect this result.   The recovery of industrial production in the United States, the outbreak of the Korean War, and the removal of the uncertainty concerning the future of sterling were among the most important of these.   It is probable that the first two factors would have effected an increase in the volume of British exports to North America even had the devaluation not occurred.   Likewise, the increase in the volume of exports to Western European countries following the devaluation, an increase that contributed to the elimination of gold payments to these countries in 1950, can be ascribed, in large part, to the liberalization of trade undertaken as part of the second intra-European payments agreement.[66]

The deterioration of Britain's payments position in 1951 brought demands in some circles for a further devaluation of the pound.   The 1951

[62] See Table 1.

[63] ECE, *Economic Bulletin for Europe,* Second Quarter, 1949, Vol. 1, No. 2, p. 26.

[64] MacDougall, "British and American Exports: A Study Suggested by the Theory of Comparative Costs," Part II, *Economic Journal,* September, 1952, p. 495.   Also see Chang, *Cyclical Movements,* chap. 4, for a much less optimistic conclusion.

[65] ECE, *Economic Survey of Europe in 1950,* p. 94.

[66] For an analysis of the influence of the various factors operating after the devaluation to improve Britain's balance of payments see Polak, "Contributions of the September 1949 Devaluations to the Solution of Europe's Dollar Problem," *I.M.F. Staff Papers,* September, 1951, and Kent, "Devaluation, One Year Later," *Lloyds Bank Review,* October, 1950.

situation was basically similar to that of the early postwar period: the accelerated defense program imposed severe strains on the British economy,[67] and it is debatable whether devaluation would have succeeded in inducing a larger volume of exports. The volume of exports was limited, for the most part, by the shortage of goods rather than by the inability to sell. Even in the case of textiles where, with the revival of production in the Far East, Britain was experiencing difficulties, it is doubtful whether a devaluation within a practical range could have offered relief. Resort to devaluation as a mechanism of adjustment should be limited to those cases in which, despite large export availabilities, actual exports are inhibited by the existence of an uncompetitive price level. It should not be used in circumstances characterized by "extreme rigidities in export availabilities" when "no relief for the payments position could conceivably result from such a move." [68]

The existence of extreme rigidities in export availabilities in 1951 led some economists to urge an appreciation of the pound. Harrod, for example, argued that an appreciation would not only improve the terms of trade but would result in a more favorable balance of payments. Although Britain might have reaped some short-term gains had she appreciated the pound in 1951, the government elected not to pursue this policy. The collapse of primary product prices and the emergence of the third great postwar payments crisis in late 1951 and early 1952 rendered talk of an appreciation academic. Though it could not possibly have been known at the time, subsequent developments justified the government's refusal to revalue the pound upward.

British Exports to the Dollar Area and Sterling Balance Releases and Other Capital Outflows, 1946–51. The heavy release of sterling balances and other capital outflows to the overseas members of the sterling area and to other soft currency countries were important factors influencing the allocation of British exports in the postwar period. These capital outflows enabled the soft currency countries to demand a larger volume of exports from the United Kingdom than would otherwise have been possible and thus inhibited an expansion of exports to the dollar area.

On December 31, 1945, Britain's sterling liabilities amounted to 3,695 million pounds. The Anglo-American Financial Agreement suggested that these balances be treated in three ways: part was to be canceled; part

---

[67] Shortages of coal and steel were especially acute.
[68] ECE, *Economic Survey of Europe in 1951*, p. 85.

to be blocked; and part to be released, subject to the same provisions covering newly earned sterling. The agreement indicated a reasonable rate of release by stipulating that releases up to 43.75 million pounds per annum could be regarded as current expenditure in computing Britain's foreign exchange requirements under the interest waiver clause.

Negotiations leading to the cancellation of the sterling balances proved futile in all but two cases.[69] The creditors argued that their own living standards were still considerably below even the reduced standard of the United Kingdom. The British argument that the debts were incurred mainly in defending the creditors against invasion fell on deaf ears. The creditors, like the Americans in 1945, found "a post mortem on relative services and sacrifices . . . extremely distasteful and dissatisfying." [70]

With some important exceptions, the British did not attempt to block any part of the sterling balances until after the convertibility crisis. Thereafter they entered into agreements with some of their major creditors [71] whereby part of the sterling balances was to be blocked in number two accounts and part, to be available for current expenditure in accordance with the prevailing monetary agreements, in number one accounts. All currently earned sterling as well as sterling releases were to be credited to the number one accounts. In addition the agreements negotiated with some sterling area creditors stipulated the amount of sterling to be released throughout the duration of the accord. This aspect of the agreements was honored more in the breach than in the observance.[72] With the older dominion creditors the United Kingdom relied on less formal agreements to regulate the utilization of the balances.

Between December 31, 1945, and December 31, 1951, the sterling balances of the overseas sterling area increased by 331 million pounds. This increase in Britain's liabilities to the overseas sterling area countries should not obscure the fact that sterling releases to specific countries contributed to Britain's difficulties during this period. For while some ster-

[69] Australia and New Zealand scaled down their balances by 26 million pounds.

[70] Keynes, "Speech before the House of Lords on December 18, 1945," reprinted in Harris, *New Economics,* p. 383.

[71] Number two accounts were ultimately established for Argentina, Brazil, Ceylon, Egypt, India and Pakistan, Iraq, Palestine, Sweden, and Uruguay.

[72] In 1948–49, for example, agreed sterling releases to Ceylon amounted to 3.5 million pounds while actual releases amounted to 7.5 million. India reduced her balances by 130 million pounds despite an agreement that India would receive no sterling releases in that period. Pakistan likewise reduced her balances by 27 million pounds despite an agreed release of 12 million pounds. See *The Economist,* September 3, 1949, p. 516.

ling area countries were adding to their balances, others were drawing them down at a rapid rate. The independent sterling area countries as a whole drew down their balances by 183 million pounds. The dependencies, on the other hand, increased their sterling balances by 514 million pounds. Even these figures do not suggest the burden of the sterling releases on Britain, for among the independent sterling area countries were some who were particularly heavy drawers. Although official data is not available, it is estimated that India and Pakistan reduced their balances by 400 million pounds, and Iraq reduced her balances by an additional 20 million pounds. Australia was the only independent sterling area country whose balances increased substantially. Moreover, this increase, which amounted to approximately 250 million pounds, was not due to current account surpluses (as was the case with the dependencies) but, rather, to the large influx of capital from the United Kingdom. Were it not for this capital inflow, Australia would undoubtedly have been, like India and Pakistan, a heavy drawer on the sterling balances.

The release of sterling balances was but one form of capital export from the United Kingdom to the rest of the sterling area in the postwar period. The British conceived of the sterling area as one "within which exchange control does not operate," [73] with the result that capital outflows, for any purpose, were virtually unimpeded.[74] These capital exports, as the accompanying table shows, played a significant role in helping the rest of the sterling area finance its postwar deficits.

Examination of the accompanying table reveals that despite a 1,222 million pound current account deficit incurred with the United Kingdom and a 226 million pound deficit incurred with the dollar area, the sterling balances of the rest of the sterling area increased by 331 million pounds between 1946 and 1951. This increase is attributable to the 467 million pound gold sale to the United Kingdom, the 299 million pound surplus the rest of the sterling area earned from non-dollar countries, and the 1,014 million pound capital influx from the United Kingdom.[75]

In addition to the net outflow of capital to the rest of the sterling area,

[73] Dalton in Hansard, V, 443, c. 1536.

[74] The United Kingdom maintained some control through the Capital Issues Committee which had to approve all new issues.

[75] The largest recipients of capital from the United Kingdom were the Union of South Africa (approximately 460 million pounds), Australia (approximately 465 millions pounds), and Southern Rhodesia, Palestine, and Iraq (111 million pounds). There appears to have been a net inflow from India during the postwar period equal to 100 million pounds. ECE, *Economic Survey of Europe in 1951*, p. 115.

TABLE 30

FINANCING OF BALANCE OF PAYMENTS DEFICITS IN THE
REST OF THE STERLING AREA [a]

(*In millions of pounds*)

	1946	1947	1948	1949	1950	1951	Total
Debits							
Independent sterling area dollar deficit	− 106	− 316	− 116	− 112	+ 24	− 62	− 688
RSA deficit with U.K.	28	− 127	− 254	− 293	− 270	− 306	− 1222
Total	− 78	− 443	− 370	− 405	− 246	− 368	− 1910
Credits							
Dependent sterling area dollar surplus	33	10	51	58	145	165	462
RSA gold sales to U.K.	82	84	55	68	100	78	467
RSA surplus with non-dollar countries [b]	− 8	− 89	152	− 12	214	42	299
Total credits	107	5	258	114	459	285	1228
Balance	29	− 438	− 112	− 291	213	− 84	− 683
Financed by							
Capital imports (+) from U.K.	− 63	307	180	279	168	143	1014
Reduction (+) of sterling balances	34	131	− 68	12	− 381	− 59	− 331
Total finance provided by U.K.	− 29	438	112	291	− 213	84	683

[a] This table shows portion of the RSA deficits financed through London.

[b] Exclusive of deficits incurred with the U.K. which are shown separately. This item is a residual.

Source: Derived from *United Kingdom Balance of Payments, 1946–1953*, Cmd. 8976.

the sterling balances of the non-dollar, non-sterling countries suffered a net reduction of 214 million pounds during 1946 and 1951 and capital outflows to these countries amounted to 155 million pounds.[76] This capital export enabled these countries to exercise a larger demand for sterling area goods than otherwise would have been possible. It is sometimes argued because a significant portion of this capital export was spent initially in the rest of the sterling area it had no effect on British exports. This view, however, is faulty; it overlooks the fact that the expenditure of sterling in the rest of the sterling area enabled those areas to exercise a larger demand for British goods.

Net capital outflows, including net changes in the sterling balances, to the non-dollar world amounted to approximately 1,052 million pounds between 1946 and 1951. While this represented but 12 percent of the total British exports to the non-dollar area, in particular years capital ex-

[76] Derived from *United Kingdom Balance of Payments, 1946–1953*, Cmd. 8976.

ports were much more significant. In 1947 and 1949, for example, net capital exports were large enough to finance approximately 50 percent and 20 percent respectively of total British exports to the non-dollar world.[77]

There can be little doubt that the large capital exports to the non-dollar countries in the postwar period intensified Britain's dollar difficulties by enabling a diversion of exports from the hard to the soft currency countries. This was particularly true in the early postwar period, when the rigidities of the export availabilities were especially strong. It is dangerous, however, to overemphasize this point. It must be recognized that a large portion of the exports sold in the underdeveloped parts of the sterling area could not be diverted to the dollar markets. Nor, in many cases, could the resources used in the production of exports for the underdeveloped areas be transferred, at short notice, to the production of goods for which a market existed in the dollar countries. A reduction or cessation of the capital exports to the underdeveloped parts of the rest of the sterling area would have thus reduced the value of "unrequited exports" but would not necessarily have increased the value of exports to the dollar countries by the same amount.[78]

Against the charge that capital exports, especially in the form of sterling releases, were excessive, the government argued that it was erroneous to regard unrequited exports as an unmitigated evil since these exports from the United Kingdom to the rest of the sterling area tended to reduce the need of the rest of the sterling area for dollar goods and hence the drain on the sterling area's reserves. Moreover, the government argued that the sterling releases aided in the reconstruction of the economies of the rest of the sterling area and thus were a positive step in the direction of a solution of the dollar shortage. Finally, the government contended that Britain did not have the moral right to deprive the sterling area countries of their freedom to draw upon the sterling balances which were, in the last analysis, debts owed to them by the United Kingdom, and that unless they were permitted to use these balances as required they would be reluctant, in periods of surplus, to contribute their exchange earnings to the hard currency pool.

[77] Derived from Cmd. 8976. It should be noted that despite the heavy outflow of capital, Britain was a net borrower during this period. Loans and disinvestments in the dollar area and in other Western Hemisphere countries amounted to 1,517 million pounds between 1946 and 1951.

[78] There is evidence to suggest that the government was reluctant to curb the sterling release for fear that this would induce unemployment in the export industries. Cf. The Economist, September 3, 1949, p. 515.

[79] See the Statement by D. Jay, Parliamentary Secretary to the Treasury, in Hansard, V, 448, c. 207.

While it would be difficult to deny that there was some validity in the government's defense, it is still more difficult to accept it completely. The argument that the less liberal release of sterling balances would have jeopardized the dollar pool arrangements is unsound in so far as the recipients of the largest releases drew on rather than contributed to the dollar pool.[80] It is also debatable whether the United Kingdom did not have the moral right to restrain the more improvident members of the rest of the sterling area, in view of the fact that she was the banker of the whole sterling area and not just for parts. Likewise, though some capital exports to the rest of the sterling area contributed toward the reconstruction of their economies, thus representing positive steps toward the correction of the dollar problem, this was by no means true of all capital exports.[81] Finally, the huge capital exports from the United Kingdom to the rest of the sterling area fed inflation in these areas and induced a larger volume of imports, not only from the United Kingdom, but from the hard currency areas as well.[82]

It would appear that the liberal release of sterling balances and the unrestricted outflow of capital to the rest of the sterling area contributed to Britain's postwar dollar difficulties. Less liberal releases and restriction of capital exports to only those contributing to the reconstruction of the economies of the recipient countries might have enabled the United Kingdom to divert part of her exports to the hard currency areas. It must be emphasized again, however, that it would be wrong to believe that every pound's worth of unrequited exports reduced the dollar exports by the same amount. The type of export the United Kingdom sold in many parts of the rest of the sterling area required resources somewhat different from those needed to produce for the dollar area.

The huge capital exports from the United Kingdom to the soft currency area contributed to Britain's difficulties in a more subtle and yet more

---

[80] The largest recipients of sterling releases were India and Pakistan, Egypt, and Palestine. Between 1946 and June, 1952, Egypt, not a member of the sterling area, received 214 million pounds, Palestine, 112 million pounds, and India and Pakistan 511 million pounds. The figure for India and Pakistan is exclusive of the sterling releases used to purchase annuities and defense stores. ECE, *Europe Since the War*, p. 115, and Bank for International Settlements, *Sterling Area*, p. 72.

[81] A good deal of the capital outflow to Australia, for example, consisted of "funk" capital.

[82] This was especially true of the capital outflow to the Union of South Africa. Hot-money flows to Australia do not appear to have had much effect on Australia's imports.

basic way. By increasing the resources at the disposal of the soft currency areas and therefore their ability to command British goods, the capital exports impeded basic adjustments that had to be made in the British economy. The soft currency areas, unable to obtain from the United Kingdom all the capital goods they desperately wanted, still drew down their balances to purchase consumer goods and thus increased the profitability of these industries. This development was not in the long-run interest of Britain. In the first place the resulting prosperity in the consumer goods industries was artificial in that its continuance depended upon the continued release, at the same rate, of the sterling balances.[83] Second, and more important, it impeded the transfer of resources from the production of consumer goods to the production of capital goods, a transfer that, given the shifts in international demand discussed above, Britain ultimately had to effect. The capital exports in the postwar period must bear part of the responsibility for the still relatively high proportion consumer goods exports bore to total British exports.

One further point should be noted. Normally, the ability to export capital signifies that savings in the capital exporting country exceeds the level of investment. This, however, was not true of Britain in the postwar period. What capital Britain succeeded in exporting was derived largely from the dollar area in the form of loans and grants and to a smaller extent from the dependent sterling area countries which earned surpluses which they invested in Britain. In short, a large part of the aid which Britain obtained from the United States and Canada was, contrary to the agreements with the North American countries, passed on to the overseas sterling area countries. The significance of the failure of the British economy to generate savings in excess of domestic investment is discussed below.

British Dollar Exports and the Increase in the Degree of American Self-Sufficiency. The increase in the degree of American self-sufficiency between the pre- and postwar period was a factor impeding the expansion of exports to the United States. Between 1936–38 and 1951 the real product of the United States increased by 98 percent while the quantum of total imports increased by but 50 percent.[84] And though British ex-

---

[83] Cripps admitted that one of the desirable aspects of the huge capital releases was that they enabled the United Kingdom to cement trade relationships that would stand Britain in good stead when the buyers' market replaced the sellers' market. It is highly debatable whether, in the long run, this could be considered desirable if the result was to impede the transfer of resources from the consumer to the capital goods industries. Cf. Cripps' remarks in Hansard, V, 448, c. 207.

[84] Council of Economic Advisers, *The Midyear Economic Review* (1952), Tables B2 and B45.

ports to the United States fared somewhat better than total exports to the United States, the increase in the volume of imports the United States derived from the United Kingdom was still considerably below the increase in American real product.

Several factors combined to effect a greater degree of American self-sufficiency in the postwar period than in the prewar period. Two of the most important were the desire, for security reasons, to reduce dependence on foreign sources of supply and the remarkable growth of American production and productivity since the outbreak of the war.[85] Had American dependence on foreign sources not declined during the war years, the large increase in the value of imports induced by the growth of American income would have made a significant contribution toward mitigating the dollar problem.

The Level of Industrial Activity in the Dollar Area and British Dollar Exports. The level of industrial activity in the United States is obviously an important factor influencing the volume and value of British dollar exports. It is noted below [86] that the fear that the United States economy is basically unstable was one of the major arguments advanced in Britain against joining a multilateral trade and payments structure in which the United States would play a dominant role. This fear was born out of the experience of the 1930s when declines in the level of industrial activity in the United States were transmitted to other countries via declines in the volume and value of American imports. Moreover, the British economy is particularly sensitive to fluctuations in the level of American industrial activities since a relatively large proportion of her total exports is accounted for by capital goods and luxury consumer goods. The significance of variations in the level of American activity as a factor influencing British exports to the United States is indicated by the fact that the slight inventory recession of 1948–49 was accompanied by a 15 percent decline in the volume of imports the United States derived from the United Kingdom.[87]

It has been argued [88] that the exporters of manufactures to the United States are likely to suffer whether America succeeds in maintaining full employment or not. Should the United States suffer a depression, manufactured imports, characterized by a high income elasticity, will suffer a

[85] See below, p. 206 ff.   [86] See below, p. 202 ff.

[87] Adler, *Pattern of United States Import Trade,* p. 136. It should be noted, however, that the total decline in dollar exports cannot be ascribed to the American recession. See above, p. 101.

[88] Cf. Balogh, "The United States in the World Economy," *Bulletin of the Oxford University Institute of Statistics,* October, 1946, p. 321.

severe decline. The maintenance of full employment, however, is contingent upon a high level of investment which, through the associated gains in productivity, will improve the competitive position of the domestic producers.

This argument is examined in detail below,[89] and it need only be said that the argument is valid if the growth of American productivity is assumed to occur in the import-substitute industries and if this growth of productivity is not associated with an equivalent expansion in money incomes. If, however, money income rises *pari passu* with the increase in productivity, the suppliers of manufactures to the American market need not suffer. Salant has suggested that this is a major reason "why we should take our secular increase of productivity in the form of rising money incomes and stable prices" rather than in the form of "stable money incomes and declining prices." [90]

American Tariffs and Other Impediments to Imports. It is sometimes argued that desirable as tariff reductions are in principle, it would be erroneous to place too much reliance on this method as a corrective for the dollar shortage. *The Economist,* for example, argued that the large tariff reductions since the inception of the Reciprocal Trade Agreements have had very little effect on the volume of American imports.[91] This argument overlooks the very important fact that American tariff reductions under the Reciprocal Trade Agreements were extremely selective and were designed, for the most part, "to minimize the adverse effect upon domestic producers." [92] This is underlined by the fact that despite the rather large tariff reductions since 1935, the average tariff on Britain's leading manufactured exports to the United States was still 35 percent in 1952.[93]

A tariff reduction will result in an increase in the value of imports if it is applied to those commodities for which American price elasticities of demand are greater than unity. In the light of the recent empirical studies, which show that the American price elasticity of demand for British exports in the interwar period was extremely high,[94] it is reasonable to assume that a sufficiently large tariff reduction, applied in a nonselective

[89] See below, p. 206.

[90] Salant, "The Domestic Effects of Capital Export Under the Point Four Program," *American Economic Review, Papers and Proceedings,* May, 1950, p. 599.

[91] *The Economist,* November 22, 1952, p. 582-3.

[92] Adler, *Pattern of United States Imports,* p. 53.

[93] News of the Week Section, *The New York Times,* May 17, 1953, p. 6.

[94] See above, p. 103.

manner would ultimately result in a rather substantial increase in the volume of American imports derived from the United Kingdom.[95]

Frequently, archaic customs regulations, restrictions such as the Buy American Act, quotas, and other barriers to imports are more significant impediments to an expansion of American imports than tariffs. It is difficult to estimate the value of imports frustrated by these non-tariff barriers. Postwar case studies [96] have demonstrated beyond doubt, however, that these obstacles are significant and that their removal is likely to lead to a substantial expansion of American imports.

While there is a clear case for a reduction of American tariffs and a simplification of American customs procedures, it is not probable that these actions alone will suffice to solve the dollar problem. The solution of Britain's dollar shortage must be sought elsewhere than in attempts to achieve a bilateral balancing of Anglo-American trade through the expansion of Britain's dollar exports.

In this section several factors, of varying degrees of importance, that influenced the expansion of British exports to the dollar area in the postwar period were examined. These factors were, individually and collectively, much less significant as far as Britain's dollar problem was concerned than the precipitous rise in the price level of American exports. Since many of the factors discussed in this section are subject to control, a knowledge of the manner in which they might have impeded adjustment in the postwar period is extremely useful.

THE DETERIORATION OF BRITAIN'S DOLLAR INVISIBLE ACCOUNTS

Reference to Table 22 reveals that the deterioration of Britain's invisible dollar accounts between the pre- and postwar periods was an important factor responsible for the increase in Britain's dollar current account deficit. Indeed, the deterioration on invisible account was responsible for 30 percent of the total deterioration on current account between 1938 and 1947, and for slightly more than 60 percent between 1938 and 1949 and 1938 and 1951.

During the last stages of the war and in the early postwar period it was widely believed that the anticipated loss of earnings on shipping and income accounts was likely to prove the most troublesome factor in the post-

[95] See Report of the ECA, *Commerce Mission,* October, 1949.

[96] *Ibid.,* appendixes J, K, L, M, N, O, P, and Q, for case studies of the effects of American tariff administrative procedures on restricting American imports.

war period as far as Britain's balance of payments was concerned. In the event, the rather rapid reconstruction of the British merchant marine and the increase in the rate of return on the remaining dollar assets prevented as great a dollar loss on these accounts as was expected.[97] The most important factor responsible for the deterioration of the invisible dollar balance was the large drain of dollars for overseas transactions of Britain's oil companies, which, according to Britain's postwar balance of payments procedures, are shown on the invisible accounts. In the early postwar years (1946–47) the heavy dollar expenditure on government account was also responsible for the unfavorable outturn on invisible accounts. This was all but stopped, however, following the introduction of retrenchment policies after the convertibility crisis.

It is not possible with currently available information to make a detailed comparison of the "traditional" items in Britain's dollar invisible accounts in the prewar and postwar periods. An unofficial estimate of Britain's invisible accounts with the United States in 1937 does offer an opportunity for a limited comparison, however. The relevant data are shown in the accompanying table.

TABLE 31

BRITAIN'S INVISIBLE ACCOUNT WITH THE UNITED STATES,
1937 AND 1948–51

(*In millions of U.S. dollars*)

	1937	1948	1949	1950	1951
Freight and shipping	34	− 72	21	26	5
Interest and dividends	50	32	56	107	− 42
Other invisibles	69		21	69	98
Total	153	− 40	98	202	61

Sources: Prewar data from *The Economist Supplement,* November 26, 1938, p. 1. Postwar data from Department of Commerce, *Survey of Current Business.*

It is apparent from the table that though there was a marked improvement in the shipping account, dollar earnings on this account, even in the best postwar years, failed to reach the prewar level and were substantially below, measured in real terms. The losses suffered by Britain's merchant marine during the war constitute only one reason for this deterioration of her dollar shipping account. The American policy of subsidizing merchant shipping and the requirement that at least 50 percent of Marshall aid be

[97] The deterioration of the income and shipping accounts was important as far as Britain's over-all balance of payments was concerned.

shipped in American bottoms were undoubtedly also important factors responsible for the deterioration.

The outturn on income account in the postwar period was satisfactory until 1951 when the first interest payment on the postwar American credit was made. The increase in the yields on the remaining British dollar assets in the postwar period precluded the decline in earnings on income account that otherwise would have occurred. As a result, the earnings on income account in 1949 were substantially the same as those in 1937, measured in monetary terms, while the earnings on income account in 1950 were twice those of 1937. It need hardly be added, however, that measured in terms of dollar imports, the earnings on income account in both these years were still below the prewar level.

The absence of detailed information concerning the traditional items subsumed under "other" invisibles for the prewar period makes it impossible to meaningfully compare these items with those of the postwar period. The table reveals, however, that these earnings, in monetary terms, were as large in 1950 as in 1937 and were somewhat greater in 1951 than in the prewar year. The real value of these earnings, in terms of dollar imports, was somewhat less in the postwar period than in 1937.

Most responsible for the deterioration of Britain's invisible dollar account between the pre- and postwar periods was the drain of dollars resulting from the overseas transactions of the oil companies. It is not possible to estimate the precise dollar drain due to these transactions, although the "other" [98] item in Britain's invisible accounts (including, in addition to the net transactions of the overseas oil companies, insurance, civil aviation, royalties, commissions, and so forth) gives some indication of its size.[99]

The drain of dollars resulting from the overseas transactions of the oil companies is attributable to the dollar payments which these companies must make for services rendered both by Americans and non-Americans. Some of the more important dollar payments which the overseas oil companies were obliged to make were for royalties or taxes to the governments granting the concessions, the purchase of local currencies which frequently had to be paid for in dollars, payments for American patents, and fees for American operated tankers. The heavy drain of dollars on oil account was thus a reflection, in part, of the dominant position of American firms in the world petroleum industry.

[98] This is not to be confused with the "other item" shown in Table 31 which consists of traditional invisible items.

[99] Britain's dollar deficit on "other" account amounted to $968 in 1946–51. Most of this deficit is attributable to the overseas transactions of the oil companies.

SUMMARY AND CONCLUSIONS

The two factors exercising the most important influence on the deterioration of Britain's current dollar accounts between the pre- and postwar periods were the precipitous rise in the American export price level and the dominant position of American firms in the world petroleum industry. The former was largely responsible for the drastic rise in the value of imports from the dollar area which occurred despite the reduction in the volume of imports. The latter was responsible for a heavy drain of dollars for overseas transactions of the oil companies and was the most important reason for the deterioration of Britain's invisible dollar accounts between the pre- and postwar periods.

It is difficult to exaggerate the importance of this conclusion. It emphasizes the fact that the sterling area's postwar dollar shortage, in so far as it was due to the deterioration of Britain's direct dollar current account, was the resultant of basic changes in the structure of the world economy rather than to the pursuit of fatuous policies on either or both sides of the Atlantic or to fortuitous adverse developments in the postwar period, as many economists concerned with the dollar problem have contended. This is not to deny, of course, that the pursuit of inappropriate policies and transitory adverse developments contributed to Britain's difficulties. On the contrary, the analysis in this chapter suggests that the liberal releases of sterling balances, the continuing of high tariff barriers, the antiquated American customs procedures, and the American inventory recession of 1948–49 did tend to inhibit the expansion of British exports to the dollar area. Nevertheless, when the factors responsible for the deterioration of Britain's dollar current account between the prewar and postwar periods are put in proper perspective, it becomes apparent that those that are subject to some degree of control were of much less significance than the more basic underlying ones discussed above.

VI   *The Rest of the Sterling Area and the Dollar Problem, 1946-51*

IN THE INTERWAR PERIOD Britain's direct current account dollar deficit was more than offset by her indirect dollar earnings from those countries that in the postwar period constituted the sterling area.   The deterioration of dollar current accounts between the pre- and postwar periods need not have resulted in a dollar shortage had Britain's dollar earnings from these countries increased *pari passu*.   As was indicated in the introduction to this study, in 1947, 1948, and 1949 the countries of the rest of the sterling area incurred heavy dollar deficits on their own accounts and in only one year, 1950, were their dollar earnings, including newly mined gold, sufficiently large to offset Britain's direct *current* account dollar deficit.   Before examining the factors responsible for this, it is necessary to review briefly some salient features of the sterling area.

THE STERLING AREA

The sterling area as it was constituted in the postwar period was an outgrowth of wartime developments and was in many fundamental respects quite different from the arrangements that existed in the prewar period when different countries, for one reason or another, found it advantageous to hold their international reserves in sterling balances, to maintain their currencies in a fixed relationship with the pound sterling, and to use London's banking facilities to discharge obligations incurred on international accounts.   The basic differences between the prewar and postwar sterling area arrangements are most clearly discerned by examining briefly the two structures.

The origins of the sterling area are to be found in the nineteenth century when, because of the dominant position of the United Kingdom in the world economy, many countries elected to hold their reserves in the form of sterling rather than in the form of gold.   This practice was so widespread that many economists frequently refer to the nineteenth century gold standard as a sterling standard.   Indeed, throughout the greater portion of the nineteenth century, sterling was more frequently used as an international currency than gold. Various reasons can explain the importance of sterling as an international currency in the nineteenth century: the dominant role played by the United Kingdom as an importer and an international lender, which mitigated the possibility of a sterling shortage; the strong inducement many countries had to accumulate sterling to service and repay their sterling loans; Britain's leading position as an exporter of manufactures; the safety of holding sterling, resulting from the relative stability of the English price level; and the full and free convertibility of sterling into gold, and hence other foreign currencies, throughout the entire period. It is not at all surprising that sterling, of all currencies, should be elevated to a position of equality with gold.

It was not until 1931, when Britain abandoned the gold standard, that countries which had hitherto kept their reserves in the form of sterling were compelled to make a choice concerning the standard to which they wished to adhere. The Commonwealth countries, with the important exception of Canada, decided to follow Britain's lead and maintain their currencies in a fixed [1] relationship with sterling. Some non-Commonwealth nations also joined what was to become known as the sterling bloc.[2]

Among the various motives that prompted these countries to follow Britain's lead were the strong political ties that bound together the members of the Commonwealth, the dominant position occupied by the United Kingdom in the trade of some of these countries, the desire of many countries to protect their competitive position in the British market, and the relative stability of the British economy as compared with that of the United States.

The outstanding feature of the sterling bloc was that it was a voluntary association of countries that, following the dictates of self-interest, decided to hold their reserves in the form of sterling [3] and to maintain their currencies in a fixed relationship with the pound. There were no formal or informal "rules of the game"; sterling bloc countries were not required, for example, to hold specified proportions of their reserves in sterling [4] nor

---

[1] It should be noted that the rates of exchange were not fixed absolutely among the sterling bloc currencies. See League of Nations, *International Currency Experience,* chap. 3.

[2] Non-Commonwealth members included Egypt, the Sudan, Portugal, Scandinavia, the Baltic countries, Iran, Hungary, Greece, and Yugoslavia. In addition Argentina and Japan fixed their exchange rates in terms of sterling although they were not regarded as members.

[3] It should be noted that many sterling area countries also maintained part of their reserves in the form of gold. *Ibid.,* p. 55.

[4] *Ibid.,* p. 54 ff.

were they required to maintain their currencies in a fixed relationship with the pound. The relative stability of exchange rates that prevailed between 1931 and the outbreak of war in 1939 was due to the pursuit of self-interest by the various associated countries. Indeed, London did nothing to maintain this stability.[5] Membership in the sterling bloc, furthermore, did not per se entail obligations. Each participating country maintained full sovereignty over its currency and the United Kingdom exercised neither direct nor indirect controls over the economic, financial, and commercial decisions of the associated members.

This is not to imply that the United Kingdom did not attempt to make the sterling bloc attractive. On the contrary, Britain used several instruments to "bind the sterling area closer to herself." These instruments consisted of

the system of imperial preference embodied in the Ottawa Agreements, the reciprocal trade pacts with non-Empire countries, . . . the securing of favorable treatment under the Argentine system of exchange control, the development of central banking in the dominions, and the preferential treatment, in the matter of international loans, extended to the Dominions and to other countries within the sterling area.[6]

They were designed to increase the attractiveness of the sterling bloc, but were not inconsistent with the informal arrangements that characterized the association.

The outbreak of war in 1939 occasioned three major changes in the sterling area mechanism. First, the composition of the area was drastically modified as non-Commonwealth countries with the exception of Egypt, the Sudan, Iraq, Iceland, and the Faroe Islands severed connections with sterling. Second, the area obtained formal status as a result of the exchange control regulations which were promulgated shortly after the outbreak of the war. Finally, the area was transformed into an exchange control system. This modification was by far the most important and was largely responsible for the sharp difference between the prewar sterling bloc and the postwar sterling area.

The major function of the wartime sterling area was to aid in the mobilization of financial and economic resources in general and in the conservation of hard currency exchange in particular. The sterling area countries attempted to achieve these objectives in three ways: (a) the United King-

5 See Brown, *International Gold Standard*, p. 1165.

6 Stewart, "Instruments of British Policy in the Sterling Area," *Political Science Quarterly*, June, 1937, p. 175.

dom and the rest of the sterling area issued exchange control regulations designed to prevent unauthorized monetary flows from sterling to non-sterling countries while maintaining the maximum degree of freedom within the area; (b) sterling area countries tacitly agreed to accumulate sterling balances rather than demand immediate payment for goods and services exported to the United Kingdom; (c) a hard currency pool was established to conserve scarce reserves and to ensure their utilization in a manner best calculated to serve the war effort.

The establishment of the hard currency pool represented a sharp break with prewar practices, for though members of the sterling bloc customarily converted their excess foreign exchange earnings and newly mined gold into sterling, there was no obligation to do so. Furthermore, the convenience of holding international reserves in the form of sterling did not imply discriminatory treatment in favor of sterling goods, and the full convertibility of sterling at the going rate of exchange assured that this result would not eventuate. Finally, sterling bloc countries were guided by the state of their individual reserves in framing their economic, financial, and commercial policies and not by the state of Britain's gold reserves, which was important to them only in that it reflected the soundness of Britain's position as an international banker. The contrary was true after the establishment of the central pool: sterling area countries were obliged to sell their hard currency earnings to London; discrimination against imports from hard currency sources and in favor of sterling goods was implicit in the operation of the central pool; [7] and sterling area countries were expected to frame their

[7] It was this feature of the dollar pool to which the Americans objected in the postwar period. Secretary of the Treasury Vinson described the operation of the dollar pool in the following manner: "The dollar pool is a wartime arrangement made by England to mobilize and conserve the dollar resources of all the countries of the sterling area. Under this arrangement, a country of the sterling area that secures a surplus of dollars from exports to the United States transfers the dollars to England for a sterling deposit in London. The dollars are allocated for essential purposes requiring payment in dollars. In practice dollars are not allocated for buying American goods which can be bought in England or anywhere in the sterling area. Some American exporters are, in effect, excluded from a large part of the world's markets. That is why we want the dollar pool brought to an end." (*Hearings before the House Committee on Banking and Currency,* 79th Congress, 2nd Session, V. 23, p. 4.)

Undersecretary of State Clayton emphasized the discriminatory aspects of the dollar pool in the following manner: "Applications [for dollars] are very critically examined from the point of view of trying to conserve all the dollars that may be in the pool for absolutely essential purchases in the United States which cannot be obtained anywhere else.

"In other words, if the applicant for dollars is able to purchase the goods or the

relevant economic policies in the light of the state of the central reserves rather than with reference to their individual sterling reserves.

The operation of the dollar pool during the war was, in principle, simple:

As a means of conserving exchange resources and to provide for their replenishment for essential war purposes, the members of the sterling area agreed to relinquish specified currencies, particularly dollars, to the pool in exchange for sterling. They also agreed to limit their demands on the pool for such currencies to amounts required for essential payments. This was reinforced by the general agreement to confine purchases outside the sterling area to items which could not be obtained within the area itself. In this system then, surpluses of dollars above the minimum requirements of the member countries accrued to the United Kingdom account.[8]

With some important modifications discussed below, the fundamental features of the wartime dollar pool were extended into the postwar period. The singleness of purpose which prevailed during the war was absent, however, and the structure was subject to severe strains and stresses. Chief among these was the manner in which the dollars were to be allocated. The heavy demand for dollars in the postwar period necessitated that restraint be practiced. This gave rise to dissatisfaction in many sterling area countries which felt that their share of dollars was not commensurate with the contributions they had made during the war period. Some countries demanded at the war's end that the dollar pool arrangements be terminated;[9] others that they be allowed to spend more dollars than the United Kingdom thought they should;[10] while still others wanted the privilege of retaining their dollar earnings to build up separate hard currency reserves.[11]

---

services in any part of the Empire for pound sterling, the application is denied, and they are required to make their purchases in pound sterling, almost without regard to price, quality, service, or what have you. In other words, the usual considerations when one goes to buy goods . . . are not given very much attention and the applicant, if he can get the commodity he wants in the British Empire for sterling, or something that is its equivalent, is required to do so." (*Ibid.*, p. 192.)

[8] U.S. Department of Commerce, *International Transactions of the United States During the War*, p. 113. Fn. 4. Also see *Federal Reserve Bulletin*, February, 1941, p. 99.

[9] India proposed the dissolution of the sterling area in 1946 when she was still a net dollar earner.

[10] Australia rejected Britain's plea to live within her own dollar earnings in 1948.

[11] It should be noted that the practice of holding separate reserves was not inconsistent with the spirit of the sterling area mechanism. In the interwar period many countries continued to hold some gold reserves in addition to the sterling reserves held in London. In the postwar period, South Africa, India, Australia, and Ceylon held independent gold or dollar reserves.

South Africa expressed her dissatisfaction by withdrawing from the pool at the end of 1947.

The principles adopted in the postwar period to govern the allocation of dollars from the pool underwent some important modifications. The need for restraint gave rise to the practice of negotiating agreements with some sterling area countries stipulating the amounts of hard currencies these countries could withdraw from the pool. The first agreements of this nature were negotiated with Egypt and Iraq immediately after the conclusion of the war. The severe drain on the reserves during the brief convertibility period led to an extension of this practice. Britain ultimately negotiated hard currency agreements with India, Pakistan, Burma, and Ceylon. In addition, an agreement of this kind appears to have been negotiated with Eire although it did not eventuate in a written accord.[12] With the older dominions, Australia and New Zealand, the United Kingdom continued to rely on informal gentlemen's agreements to govern withdrawals from the dollar pool.

The limitations imposed upon the newer dominions with respect to their rights to draw on the dollar pool violated the spirit of the sterling area and were not designed to foster the harmony necessary for the successful operation of the system. Recognition of this ultimately led to the abandonment of this practice; by late 1950 all sterling area countries were treated equally with respect to their rights to draw on the dollar pool.

A unique position was occupied by the Union of South Africa in that during the war she agreed to sell to the Bank of England all gold in excess of that retained by the Reserve Bank of South Africa,[13] with the proviso that annual gold sales would not fall below 80 million pounds. Immediately after the conclusion of the war the United Kingdom and the Union of South Africa entered into an agreement whereby the Union undertook to continue selling to the Bank of England 80 million pounds of gold per annum over a period of two years. These gold sales did not represent net contributions to the hard currency pool, however, as the Union was able to draw on the pool to meet her own hard currency obligations. Indeed, in 1946 and 1947 the Union, on balance, drew an amount equal to approximately 110 million dollars.

In November, 1947, a new agreement was negotiated covering the Union of South Africa's position in the dollar pool. Under the provisions of this agreement, the Union extended an 80 million pound gold loan to the

12 See *The Economist,* November 15, 1947.
13 The Reserve Bank of South Africa was building up an independent gold reserve during the war.

United Kingdom in lieu of the former obligation to sell gold to the Bank of England. In addition, the Union was deprived of the right to draw on the central pool. Henceforth, the Union would be responsible for her own hard currency obligations, although provisions were made that London would continue to act as international banker. This last provision meant simply that the Union would recompense the Bank of England in gold for any net payments in sterling or other currencies that the bank was called upon to make on the Union's account to foreigners. Under this provision, the Union sold to the Bank of England 78 million pounds of gold between January 1, 1948, the effective date of the accord, and March 31, 1949, at about which time the Union experienced a severe sterling shortage and requested the United Kingdom to repay the gold loan in sterling. Since the life of the Gold Loan Agreement was limited to the duration of the loan, repayment necessitated a new accord.

A new agreement was negotiated with the Union of South Africa in January, 1950, that provided for the revision of the Union of South Africa's import control mechanism by introducing "universal" import permits for "essential" imports. These permits were sold against gold which the Union agreed to use in purchasing from London any soft currencies required to obtain these "essential" imports. Thus as long as the "essential" imports were obtained from soft currency sources the United Kingdom was enabled to earn gold from the Union through the sale of the requisite soft currencies.[14]

It is evident even from this brief discussion of the Union of South Africa's position in the sterling area that it would not be correct in discussing the area's problems to assume that the Union was a full-fledged member. Nor would it be correct to ignore her completely. South Africa occupied a "half-way house" in the postwar period. Her dollar deficits did not eventuate in a direct drain on the reserves of the area as did the deficits of, for example, Australia and India. On the other hand, the larger the gold payments made by the Union to the dollar area or to other non-sterling countries, the less gold the United Kingdom and other sterling area countries could potentially earn from the Union. In view of the fact that the Union is the largest gold producer in the sterling area and that in the period under discussion she tended to discriminate in favor of sterling countries, it is evident that Britain and the rest of the sterling area had important stakes in South African developments.

Thus far attention was focussed on the modifications made in the post-

[14] See Franklin, "South Africa's Balance of Payments and the Sterling Area, 1939–1950," *Economic Journal*, June, 1951.

war period with respect to the operation of the dollar pool. It is also necessary to review briefly other aspects of the postwar sterling area machinery. It is noted below that the failure to develop adequate machinery to cope with the general sterling area problems was a factor responsible for the severity of the sterling area's postwar dollar shortage.

The sterling area is a typically British institution in the sense that it lacks a formal constitution or well-defined rules of action. In the postwar period it also lacked the rudimentary machinery necessary to coordinate the activities of the associated members. In the early postwar years, the only semblances of permanent sterling area machinery were the Sterling Area Statistical Committee, composed of representatives of all associated countries, and the Commonwealth Liaison Committee. The function of the former committee was to disseminate information concerning the balance of payments positions of the associated members, gold and dollar reserve position, and so forth. The function of the latter was to act as "a forum where policy matters can be discussed and general approval secured for decisions." Neither of these committees had real policy making functions, nor did they attempt to deal with the over-all problems facing the sterling area. The absence of effective policy making machinery necessitated resort to ad hoc conferences of high-level sterling area officials which were convened at irregular intervals to cope with specific sterling area problems as they arose.[15] While effective to a degree, this method of coping with problems was not conducive to the formulation of long-run plans and policies that were obviously required in the face of a persistent dollar problem. It is argued below that a more effective method of coordinating the policies of the associated sterling area countries would have mitigated somewhat the dollar shortage.

THE REST OF THE STERLING AREA AND THE POSTWAR DOLLAR DEFICIT

The rest of the sterling area (RSA) contributes to the dollar pool when it earns a surplus with the dollar area, or when it sells newly mined gold to the United Kingdom and earns a surplus of convertible or partially convertible currencies. It draws upon the dollar pool when it incurs a deficit with the dollar area or with countries which enjoy complete or partial con-

---

[15] The first high-level conference was convened immediately after the suspension of convertibility. Other conferences were held in July, 1949, to adopt concerted action in order to stay the drain on the reserves; in September, 1950, to allow for a relaxation of import restrictions in the light of favorable reserve developments; and in January, 1952, to deal with the crisis which resulted primarily from the collapse of primary product prices.

vertibility of sterling privileges.   While it is not possible with the currently available information to isolate the net contribution (drain) of the rest of the sterling area to the dollar pool as a result of surpluses (deficits) earned (incurred) in non-dollar convertible currencies, information is available concerning the rest of the sterling area's direct dollar deficits (surpluses) and gold sales to the United Kingdom.   The relevant information for the period between 1946–51 is shown in Table 32 which also includes, for reference, Britain's direct current account dollar deficit.

TABLE 32

ALLOCABLE CONTRIBUTIONS (DRAWINGS) OF THE REST OF THE STERLING AREA TO (FROM) THE DOLLAR POOL

(*In millions of dollars*)

	1938	1946	1947	1948	1949	1950	1951
Independent sterling area dollar deficit	– 80	– 427	– 1272	– 469	– 461	65	– 174
Dependent sterling area dollar surplus		134	40	206	202	408	462
RSA gold sales to the United Kingdom	550	334	342	222	234	281	
RSA contribution (+) to dollar pool	470	41	– 890	– 41	– 25	754	506
Britain's dollar deficit	– 442	– 1211	– 2059	– 1016	– 1093	– 224	– 1192

Sources: 1938 data from ECE, *Economic Bulletin for Europe,* Second Quarter, 1949, p. 14.   These data refer to the current account of the sterling area with the United States and Canada and are thus not strictly comparable with the postwar data that refer to the current accounts of the sterling area with the postwar dollar area. Data for 1946–51 from *The United Kingdom's Balance of Payments, 1946–1953,* Cmd. 8976.

Examination of the table reveals (a) that the independent rest of the sterling (ISA) incurred a deficit with the dollar area in every year but 1950, (b) that though the dependent rest of the sterling area earned substantial (and after 1947, increasing) surpluses from the dollar area these did not suffice to offset the dollar deficit incurred by the independent rest of the sterling area except in 1951, (c) that the gold sales of the rest of the sterling area to the United Kingdom manifested a downward trend between 1946 and 1951, (d) that even in 1950 the *real* contribution of the rest of the sterling area to the dollar pool was less than that made in 1938, and (e) that except for 1950 the net contribution of the rest of the sterling area to the dollar pool was insufficient to offset Britain's direct current account deficit with the dollar area.

The contrast between the pre- and postwar roles of the rest of the sterling area is striking; whereas in the prewar period the rest of the sterling area's earnings of gold and dollars sufficed to offset the direct dollar deficit of the United Kingdom, in the postwar period the rest of the sterling area either added to the demand for dollars or, except for 1950, failed to contribute enough to offset Britain's current account deficit incurred with the dollar area. Three factors were responsible for this development: the increase in Britain's direct dollar deficit, the failure of the dollar price of gold to rise,[16] and the large increase in the independent rest of the sterling area dollar deficit.

The decline in the real value of gold caused by the rise in the price levels of internationally traded goods, while the official dollar price of gold remained unchanged, was a particularly important factor in the deterioration of the rest of the sterling area's dollar and gold accounts. Had the price of gold risen *pari passu* with the prices of other commodities, the rest of the sterling area's annual contribution to the pool, all other things equal,[17] would have increased by at least 300 million dollars and probably by more in view of the incentive a rise in the dollar price of gold would have provided the producers. This is not to infer, however, that it would have been wise to increase the dollar price of gold in the postwar period. The complex issues involved are discussed below. The third factor mentioned above as being responsible for the change in the role the rest of the sterling area played in the pre- and postwar periods, the increase in the dollar deficits of the independent rest of the sterling area, requires further investigation.

The independent rest of the sterling area consists of the dominion members of the sterling area and the non-Commonwealth members. The accompanying table [18] shows the merchandise account of each independent

---

[16] Absolute production of gold declined by much less than the item RSA gold sales to the U.K. implies. Indeed, gold production of the rest of the sterling area was consistently above 500 million dollars in the postwar period. A substantial part of this gold, mined in South Africa, was not sold to the United Kingdom but was used to cover South Africa's direct dollar deficit.

[17] This assumption is tenuous, however. It is probable that had the dollar price of gold been allowed to rise the imports of the rest of the sterling area would have risen also. See the discussion below, p. 220 ff.

[18] This table is not strictly comparable to Table 32 (which was derived from Britain's balance of payments statement) for several reasons, some of which were previously noted on p. 80. In addition to the reasons cited there, lack of correspondence between the tables is due to the inclusion in Table 33 of the Union of South Africa and the exclusion of the Union in the British balance of payments table.

member of the rest of the sterling area with the United States and Canada in the pre- and postwar periods.

The outstanding features shown in the table are: (a) the tremendous increase in the value of the independent sterling area's (ISA) dollar imports between the prewar period and 1947, which was associated with a much more moderate increase in the value of independent sterling area

TABLE 33

INDEPENDENT STERLING AREA DOLLAR DEFICIT ON MERCHANDISE ACCOUNT WITH THE UNITED STATES AND CANADA

(In millions of dollars, f.o.b. prices)

	Prewar [a]	1946	1947	1948	1949	1950	1951
Burma							
Imports	4.8	2.4	6.8	4.2	2.2	1.0	4.3
Exports	1.0	1.0		2.0	1.0	1.0	2.0
Balance	− 3.8	− 1.4	− 6.8	− 2.2	− 1.2		− 2.3
Ceylon							
Imports	1.8	12.2	50.8	21.1	30.8	10.7	22.7
Exports	24.3	35.7	41.4	64.0	46.4	83.8	65.7
Balance	22.5	23.5	− 9.4	42.9	15.6	73.1	43.0
India [b]							
Imports	46.7	230.1	444.0	331.9	327.6	244.0	500.0
Exports	87.1	265.7	296.3	298.6	265.0	296.4	336.6
Balance	40.4	35.6	− 147.7	− 33.3	− 62.8	52.4	− 163.4
Pakistan							
Imports				24.7	63.9	39.1	42.6
Exports				27.4	28.9	33.1	46.4
Balance				2.7	− 35.0	− 6.0	3.8
Australia							
Imports	96.5	121.7	295.9	152.5	178.1	135.9	225.9
Exports	32.8	164.3	139.5	156.6	125.0	173.9	396.4
Balance	− 63.7	42.6	− 156.4	4.1	− 53.1	38.0	70.5
New Zealand							
Imports	33.0	44.1	114.2	52.4	57.1	37.5	70.0
Exports	16.6	46.7	38.4	42.0	33.3	76.3	127.1
Balance	− 16.5	2.6	− 75.8	− 10.4	− 23.8	38.8	57.1
Southern Rhodesia							
Imports	2.5	11.1	15.7	8.8	9.5	5.5	10.9
Exports	4.6	3.9	3.7	6.3	6.5	7.4	9.9
Balance	2.1	− 7.2	− 12.0	− 2.5	− 3.0	1.9	− 1.0
Union of South Africa							
Imports	95.9	296.9	480.6	575.3	343.7	162.6	299.8
Exports	26.7	158.2	115.3	139.0	120.2	146.6	142.9
Balance	− 69.2	− 138.7	− 365.3	− 436.3	− 223.6	− 16.0	− 156.9

The reason for the inclusion of South Africa despite her departure from the dollar pool is given on page 127.

TABLE 33 (*Continued*)

	Prewar [a]	1946	1947	1948	1949	1950	1951
Iceland							
Imports	.6	14.7	18.2	22.0	9.1	6.6	7.6
Exports	1.5	5.9	3.1	4.1	2.3	4.6	8.5
Balance	.9	− 8.8	− 15.1	− 17.1	− 6.9	− 2.0	.9
Ireland							
Imports	16.8	36.1	106.4	46.2	71.6	57.8	73.8
Exports	1.6	2.2	2.8	2.8	1.8	2.6	8.5
Balance	− 15.2	− 33.9	− 103.6	− 43.4	− 69.8	− 55.2	− 65.3
Iraq							
Imports	2.8	9.9	16.4	13.3	13.6	9.7	29.8
Exports	5.7	15.5	6.7	11.3	7.0	13.7	21.8
Balance	2.9	5.6	− 9.7	− 2.0	− 6.6	4.0	− 8.0
Total Independent RSA							
Imports	301.5	778.2	1549.0	1252.4	1107.2	710.4	1287.4
Exports	201.9	699.1	647.2	754.1	637.4	839.4	1165.8
Balance	− 99.6	− 79.1	− 901.8	− 498.3	− 469.8	129.0	− 121.6

[a] Prewar data for the United States consists of the average imports and exports for 1936–40; for Canada average imports and exports for 1935–39.

[b] Includes Pakistan up to 1948.

Sources: Department of Commerce, *Statistical Abstract of the United States,* 1942, p. 858 ff and *Canada Year Book,* 1952–53.

exports to the dollar area and which resulted in a ninefold increase in the dollar merchandise deficit during this period; (b) the reduction in the value of imports the independent sterling area derived from the dollar area between 1947 and 1950 only to be succeeded by a precipitous rise in the value of dollar imports between 1950 and 1951; and (c) the expansion of the value of exports to the dollar area between 1947 and 1951 which was interrupted, however, by a decline in the value of dollar exports between 1948 and 1949.   The diverse movements of dollar imports and exports led to a replacement of the 902 million dollar deficit in 1947 by a 129 million dollar surplus in 1950, which, in turn, was replaced by a 122 million dollar deficit in 1951.   To examine the factors responsible for these developments in greater detail, attention is focussed, in turn, on the reasons for the increase in the value of imports between the pre- and postwar periods, on the causes for the fluctuations in the value of imports the independent sterling area derived from dollar sources in the postwar period, and on the factors that influenced the independent sterling area's dollar exports in the postwar period.

The Increase in the Value of Dollar Imports into the Independent Sterling Area, Prewar to 1947.   Table 33 reveals that the deterioration of the independent sterling area's dollar merchandise account between the pre- and postwar periods was due to an increase in the value of dollar imports which was greatly in excess of the expansion in the value of dollar exports. As in the case of the deterioration of Britain's dollar accounts between the pre- and postwar periods, an explanation of the factors responsible for the increase in the value of dollar imports will contribute toward explaining the reasons for the postwar dollar shortage.

The increase in the value of imports the independent members of the sterling area derived from the dollar area is attributable to two factors: the rise in the American export price level and, more important, the large increase in the volume of imports derived from the dollar area (see Table 34).

TABLE 34

VOLUME OF IMPORTS FROM THE UNITED STATES BY SELECTED
MEMBERS OF THE STERLING AREA

(1938 = 100)

	1948	1951
Australia	82	114
India and Pakistan	476	831
Iraq, Burma, and Ceylon	321	416
Ireland	61	75
New Zealand	64	116
Union of South Africa	386	182

Sources: ECE, *Economic Survey of Europe Since the War*, pp. 306, 313.

Three factors were most important in this increase in volume: the decline per capita in primary production in non-dollar countries, necessitating the placing of heavier reliance on dollar sources of supply; the increased tempo of industrialization in the independent sterling area countries, which resulted in an increase in the demand for capital good imports from the United States as well as from the United Kingdom; and Britain's inability to meet the sterling area countries' expanded and somewhat altered demand for textile imports, which increased the volume of textile imports derived from the United States. Of these three factors the first two were the most important; the last factor has already proved to be a reflection of transitory difficulties.

The impact of the decline of agricultural production in the non-dollar areas on the dollar imports of the independent sterling area is apparent from an examination of India's postwar imports. In the interwar period India imported large quantities of grain from Far Eastern sources. The decline in rice exports from Burma and Siam in the postwar period [19]

[19] The export of rice from Burma and Siam in the early postwar period was well below 50 percent of the prewar level.

necessitated the placing of heavier reliance on wheat, which was obtainable, for the most part, from dollar sources.[20]   Between 1938 and 1948 the volume of foodstuffs (predominantly grain and flour) India derived from the United States increased by thirteenfold while the increase between 1938 and 1951,[21] when India suffered from a severe drought and locust plague, was much greater.   The increase in the value (and volume) of food imports India derived from the dollar area between the pre- and postwar periods was thus a major factor contributing to the increase in the total value of dollar imports.[22]

Though the increased reliance of India on American sources for food imports was the most spectacular, other independent sterling area countries derived a larger volume of food imports from the dollar sources in the postwar period than in the prewar period.   Between 1938 and 1948 the volume of food imports derived from dollar sources by the Union of South Africa,[23] Iraq, Burma, and Ceylon increased, in some cases significantly.

The importance of placing heavier reliance on dollar sources for the food imports of the independent sterling area countries as a factor in the sterling area's postwar dollar problem cannot be gainsaid.   It is unfortunate that one of the factors responsible for this development was the neglect of primary production by the primary producing countries as a result of their strong desire to industrialize.   This development thus points up the necessity for international cooperation designed to guarantee that some of the fruits of economic progress are passed on to the primary producers and to eliminate the violent price fluctuations which characterized primary production formerly.   Unless plans toward these ends are introduced, it is almost inevitable that primary producers will attempt to solve their particular problems by diversifying their economies and generally creating

[20] India also placed heavier reliance on Australian wheat in the postwar period and this was one of the factors responsible for the decline of Australian wheat exports to the United Kingdom.   It was noted above that the decline in wheat imports from Australia resulted in a larger volume of wheat imports into the United Kingdom from dollar sources of supply.

[21] A substantial part of India's "emergency" wheat imports from the United States in the latter year was financed through the wheat loan granted her by the United States.

[22] Between 1938 and 1948 the value of Indian grain imports derived from the United States increased by 66 million dollars.   The increase between 1938 and 1951 was even greater although, as was noted above, the payments for these imports did not impose a burden on the sterling area reserves.

[23] After 1948 the Union of South Africa imposed rigorous restrictions against dollar food imports and succeeded in reducing the volume of imports derived from the United States below the prewar level.

conditions which they feel will make them less susceptible to vicissitudes over which they have no control. The adoption of this latter course of action may result in a permanent shortage of primary production in the non-dollar world.

The increased tempo of industrialization in the independent sterling area was the second major factor responsible for the increase in the volume of dollar imports into these countries in the postwar period. The consequences of this development on the sterling area's dollar problem are evident from the accompanying table which shows the increase in the quantum of capital good imports selected countries of the independent sterling area derived from the United States between the prewar and postwar periods.

TABLE 35

OUTER STERLING AREA COUNTRIES' IMPORTS OF SELECTED
CAPITAL GOODS FROM THE UNITED STATES

(*In millions of U.S. dollars, 1948 prices*)

	Metals and Manufactures	Machinery	Transport Equipment [a]	Chemicals
Australia				
1938	9.9	28.0	8.4	5.2
1948	12.9	25.8	16.2	5.6
1951	19.0	35.5	30.1	8.9
India [b]				
1938	6.5	13.6	4.6	6.3
1948	35.2	63.3	38.0	38.2
1951	15.1	41.4	27.8	26.0
Iraq, Burma, and Ceylon				
1938	1.7	3.2	.7	.8
1948	1.6	7.9	3.7	1.7
1951	16.3	5.1	3.2	3.5
New Zealand				
1938	2.0	12.8	2.1	1.2
1948	3.8	11.2	1.8	1.9
1951	4.1	9.9	9.2	3.1

[a] Exclusive of personal cars.

[b] Including Pakistan.

Source: United Nations, ECE, *Economic Survey of Europe Since the War,* Table LV, p. 313.

The increase in the volume of capital good imports the outer independent sterling area countries derived from the United States was not due, moreover, to the inability to obtain the prewar volume from the United Kingdom. On the contrary, Table 36 shows that capital good imports from the United Kingdom, the major supplier in the prewar period, increased between the pre- and postwar periods.

TABLE 36

OUTER STERLING AREA COUNTRIES' IMPORTS OF SELECTED
CAPITAL GOODS FROM THE UNITED KINGDOM

(*In millions of U.S. dollars, 1948 prices*)

	Metals and Manufactures	Machinery	Transport Equipment [a]	Chemicals
Australia				
1938	55.1	65.6	42.5	20.2
1948	52.2	108.4	63.4	20.7
1951	104.9	199.2	179.2	41.3
India [b]				
1938	43.0	85.2	20.7	27.6
1948	50.0	174.8	43.7	42.7
1951	60.6	180.5	81.7	58.8
Iraq, Burma, and Ceylon				
1938	15.3	13.1	7.6	5.1
1948	28.3	37.5	22.2	10.9
1951	22.1	27.9	19.3	16.8
New Zealand				
1938	30.9	26.0	15.1	8.0
1948	30.8	44.1	21.9	7.5
1951	42.7	53.7	43.0	14.9

[a] Exclusive of personal cars.
[b] Including Pakistan.

Source: United Nations, ECE, *Economic Survey of Europe Since the War*, Table LV, p. 308.

Though the volume of capital good imports derived from Britain increased, it is evident that the United Kingdom was unable to supply the independent sterling area countries with capital goods in the quantities which they desired. It was this inability which led to the increase in the volume of capital good imports from the United States. Since it is not probable that the development programs of the outer independent sterling area countries will be reduced in the future, the moral that emerges is inescapable: if the dollar imports of the independent sterling area are to be kept within manageable proportions, it is imperative that the United Kingdom adapt her economy to supply these countries with the capital goods they desperately want at prices and delivery dates competitive with those prevailing in the United States. If Britain is unable to meet the demands of the independent sterling area countries for capital goods, they will inevitably attempt to derive them from other sources. The industrialization of the independent sterling area thus presents Britain with both an opportunity and a challenge. The adaptability of the British economy will determine, in large part, whether it is a boon or a bane.

The increase in the volume of textile imports some members of the oversea independent sterling area derived from the United States was a third important factor responsible for the large increase in the value of dollar imports into the independent sterling area in the postwar period. Between 1938 and 1948 the value of textiles South Africa derived from the United States increased by 99 million dollars, while the increase in the value of dollar textile imports into India amounted to 15 million dollars.[24] The major factor responsible for this development was the competitive advantage the United States enjoyed with respect to the production of artificial fibers. By 1951 the volume of textile imports derived from the United States was severely reduced from the 1948 level, although it remained higher than the prewar level for some overseas independent members of the sterling area.

The increase in the value of imports the independent members of the sterling area derived from the dollar area between the pre- and postwar periods, as in the case of the United Kingdom, was due to deep-seated structural changes in the world economy. The rise in American export prices and the per capita decline of primary production in non-dollar countries, placing heavier reliance on dollar sources of supply, were developments over which neither the United Kingdom nor the rest of the sterling area had control. The increased tempo of industrialization in some sterling area countries, which played an important role in increasing the value of dollar imports into the independent sterling area countries, was technically subject to control although politically it was not. The extreme poverty of some of these countries combined with increasingly restive populations, goaded on by the example of Soviet industrialization, rendered unfeasible attempts to moderate development plans which were, on the whole, not too extreme.

Fluctuations in the Value of Dollar Imports into the Independent Sterling Area. The accompanying table reveals that, excluding dollar imports into the Union of South Africa after 1947, the value of imports the independent sterling area derived from dollar sources in the postwar period was subject to biennial fluctuations. The value of dollar imports rose in

[24] The volume of textile imports the Union of South Africa derived from the United States increased by ninefold between 1938 and 1948 while the volume of textile imports India derived from the United States increased by rather more than sixfold. The volume of textile imports from the United States into Australia, New Zealand, Iraq, Burma, and Ceylon also increased between 1938 and 1948, although in most of these countries the value of dollar textile imports even in 1948 was rather low.

1947, 1949, and 1951 and declined in 1948 and 1950. These fluctuations of the value of dollar imports had an important bearing on the postwar dollar problem.

TABLE 37

VALUE OF INDEPENDENT STERLING AREA DOLLAR IMPORTS

(*In millions of U.S. dollars*)

Year	Dollar Imports [a]
1946	778
1947	1549
1948	677
1949	764
1950	547
1951	987

[a] Excluding, after 1947, the dollar imports into the Union of South Africa.

Source: Department of Commerce, *Statistical Abstract of the United States*, 1952 and Dominion Bureau of Statistics, *Canada Yearbook*, 1952–53.

As in the case of Britain's dollar imports, the biennial fluctuations of dollar imports into the independent sterling area is attributable, primarily, to the degree of stringency with which import restrictions against dollar goods were applied. This, in turn, was largely a function of the state of reserves; an increase in the reserves was the signal to relax import restrictions, while a depletion of the reserves resulted in a tightening of the import restrictions.[25] Thus, the independent sterling area countries imposed severe restrictions on dollar goods following the precipitous drain on the reserves during the brief convertibility period, relaxed these restrictions in the course of 1948 as the reserve position improved, agreed to limit dollar imports to 75 percent of the 1948 levels in July, 1949, to stay the drain on the reserves, and tended to relax these restrictions in 1951. The relaxation of import restrictions in 1951 was undertaken without Britain's blessing; indeed, Britain continued to impose vigorous restrictions against dollar goods in 1951, arguing that the 1950 improvement in the reserves was due to transitory developments.

The biennial fluctuations in the value of dollar imports reflect in large part the inadequate sterling area machinery in the postwar period. The ad hoc conferences were not designed to formulate long run policies which would eliminate the "discontinuity of joint action [and] the time lag which inevitably occurs between taking decisions on import policy and seeing the effects of these decisions on the balance of payments." The postwar ma-

[25] It is argued below that the state of the central reserves affected the relevant economic policies of the outer sterling area countries differently from the manner in which it affected the policies of the United Kingdom.

chinery was simply not designed to supply "member governments with . . . a steady disincentive to dollar spending" which was necessary to "mitigate the shortage over a number of years." [26]

Dollar Exports of the Independent Sterling Area. The increase in the value of independent sterling area exports to the dollar area between the prewar period and 1947, though substantial, was very much less than the increase in the value of dollar imports into the independent sterling area. This failure to increase *pari passu* may be attributed mainly to the expansion in the volume of dollar imports that greatly exceeded the increase in volume of dollar exports; changes in the independent sterling area terms of trade vis-à-vis the dollar area between the prewar period and 1947 do not appear to be important.

Between 1947 and 1948 the value of independent sterling area dollar exports increased moderately, largely through an increase in the price level of independent sterling area exports. It was interrupted, however, by a rather precipitous decline in the value of dollar exports between 1948 and 1949.[27] Between 1949 and 1951 there was a sharp increase in the value of independent sterling area exports to the dollar area.

The factors responsible for the fluctuations in the value of independent sterling area exports to the dollar area between 1947 and 1951 are familiar: the decline between 1948 and 1949 was due mainly to the American inventory recession and to the widespread anticipation of a sterling devaluation; the spectacular increase between 1949 and 1951 was a reflection of the rise in primary product prices following the outbreak of the Korean War.

The reduction in value between 1948 and 1949 was one of the major factors in the 1949 crisis. Responsible for this development were (a) the inventory recession in the United States, (b) the speculative pressures against the pound, and (c) shunting operations made possible by the existence of cheap sterling in the world markets.

The adverse effects of an American recession on the exports of the independent sterling area are particularly severe since the exports of these countries are predominantly primary products, for which the American income elasticity of demand is high. Furthermore, the relative importance of the United States as an importer of commodities of the independent sterling area countries causes even a relatively slight recession in the United

[26] Fleming, "Regional Organization of Trade and Payments," *American Economic Review, Papers and Proceedings,* May, 1952, p. 350.

[27] If South African dollar exports are excluded, the decline in the value of independent sterling area dollar exports between 1948 and 1949 amounted to 100 million dollars.

States to have pronounced effects on the price level of independent sterling area exports. These countries are thus adversely affected by an American recession in two distinct but related ways: the *volume* of their exports to the United States is reduced, and the *unit values* of the remaining exports suffer a decline (see Table 38).

TABLE 38

QUANTITY AND VALUE OF SELECTED STERLING AREA EXPORTS
TO THE UNITED STATES IN 1948 AND 1949

Commodity	Principal Exporters	QUANTITY		VALUE [c]	
		1948	*1949*	*1948*	*1949*
Rubber [a]	Malaya, Ceylon	1144.6	793.3	218.6	132.1
Wool [a]	Australia, New Zealand, India, Pakistan, South Africa	161.6	104.7	142.0	108.2
Jute & man. [a]	India, Pakistan	695.9	592.3	163.0	133.1
Tin [a]	Malaya	76.9	77.0	77.7	77.3
Diamonds [b]	South Africa	8.8	4.2	77.1	46.9
Lead, raw [a]	Australia	60.9	36.7	9.9	6.3

[a] Millions of pounds.
[b] Millions of carats.
[c] Millions of U.S. dollars.
Source: ECE, *Economic Survey of Europe in 1950*, p. 196.

The manner in which speculative pressures against a currency adversely affect exports is well-known. The expectation of a currency devaluation induces importers to postpone placing orders until the devaluation is effected or the expectations reversed. Since other factors were operating in the latter part of 1948 and the early part of 1949 to reduce the value of independent sterling area exports to the United States, it is extremely difficult to isolate the effects of this single factor. The widespread belief in the United States that the pound was overvalued and that a devaluation was imminent undoubtedly increased the importance of the speculative factor in reducing the value of independent sterling area exports.

The third factor mentioned above as being important in reducing the value of independent sterling area dollar exports to the United States in 1949 was the shunting operations which were made possible by the existence of cheap sterling on world markets. Though the technique of shunting operations was frequently quite complex, the end result was simple. Transferable and bilateral account countries, anxious to convert part of their sterling balances into dollars, purchased sterling area goods for the purposes of resale to the United States. The American importers were able to purchase these goods for dollars at substantial discounts from the prevailing sterling area prices. Operations of this kind were made possible by the inconvertibility of sterling at a time of a general dollar shortage. There were two ways in which shunting operations could be eliminated: restoration of sterling convertibility and the successful pursuit of policies designed to make the pound as scarce as the dollar. Barring either of these developments it was extremely difficult to avoid the loss of dollar earnings from the shunting operations.

It is not possible with the currently available information to estimate the loss of dollars to the independent sterling area from shunting operations; however, available evidence indicates that this loss was significant. A Department of Commerce study concluded that in 1948 approximately 7 percent of the American import of Australian wool was purchased through third countries other than the United Kingdom.[28] It is unlikely that the cheap sterling transactions were limited to Australian wool.

The large increase in the value of independent sterling area exports to North America between 1949 and 1951 is attributable, in large part, to the recovery of industrial activity in the United States, the increased need for primary product imports following the outbreak of the Korean War, and, most important, the steep rise in the prices of some of the more important dollar exports of the independent sterling area.[29] The significance of this last factor in increasing the value of independent sterling area exports to the United States between 1949 and 1951 is apparent from the accompanying table, which shows the course of the price movement of selected pri-

TABLE 39

UNITED STATES PRICES OF SELECTED INDEPENDENT
STERLING AREA EXPORTS

(*Oct.–Dec., 1949 = 100*)

	Jan.–June, 1950	*Jan., 1951*	*June, 1951*	*Dec., 1951*
Jute	112	121	203	161
Lead	84	131	131	146
Rubber (natural)	140	432	389	306
Tea	96	180	179	153
Tin	87	193	135	117
Wool	108	259	205	134

[28] Martin, "Indirect Sales of Australian and New Zealand Wool to the United States in 1949," *World Trade in Commodities,* June, 1950, V. 8, part 19, no. 24.

[29] The effect of the devaluation on the exports of the independent sterling area to the dollar area is rather uncertain. On a priori grounds it would appear that the devaluation was not a very important factor influencing the volume of independent sterling area exports to the United States in view of the fact that these exports were predominantly primary products, for which the American price elasticity of demand is likely to be rather small. In any event, it is fairly certain that the revival of industrial activity and the outbreak of the Korean War were much more important influences than the pound devaluation.

mary products in the United States during this period. It need hardly be added that with the ultimate collapse of these prices the exports of the independent sterling area suffered severely.

THE DEPENDENT MEMBERS OF THE STERLING AREA (DSA)

The dependent members of the sterling area earned a merchandise surplus with North America in every postwar year, but it was not until 1951 that the real value of the surplus equaled or exceeded that earned in the prewar period. The accompanying table shows the merchandise

TABLE 40

MERCHANDISE TRADE OF THE DEPENDENT STERLING AREA
WITH THE UNITED STATES AND CANADA

(In millions of U.S. dollars, f.o.b. prices)

	Prewar[a]	1946	1947	1948	1949	1950	1951
British Guiana							
Imports	2.4	10.6	18.1	14.5	10.6	6.7	9.9
Exports	6.4	13.1	13.6	16.7	23.5	23.1	26.9
Balance	4.0	2.5	− 4.5	2.2	12.9	16.4	17.0
British Malaya							
Imports	11.8	17.8	73.2	91.3	43.0	23.8	68.6
Exports	199.2	135.0	301.3	291.1	211.7	338.8	483.4
Balance	187.4	117.2	327.8	199.8	168.7	315.0	414.8
Hong Kong							
Imports	18.8	51.0	95.9	92.5	131.3	110.7	40.8
Exports	6.4	1.7	3.4	5.5	7.3	7.6	12.2
Balance	− 12.4	− 49.3	− 92.5	− 87.0	− 124.0	− 103.1	− 28.6
Gold Coast							
Imports	3.7	4.6	12.1	8.3	8.2	6.2	8.7
Exports	14.0	28.7	58.7	84.2	57.5	70.3	95.4
Balance	19.3	24.1	46.6	75.9	49.3	64.1	86.7
Nigeria							
Imports	2.7	7.4	24.1	10.4	8.0	6.0	9.9
Exports	7.7	16.9	33.5	36.0	33.1	36.3	49.9
Balance	5.0	9.5	9.4	25.6	25.1	30.3	40.0
Other dependent countries							
Imports	39.0	132.9	229.0	125.7	103.8	72.6	103.7
Exports	29.0	78.0	68.8	77.2	99.2	104.4	129.0
Balance	− 10.0	− 54.9	− 160.2	− 48.5	− 4.6	31.8	25.3
Total DSA							
Imports	78.4	224.3	452.4	342.7	305.9	226.0	241.6
Exports	263.7	273.4	479.0	510.7	432.3	580.5	796.8
Balance	184.3	49.1	26.6	168.0	126.4	354.5	555.2

[a] 1935–39 average.

Source: Derived from Department of Commerce, *Statistical Abstract of the United States,* 1952, p. 858 ff. and Dominion Bureau of Statistics, *Canada Year Book,* 1952–53.

trade of the dependent territories with the United States and Canada in the prewar period and in each of the postwar years.

The picture that emerges from this table is a familiar one. In the early postwar period, a greater expansion in the value of dollar imports than in the value of dollar exports drastically reduced the traditional dollar merchandise surplus of the dependent sterling area. The imposition of severe import restrictions against dollar goods following the 1947 crisis, together with the continued and sustained expansion in the value of exports, eventuated in an increase in the dollar surplus in 1948. This improvement was shortlived, however, when, as a result of the operation of the factors discussed above, the value of the dependent sterling area's dollar exports was reduced.[30] Between 1949 and 1951 the dramatic expansion in the value of dollar exports, caused primarily by the precipitous rise in the price level of primary products consequent upon the outbreak of the Korean War, resulted in a merchandise dollar surplus which exceeded the prewar surplus by threefold, measured in monetary terms, and was considerably above the prewar surplus in real terms.

The importance of these developments to the postwar dollar shortage of the sterling area is apparent from Table 41 which shows the proportion of Britain's merchandise dollar deficit that the trade surplus of the dependent sterling area covered in the prewar and in the postwar periods.

TABLE 41

PROPORTION OF BRITAIN'S MERCHANDISE DOLLAR DEFICIT
COVERED BY THE DOLLAR TRADE SURPLUS OF
THE DEPENDENT STERLING AREA

Year	Percentage
1935–39	27
1946	4
1947	2
1948	23
1949	14
1950	143
1951	86

Source: Derived from the Official Trade Statistics of the United States and Canada. Import and export figures used to derive the trade balances of both the United Kingdom and the dependent sterling area are valued f.o.b.

The decline in the relative importance of the dependent sterling area's dollar surplus in the early postwar period was due to the increase in the dollar deficit of the United Kingdom and to the decline in the surplus of

[30] The reduction in the surplus of the dependent sterling area occurred in the face of a further reduction in the value of dollar imports.

the dependent sterling area.   This latter development, in turn, is attributable, in large part, to the increase in the volume of imports the dependent sterling area derived from North America; between 1938 and 1948 the volume of imports the British dependencies derived from the United States increased by 222 percent.[31]

This increase in the volume of dollar imports between 1938 and 1948 reflected the low levels of production in the non-dollar world, the necessity to repair the damage suffered by some dependencies during the war,[32] and other transitional difficulties.   By 1951 the need to place heavier reliance on the United States for food and textile imports was the major reason for the increase in the volume of imports the dependencies derived from the dollar area.   Table 42 shows the increase in the volume of selected imports the dependencies derived from the United States between 1938 and 1948 and between 1938 and 1951.

TABLE 42

SELECTED IMPORTS OF THE DEPENDENT STERLING AREA
FROM THE UNITED STATES

(1938 = 100)

	1948	1951
Chemicals	374	115
Food, drink, and tobacco	183	252
Machinery	187	118
Metals and manufactures	153	81
Textiles	1400	450
Total imports	222	142

Source: Derived from United Nations, ECE, *Economic Survey of Europe Since the War,* p. 313.

The extent to which the dependencies' imports from the United States will remain large or increase in the future will depend in large part upon Britain's ability to supply these countries with the capital goods they are sure to desire as well as on the future availability of food imports from non-dollar sources.   If Britain succeeds in adapting her economy to the point where she can supply the dependent territories with the types of goods they inevitably will demand at prices and delivery dates competitive with those prevailing in the United States, she will be able to maintain her position as the major supplier to these countries.   Should Britain fail,

[31] United Nations, ECE, *Economic Survey of Europe Since the War,* p. 313.

[32] This factor was especially important for Malaya, where in 1948 the volume of imports from the United States increased by 355 percent over the 1938 level.   A substantial part of this increase is attributable to the expansion of capital good imports.

however, it is not probable that the dependencies will agree to postpone much longer their development schemes. Capital good imports will be obtained—if possible from Britain, if necessary from the United States.

In the postwar period, the dependencies reassumed in large part the role they played in the prewar period in the equilibration of dollar-sterling accounts. The economies of these countries make them particularly suitable for this role. It must be emphasized, however, that Britain cannot assume that these countries will continue to supply her with dollars in the future. The import restrictions imposed by the dependencies in the postwar period were in the main more stringent than those imposed either by the United Kingdom or the independent sterling area countries. The component of the sterling area comprising the dependent territories was the only one which succeeded in living within its means in the postwar period. Indeed, the surpluses which the dependencies earned in their dealings with the rest of the world offset in part the deficits of other sterling area components. It must be emphasized, however, that it is not probable that the dependencies will remain content to accumulate sterling balances. These countries are among the poorest in the world. Economically, there is no justification for their being capital exporters as they in effect were in the postwar period.[33] The time cannot be too far off when these countries will wish to spend their foreign exchange earnings to alleviate their poverty. Britain can earn these surpluses only if she is capable of supplying the dependencies with the types of goods they are likely to demand.

THE DETERIORATION OF THE DOLLAR INVISIBLE ACCOUNTS OF THE REST OF THE STERLING AREA (RSA)

The deterioration of the rest of the sterling area's dollar invisible accounts between the prewar and the postwar periods was important in contributing to the postwar dollar shortage. A comparison of the pre- and postwar accounts reveals that whereas in the prewar period the rest of the sterling area achieved a balance on dollar invisible account,[34] in the postwar period the rest of the sterling area incurred substantial dollar deficits on this account. The relevant data for the postwar period is reproduced in Table 43.

[33] During the period December, 1945, to December, 1951, the sterling assets of the dependencies were increased by 514 million pounds. And although some part of the increase of these holdings may have eventuated as a result of a prior flow of capital from Britain, there is evidence to suggest a substantial portion was derived from earnings.

[34] Conan, *Sterling Area*, p. 183.

TABLE 43

INVISIBLE ACCOUNTS OF THE REST OF THE STERLING AREA
WITH THE UNITED STATES AND CANADA

(*In millions of U.S. dollars*)

	1948	1949	1950	1951
Foreign travel	13	25	39	39
Transportation	– 36	– 50	– 36	– 121
Interest, profits, and dividends	– 114	– 120	– 146	– 136
Other services	– 23	– 1	– 9	– 4
Total	– 160	– 146	– 152	– 222

Sources: Canadian data from IMF, *Balance of Payments Yearbooks* and IMF, *International Financial Statistics;* United States data from Department of Commerce, *Survey of Current Business.*

The absence of detailed information for the prewar period precludes the possibility of analyzing the factors responsible for the deterioration of the rest of the sterling area's dollar invisible accounts. The deterioration was probably due to an increase in the deficit on shipping and income accounts. The expansion of the British fleet should enable, if it has not already done so, the reduction or elimination of the shipping account deficit. The deficit on income account, however, is likely to remain large.

THE STERLING AREA MECHANISM AND THE INTERNATIONAL ACCOUNTS OF THE REST OF THE STERLING AREA

The discussion to this point has been limited to the factors responsible for the deterioration of the rest of the sterling area's dollar accounts in the postwar period. Now attention is focused on a broader issue: the extent to which the sterling area mechanism, per se, contributed to the balance of payments difficulties.

The two outstanding features of the sterling area were the relative, although by no means absolute, freedom of trade and capital movements within the area and the maintenance of a hard currency pool to which the dollar earners of the sterling area contributed and from whence the net dollar spenders derived the hard currency necessary to discharge current account deficits. These two features of the postwar sterling area constituted, at one and the same time, the major source of strength of the sterling area and one of its prime weaknesses.

The practice of pooling hard currency earnings and financing deficits through drawings on the resources of the central pool contributed to the inflationary pressures in the overseas sterling area countries by effecting a partial divorcement between the financial, economic, and commercial policies pursued by these countries and the direct responsibility for the financing of the possible ensuing deficits on international account.[35] The partial substitution of group for individual responsibility, implicit in the operation of a central pooling system, would not by itself be unfeasible if the associated countries were bound together by a strong community of interest, if the economic, financial, and commercial policies of the affiliated countries were framed with reference to similar objective criteria, or if effective control from the center prevented some countries from pursuing policies at variance with the group's welfare. None of these conditions prevailed in the postwar period. An examination of the economic aspirations of the sterling area countries reveals marked conflict; the state of the central reserves exercised a varying influence on the policies of the associated countries and the sterling area retained to a large degree the decentralized features of the prewar sterling bloc.

Ordinarily, one of the most effective restraints on a country living beyond its means (measured in terms of its productive capacity and its ability to obtain autonomous loans) is the ensuing international deficits which must eventually be financed by a reduction of its reserves. Provided a country is not "working off" excess reserves, the need to stay the drain on the reserves must lead to the introduction of restrictive policies designed to reduce the level of domestic expenditure to a point where it can be satisfied by the resources made available from domestic production and autonomous loans. It is this necessity which precludes an open economy from pursuing more inflationary policies than its neighbors.

The central pooling of hard currencies initiated by the sterling area countries during the war and projected into the postwar period seriously weakened the restraints normally imposed by balance of payments disequilibria. For under this system, the state of the central reserves, rather than that of the individual members, had to play the decisive role in the formulation of the relevant economic and commercial policies. There were two factors in the postwar period that militated against this arrangement. The first was that while the central pool reserves, almost constantly at precariously low levels, dictated policies of restraint, the sterling reserves of the self-governing outer sterling area countries were extraordinarily large and imparted an inflationary bias into the system (see Table 44). The second factor was the determination of the overseas independent sterling

---

[35] For a fuller discussion of the material discussed on pp. 147–49, see Zupnick, "The Sterling Area's Central Pooling System Reexamined," *The Quarterly Journal of Economics,* February, 1955.

TABLE 44

STERLING RESERVES OF THE OVERSEAS INDEPENDENT
STERLING AREA COUNTRIES

(*In millions of U.S. dollars*)

	1937	1946	1948	1950
Australia	291	677	1126	1432
Burma	68		213	143
Ceylon			113	119
India [a]	316	4905	3099	1752
Iraq	26	179	139	117
Ireland	57	170	192	228
New Zealand	68		213	143
Pakistan			787	479

[a] Prior to 1948, India's reserves include those of Burma, Ceylon, and Pakistan.
Source: Derived from IMF, *International Financial Statistics.*

area countries to diversify their economies at almost any cost in order to
render them less susceptible to vicissitudes over which they have no control and which were largely regarded as being responsible for these countries' failure to share the fruits of economic progress in the interwar period.
This strong desire for diversification through industrialization reinforced
the inflationary bias imparted to the system by the huge sterling reserves
of the associated countries by making them more prone to frame their
economic, financial, and commercial policies with reference to the state
of their own reserves rather than to the state of the central reserves.

There can be little doubt, in view of the rather large current account
deficits of the overseas independent sterling area countries in the postwar
period, that this feature of the sterling area mechanism contributed to the
sterling area's payments difficulties. A mechanism that assured greater
individual responsibility would undoubtedly have produced more favorable
results.

It is difficult to suggest, however, how a greater degree of individual
responsibility can be introduced within the framework of the postwar sterling area. The dollar pool was established precisely for the purpose of
enabling the dollar deficits of some countries to be offset by the surpluses
of others.[36] The aim of the dollar pool was thus to substitute group responsibility for individual responsibility. This in itself would not constitute
a weakness if the members of the group felt, or were made to feel, that
their own welfare was contingent upon that of the group as a whole, but it

[36] Sargent argued that this feature of the sterling area mechanism was the chief
advantage of membership. "Britain and the Sterling Area," Worswick, *British Economy,* p. 548.

was precisely this that was lacking in the postwar period. Aside from the "crisis" periods, the attitude of the members of the group was often one of "getting while the getting was good." The United Kingdom must bear part of the responsibility for this development. All too frequently Britain's failure to consider the associated members full partners created a good deal of dissatisfaction. Even in so important a matter as exchange devaluation, she failed to notify the sterling area countries more than a day or two before the event.[37] It is true, however, that in the late postwar period Britain did attempt to create better feeling by holding more frequent consultations with the associated members of the sterling area. It is difficult to say with any degree of definitiveness how far this development should be ascribed to the fact that during this period the overseas independent members of the sterling area were net contributors to the dollar pool rather than net drawers on the dollar pool and that unofficial critics of the operation of the sterling area in the independent sterling area were becoming more vociferous.[38] It is also difficult to say, at this stage, whether this by itself will prove sufficient to obtain the "group oriented" interest which is so vital to the continued successful operation of the sterling area.

THE FUTURE OF THE STERLING AREA

The postwar sterling area, like its predecessor the sterling bloc, is based on utilitarian considerations. Any question concerning the future of the area can be best resolved by considering the advantages and disadvantages of the sterling area mechanism to the United Kingdom and to the overseas independent members.

The advantages of the sterling area to the United Kingdom are evident. The existence of an area from whence the United Kingdom can derive a substantial portion of her food and raw material imports without undue concern about the financing of such imports [39] is obviously of prime importance to a country so dependent upon imports. Likewise, the impor-

---

[37] The Finance Minister of India stated at the time: "I cannot help thinking that in a matter which so vitally affects the whole economy of every country in the sterling area, steps should have been taken to arrange for a secret meeting of the Finance Ministers of the Commonwealth before a decision was reached regarding these matters; the need for devaluation, the extent of the devaluation and the time of devaluation." Quoted in Conan, *Sterling Area*, p. 161.

It should, of course, be noted that Britain was not entirely at fault. In matters like devaluation utmost secrecy is required.

[38] See "Strains Within the Sterling Area," *The Economist*, November 10, 1951, p. 1145.

[39] See below, p. 153, for necessary qualifications.

tance of a large area in which Britain's exports receive preferential treatment, a result of the discriminatory aspects of the sterling area mechanism, cannot be gainsaid. Finally, the stability of exchange rates within the sterling area is an extremely attractive feature to so important a trading nation as the United Kingdom.

The major disadvantages of the sterling area as it was constituted in the postwar period resulted from the operation of the dollar pool and the relative freedom of capital flows from the United Kingdom to the rest of the sterling area.[40] Examination of the sterling area dollar accounts reveals that the dollar deficit of the overseas independent members of the sterling area were important contributory factors in the postwar dollar shortage. Indeed, as Table 45 shows, the dollar aid and loans the United Kingdom obtained between 1946 and 1951 in conjunction with the dollar earnings of the dependent members of the sterling area more than sufficed to cover Britain's direct dollar deficit on current and capital accounts as well as the dollar deficits the whole sterling area incurred with non-dollar countries.

Given the precariously low level of the reserves and the shrinking of dollar aid and loans, it is evident that the United Kingdom cannot in the future tolerate a drain of dollars to the independent sterling area comparable to that which occurred between 1946 and 1951. The conclusion that emerges is similar to the one reached above; either the independent sterling area countries must develop a greater degree of responsibility for their drawings on the dollar pool, or arrangements will have to be evolved that will preclude the possibility of the independent sterling area's imposing as severe a burden as in the period under discussion. The dollar pool should not be regarded as sacrosanct; utilitarian considerations dictated its creation and the same considerations may seal its doom.

The second major disadvantage to Britain of the sterling area as it was constituted in the postwar period was the freedom with which capital flowed from the United Kingdom to the rest of the sterling area. It was noted above that the current account deficits of the rest of the sterling area [41] with the United Kingdom between 1946 and 1951 amounted to

[40] Capital flows to outer sterling area countries were not completely free in the postwar period. The Capital Issues Committee must approve all new flotations and on at least one occasion—in 1949—the Committee threatened to withhold permission from South Africa in order to obtain better terms on a proposed gold agreement.

[41] It is not possible with the currently available information to discuss the independent sterling area and the dependent sterling area separately in this context.

TABLE 45

INCURRING AND FINANCING OF THE STERLING AREA
DOLLAR DEFICIT, 1946–51

(*In millions of dollars*)

U.K. direct dollar deficit	7101	
Whole sterling area dollar payments to non-dollar countries	1612	
Total British and unallocated dollar deficit	8713	
Dependent sterling area dollar surplus	1452	
Dependent sterling area gold sales to U.K.	153	
Total contribution of dependent sterling area to dollar pool	1605	
Britain's [a] and dependencies' dollar deficit		7108
American 1946 credit	3750	
Canadian 1946 credit	1159	
ERP loans and grants to U.K.	2694	
U.K. drawings on IMF	300	
U.K. gold loan from Union of South Africa	325	
Total of dollar, grants, loans, and credits	8228	8228
Depletion of gold and dollar reserves		143
Total "compensatory" dollar finance		8371
Drain of dollars to independent sterling area [b]		1263

[a] This item includes the unallocated dollar deficit incurred by whole sterling area vis-à-vis non-dollar countries.

[b] This item is derived by subtracting Britain's and the dependencies' dollar deficit, as defined, from the total "compensatory" dollar finance.

Source: *United Kingdom Balance of Payments, 1946 to 1953*, Cmd. 8976.

1,222 million pounds. The rest of the sterling area effected multilateral settlements equal to 540 million pounds.[42] The remainder, or 683 million pounds, is equal to the "unrequited" exports made possible by the outflow of capital from the United Kingdom to the rest of the sterling area in the postwar period. Quite aside from the question as to whether these "unrequited exports" could have been diverted to the dollar area, the extremely large capital outflow imposed a rather heavy burden on the United Kingdom. In the interwar period some critics argued that huge capital outflows was one of the major factors responsible for the neglect of Britain's domestic industrial machine. In view of the overriding necessity for a high level of domestic capital formation, it is questionable whether it is in Britain's ultimate interest to engage in capital exports of even the magnitude occurring in the postwar period. It should be noted in this context that a large part of the capital which Britain succeeded in exporting in the

[42] The total sterling area earned a net gold and dollar surplus (including gold sales to the United Kingdom) equal to 241 million pounds and a surplus with non-dollar countries, exclusive of the United Kingdom, of 299 million pounds. See above, p. 110.

postwar period was derived not from an excess of domestic savings over domestic investment but rather from the dollar area in the form of loans and grants and, to a smaller extent, from the dependent countries which earned surpluses that they invested in Britain. Since neither of these sources is likely to be important in the future, a continuation of capital exports even on the scale achieved between 1946 and 1951 will necessitate either an increase in the level of British savings or a reduction in the level of capital formation. The former development is not probable while the latter would be disastrous.

There is, of course, the obverse side of the coin. Thus far attention has been focused on the sterling area mechanism from Britain's vantage point. It is also necessary to examine the mechanism from the viewpoint of the other sterling area countries. If the period between 1946 and 1951 is taken as a whole, there can be little doubt that the postwar sterling area arrangements were favorable to the outer independent members. These countries were not only the recipients of large amounts of capital but were, as was indicated above, net drawers on rather than contributors to the dollar pool. This procedure of examining the period between 1946 and 1951 as a unit is somewhat misleading; it tends to obscure some factors that may make the sterling area mechanism less attractive to the overseas members than appears at first sight. These factors are apparent if the period between 1946 and 1951 is subdivided into two parts; from 1946 to the end of 1949 and the year and one half between January, 1950, and June, 1951. In the first of these periods, the huge dollar deficits the independent sterling area incurred in trade with the dollar area more than offset the gold sales to the United Kingdom, with the result that the independent sterling area, as a group, was a net drawer on the dollar pool. The position of the independent sterling area with respect to the dollar pool changed radically, however, in the period between 1950 and June, 1951. The precipitous rise in the price level of primary products, the increase in American primary product imports induced in part by the stockpiling policies pursued after the outbreak of the Korean War, and the imposition of severe import restrictions against dollar goods in July, 1949, earned the independent sterling area substantial surpluses in trade with the dollar area. The dollars earned from the dollar area supplemented the gold sales of the independent sterling area with the result that in this period the overseas independent members of the sterling area were large contributors to the dollar pool.

At first sight it would appear that these developments were extremely favorable. Indeed, there was wide hope at the time that after the severe transitional difficulties a basis for the reestablishment of a multilateral payments structure not unlike that of the prewar had at last been achieved. There was, however, one important slip between the cup and the lip. The United Kingdom failed to develop a sufficiently large export surplus with the independent sterling area, with the result that the circuit was not closed. The independent sterling area sold the dollars and gold to the United Kingdom not against British exports but against sterling, causing the increased dollar earnings [43] of the independent sterling area to eventuate in an increase in sterling liabilities.[44]

This development posed serious problems. On the one hand the failure of the United Kingdom to earn the gold and dollars sold by the independent sterling area to the dollar pool created a dangerous threat to the gold reserves. Since unblocked sterling balances [45] are, through the operation of the dollar pool mechanism, fully convertible into dollars, the huge accumulation of these balances created a situation whereby, in the absence of self-restraint, the gold reserves could be rapidly depleted. On the other hand, the independent sterling area found the forced loans they were making to the United Kingdom extremely distasteful, thereby strengthening the possibility of their converting these sterling balances into dollars. Indeed, it was during this period when the independent sterling area was selling its gold and dollars to the United Kingdom against sterling that the most ominous rumblings about the operation of the sterling area mechanism were heard.[46]

Though the situation created by the increase in the gold and dollar earnings of the independent sterling area was short-lived,[47] the period revealed an important weakness in the United Kingdom-independent sterling area relationship. During the period under discussion, the United King-

[43] Including the newly mined gold sold to the United Kingdom.

[44] The sterling liabilities of the overseas independent sterling area increased by 424 million pounds between January, 1950, and June, 1951. It should be noted that part of this increase is attributable to the capital outflows from the United Kingdom during this period and to the receipt of sterling from "third" countries.

[45] All currently earned sterling was freely available for expenditure.

[46] See "Strains Within the Sterling Area," *The Economist,* November 10, 1951, p. 1145.

[47] With the collapse of primary product prices, the independent sterling area incurred rather large deficits with the dollar area after the middle of 1951. These deficits were met entirely by drawing down the sterling balances. Between June, 1951, and June, 1952, the sterling balances of the independent sterling area were drawn down by 663 million pounds. *United Kingdom Balance of Payments,* Cmd. 8976, Table 27.

dom could not supply to independent sterling area countries the type of goods they wanted in sufficiently large quantities. This inability was a factor responsible for the large independent sterling area dollar deficits in the period between 1946 and 1949 and was important in preventing the reemergence of a true multilateral payments structure during 1950 and the first half of 1951, when the independent sterling area had substantial dollar surpluses. The conclusion that emerges from this consideration is clear; either the United Kingdom will effect the necessary adaptations to enable her to meet the needs of the independent sterling area, or the basis for the reestablishment of the type of multilateral structure that existed in the prewar period will be irrevocably destroyed, even should the independent sterling area earn a substantial amount of dollars. Certainly, the independent sterling area countries are not likely to acquiesce to arrangements that result in their accumulating idle sterling balances in return for their gold and dollars.

There was still another factor that tended to make the sterling area mechanism somewhat less attractive to the independent sterling area than appears at first sight. It was noted above that during the period, 1946 to 1951, the drawings of the United Kingdom on the dollar pool to meet her direct dollar deficit was somewhat less than the net contribution of the dependent sterling area to the dollar pool and the aid which the United Kingdom obtained in one form or another. If the dollar aid is excluded, however, it becomes apparent that the dollar deficits of the United Kingdom represented the largest drain on the dollar pool. Since it is unlikely that aid in the future will approximate that in the immediate past, the possibility is strong that the United Kingdom may become by far the largest drawer on the resources of the dollar pool. It is doubtful whether the pooling arrangements will appear attractive to the associated overseas members under these circumstances.[48]

The analysis of the modifications that may have to be effected to make the sterling area mechanism palatable to the two major components of the sterling area leads to disquieting conclusions concerning the probable future of the area. Thus it was noted above that the major drawbacks of the postwar sterling area mechanism to the United Kingdom were the almost unimpeded movement of the capital to the rest of the sterling area and the virtually free access the rest of the sterling area had to the dollar pool. Any modifications designed to impede capital movements to the rest of

[48] See the review by Bell in *American Economic Review*, September, 1953, p. 696.

the sterling area or to limit the rest of the sterling area's freedom to draw on the dollar pool may well lead to the destruction of two of the most important cohesive factors.   There can be little doubt that, in the long run,[49] the major advantages the rest of the sterling area can draw from continued participation in the sterling area are the ability to obtain capital and the necessary finance to meet hard currency deficits, should the dollar shortage persist.   Should the sterling mechanism be modified to the disadvantage of the rest of the sterling area in respect to these two factors, it is doubtful that it will remain sufficiently attractive to the associated overseas members.

This conclusion is not appreciably vitiated by considering the other cohesive forces which are generally cited in literature on the sterling area. Among the more important of the alleged ties are the large volume of intra–area trade, the relative stability of the British market for outer sterling area exports, and the force of habit of association and the feeling of belonging together.   Without deprecating the importance of these ties, it is not difficult to show that the case for the continuance of the sterling area arrangements based on these considerations has been exaggerated.

In the postwar period, intra-area trade has been extremely significant. It must not be overlooked, however, that the large volume of this trade was due, at least in part, to the discriminatory import restrictions maintained by sterling area countries.   Were it not for these restrictions it is questionable whether intra-area trade would have been as large as it actually was.   This consideration is especially important in view of the fact that there has been a steady dismantling of the discriminatory controls since 1954.   Should this development continue, it will remove an important factor contributing to the large volume of intra-area trade.

The importance of the large volume of intra-area trade as a cohesive factor is deceptive on still other counts.   It is frequently stated, for example, that intra-area trade accounted for 50 percent of total sterling area trade in the postwar period.   This statement, however, ignores the fact that the importance of intra-area trade varied from country to country and the further fact that some sterling area countries could have sold their exports to non-sterling countries without much difficulty.   Of the sterling

---

[49] In the early postwar period the existence of huge sterling balances was an important cohesive factor.   Its importance has waned, however, with the reduction of the sterling balances of the independent sterling area.   Moreover, by 1957 it is expected that the balances will have been all but eliminated; the remaining balances will, at that date, be required for working reserves.

area countries, only New Zealand and Ireland are overwhelmingly dependent on sterling area trade. In the postwar period, both of these countries sold approximately 90 percent of their exports to the United Kingdom. Moreover, given the nature of their exports, it is not probable that they could have developed alternative markets. At the other extreme are countries like the Union of South Africa and Iraq which, though they found their chief market in the United Kingdom in the postwar period, would have experienced no difficulty in finding alternative markets. The Union of South Africa could have readily sold her gold exports to the United States while markets for Iraq's petroleum existed on the continent. In between these extremes are countries which could, if necessary, develop alternative markets, albeit not without difficulties. Australia, could sell her wheat to the Continent rather than to the United Kingdom and India, while India and Pakistan could develop Japan and the Continent as markets for their cotton.

In discussing the large volume of intra-area trade as a cohesive force, it should not be overlooked, moreover, that even in cases where the dependence of outer sterling area countries on the British market is great, the United Kingdom frequently has no practicable alternative source of supply. It is true, for example, that Australia and New Zealand are heavily dependent on Britain as a market for their wool exports. If Britain did not buy wool from these countries, however, it would have to obtain its wool from either Argentina or Uruguay, the only two important wool exporters outside the sterling area. It is questionable that Britain would willingly increase her dependence on these two countries. Likewise, the monopoly which Pakistan and India enjoy in the production of jute and jute products precludes Britain from obtaining these supplies from other sources. The dependence of outer sterling area countries on the British market is thus to some extent offset by Britain's dependence on these countries as sources of supply.

These considerations should not be interpreted to mean that the large volume of intra-area trade is of no importance as a cohesive force. They are designed, rather, to suggest that the significance of this tie has been overexaggerated in the literature and that in the absence of other cohesive factors, it is not probable that this alone will suffice to maintain the sterling area arrangements.

The second cohesive factor cited above—the relative stability of the British market for outer sterling area exports—appears to be much more significant. In the past the American economy has been notoriously unstable and this had had disastrous consequences for outer sterling area countries. By contrast, the British economy has been relatively stable with the result that the fluctuations of overseas sterling area exports to the United Kingdom have been very much less severe than those of sterling area exports to the United States. Indeed, as was noted above, many countries chose the sterling standard after 1931 largely because of considerations of stability. There can be little doubt that in so far as this factor is concerned, the sterling area arrangements are likely to remain attractive to outer sterling area countries. The future strength of this factor, however, will depend in very large part upon how the American economy behaves. Should the United States succeed in avoiding the instability which characterized her economy in the past, the importance of this factor will diminish.

Long association and the feeling of belonging together are, on the other hand, alone unlikely to be important cohesive forces. If all other things were equal, the fact that the current sterling area countries have a long history of association during which a strong feeling of unity developed, would, of course, be extremely significant. It is questionable, however, whether the sterling area countries will place much weight on this factor if the costs of membership in the sterling area are high. Sir Douglas Copland stated the case succinctly:

It would be foolish for a country like Australia to refrain from seeking American capital . . . because of an unwillingness to break the traditional relationship in trade and financial policy with the United Kingdom. The alternative is to incur a continued shortage of capital that will hamper development in Australia, to sustain and perhaps to intensify restrictions on trade, to narrow the channels of Australia's overseas trade, and thus to limit the range of our economic achievement. . . . To be influenced by those who seek to excuse their own timidity by raising the cry of loyalty to the sterling area, will be to take Australia out of the main stream of development.[50]

Although Copland is one of the most severe critics of the postwar sterling area arrangements, his is by no means a voice in the wilderness. The sentiments expressed by Copland have been echoed in practically every sterling area country in the postwar period, and there can be very little doubt that if the drawbacks of membership should outweigh the advantages, few sterling area countries would be deterred from severing their bonds with sterling because of the long tradition of association and the

[50] Copland, "Factors Determining the Efficiency of Australian Production," in R. F. Holden and others, *Australian Production at the Crossroads*.

feeling of belonging together. Membership in the sterling area—and before that in the sterling bloc—has always been based on convenience and self-interest. Should the costs of membership outweigh the advantages, the sterling area, at least as it existed in the postwar period, will not survive.

This is not to imply, of course, that sterling will cease to be used as an international currency or even that some countries will not continue to hold a major part of their reserves in sterling. Sterling's supremacy in the pre-World War I period was due in no small part to London's well-developed money market. Holding sterling balances and financing overseas trade through the use of sterling bills of exchange will undoubtedly remain a convenience for some countries. Britain's diminishing importance as a capital exporter and as a supplier of the types of goods the outer sterling area countries are most likely to demand, however, are likely to reduce the significance of this consideration.

Although the conclusion that emerges from the preceding discussion is somewhat disquieting, it should not be surprising. The prewar sterling bloc came into existence because of the strong position of the United Kingdom in the world economy. The war and postwar sterling area was in large part a defensive mechanism. With the serious waning of Britain's economic power and the reduced need for defensive arrangements, it is almost inevitable that Britain will have to relinquish the position of leadership that is implied by her being the center of an important currency area, based not on force but volition.

VII *Dollar Payments to Non-Dollar Countries, 1946-51*

HAVING CONSIDERED the factors responsible for the deterioration of Britain's and the rest of the sterling area's direct dollar accounts between the prewar and postwar periods, attention in this chapter is focused on the dollar payments effected on whole sterling area account to non-dollar countries. These payments accounted for 19 percent of the total sterling area's dollar deficit between 1946 and 1951, while in particular years the proportion of the dollar deficit accounted for by sterling area gold and dollar payments to third countries was substantially higher.

The larger drain of gold and dollars to third countries serves as a salutary reminder that the postwar dollar problem was not a peculiarly sterling area phenomenon. Indeed, to a lesser or greater extent, virtually every country outside the Soviet orbit suffered from a dollar shortage in the postwar period. As in the case of the sterling area, the precipitous rise in the American export price level between the prewar and postwar periods, the decline of primary production in non-dollar countries, necessitating the placing of heavier reliance on dollar sources of supply, and the huge postwar demand for capital goods, obtainable, in large part, only in the dollar area, were the chief factors responsible for the general postwar dollar shortage. However, the sterling area's postwar dollar problem accentuated the difficulties of the third countries. In the interwar period these countries relied, in varying degrees, on their dollar earnings from the sterling area to discharge their own direct dollar deficits. The United Kingdom's failure to earn enough gold and dollar surpluses from the rest of the sterling area in the postwar period to offset her own direct dollar deficit jeopardized the position of the third countries which traditionally earned dollars from the United Kingdom. Their frequently successful attempts to continue earning the requisite dollars from the sterling area contributed, in turn, to the sterling area's postwar dollar problem.

The success third countries enjoyed in the postwar period in earning dollars from the sterling area was a function of their bargaining positions vis-à-vis the sterling area. Generally speaking, those countries which specialized in the production and export of "essential" commodities were in a position to demand and obtain dollars in payment for these exports. Thus, despite the fact that the sterling area earned consistently high surpluses from Western Europe in the period under discussion, the drain of gold and dollars to particular countries in this group—notably Belgium, Switzerland, and West Germany—imposed a heavy drain on sterling area reserves. These countries [1] were in the fortunate position of being able to supply the United Kingdom and the rest of the sterling area with goods which were otherwise obtainable only in the dollar area and were thus able to demand at least partial payment in dollars.

Britain's postwar financial relations with the non-dollar countries frequently took on the character of a tug of war. The British were intent upon minimizing the drain of gold and dollars to these countries, while continuing to derive from them essential imports. These countries, in turn, were equally intent upon maintaining their dollar earnings from "third sources" at as high a level as possible. This conflict of interests can be put in another way; faced with the postwar world shortage of dollars, the British were intent upon generalizing the problem as much as possible. Other non-dollar countries, on the other hand, attempted to particularize it, to shift the burden of the shortage, as much as possible, to the sterling area. The gold and dollar payments the sterling area made to third countries in the postwar period is a measure of the success enjoyed by these countries.[2]

The gold and dollar payments the sterling area made to third countries were intimately related to the evolution of Britain's postwar payments machinery. It is thus necessary to examine this evolution to understand the manner in which this particular drain on the sterling area's reserves eventuated. A word of caution is necessary. A comprehensive analysis of Britain's postwar payments machinery would require a study of its own which it is neither possible nor desirable to undertake at this juncture. All that is required for the purposes at hand is a broad sketch of the developments; greater detail would undoubtedly contribute to clarity but would not appreciably alter the major picture.

---

[1] In the case of Belgium this includes the associated monetary area.

[2] The threat of losing dollars to the OEEC countries was a major factor responsible for Britain's policy of retaining import control against OEEC goods while making liberal sterling releases. It was felt that the sterling releases could be more readily controlled than sterling accruing to OEEC countries as a result of an increase in imports.

POSTWAR PAYMENTS ARRANGEMENTS

The development of Britain's postwar payments machinery with non-dollar countries falls into four distinct phases. In the first phase, occupying in point of time about a year after the cessation of hostilities, the United Kingdom attempted to reconstruct the payments machinery with non-dollar countries in a manner designed to maximize trade but minimize the need for dollar payments. Under the circumstances it was believed that these two desiderata were interdependent; the British authorities argued that with the over-all dollar shortage, maximization of trade was contingent upon removing the dollar from non-American trade, and payments arrangements in this phase reflect this belief. In the second phase, which coincided with the implementation of the convertibility agreement, Britain undertook, with some exceptions, to allow free and unrestricted transferability of currently earned and newly released sterling.[3] The large drain on Britain's reserves brought this phase to an end and ushered in the third phase, during which Britain reverted, in part, to her original desire to remove the dollar from non-American trade and to extend the area of transferability to whatever limits were compatible with this end. In the fourth phase, which coincided with Britain's participation in European regional payments schemes, the United Kingdom took an important step toward the reestablishment of sterling convertibility.

Preconvertibility Payments Machinery. The evolution of Britain's payments machinery can be understood only in the context of the developing economic scene. Immediately after the end of the war, effective demand for goods exceeded the ability to produce in virtually every country. Moreover, as a result of the serious impairment to the non-dollar world's productive capacity and the reduced levels of primary production in non-dollar countries, many of the commodities which were in shortest supply were obtainable only from the dollar area. This gave rise to a competitive scramble for the available dollars and to a jealous guarding of those dollars and other hard currencies that were earned. Wherever possible, countries demanded payments in dollars for their exports while attempting to discharge their trade debts in soft currencies.

Few countries were willing to hold substantial balances of another's currency for any length of time. In general, if a country could not use these soft cur-

---

[3] Since the free transferability extended to the American account countries, the freedom of transferability, in effect, meant the restoration of convertibility as far as current sterling was concerned.

rencies for essential imports, it tried to get gold or dollars for them. At the same time, each country tried as often as it could to sell its own products for dollars, either by directing its exports to hard currency countries, or if the goods it had to offer were scarce enough, by insisting that [the] customers pay for them in dollars. A country that exported more to another than it imported from that country usually could not use the excess to pay its debts to a third country from which it might have bought more than it sold. So trade in the [early] post war period tended to revert to bilateral barter, mitigated by the willingness of some countries to grant credit to the others or by a limited use of gold and dollars to pay trading debts.[4]

Britain played an active role in the negotiation of bilateral monetary agreements in the early postwar period. Her goal was to maximize non-dollar trade by reducing to the minimum the possibility of losing gold and dollars through this trade. The central features of the bilateral monetary agreements were the establishment of an official rate of exchange, mutual promises of cooperation with respect to exchange control matters, and the creation of overdraft facilities. This latter provision was designed to reduce the need for dollar payments in discharging trade debts incurred with non-dollar countries.

Britain's success in eliminating the dollar from "third country" trade varied with the circumstances. The early monetary agreements negotiated with Denmark, Sweden, and Norway, for example, provided for unlimited overdraft facilities. Those negotiated with Belgium, Switzerland, Portugal, Spain, and the Netherlands, on the other hand, stipulated specific "swings," accumulations beyond which were to be fully convertible into gold. It is of some interest to examine the provisions of one of these "gold point" agreements in greater detail.

The monetary agreement negotiated with Belgium in October, 1944, provided for the accumulation by the respective central banks of an amount of the other country's currency up to five million pounds or its franc equivalent. Any accumulation beyond this amount, however, was to be freely convertible into gold or dollars. The agreement also provided for the administrative transferability of the other country's currency. This latter provision meant that currencies could not be transferred unless prior consent was obtained from the exchange control authorities of the country whose currency was to be transferred. This concept of administrative transferability, which was to play a leading role in the post-convertibility payments machinery, was formulated to prevent a loss of gold or dollars through the transfer of a currency to a country whose holdings of that currency were near the agreed "gold point."

[4] Diebold, *Trade and Payments in Western Europe*, p. 17.

Though these bilateral monetary agreements had obvious shortcomings, they played an important role in preventing "third country" trade from being reduced to a trickle. In the circumstances prevailing in the early postwar period any arrangement that provided for some extension of credit, no matter how limited, and a partial removal of gold and dollars from third country trade was desirable. Had Britain succeeded in her attempt to remove the dollar completely from non-dollar trade there undoubtedly would have been a greater expansion of non-dollar trade than actually occurred.

Britain's Payments Arrangements during the Convertibility Period. As a quid pro quo for an American line of credit, Britain undertook to remove "all restrictions on payments and transfers" from the United Kingdom to any other country and to make the sterling receipts of all sterling area countries arising out of current transactions "freely available for current transactions in any currency areas without discrimination." The implementation of these provisions of the Anglo-American loan agreement necessitated drastic changes in Britain's payments machinery.

The United Kingdom effected the necessary changes through the American accounts and the transferable accounts system. American accounts were established for eighteen countries, mainly in the Western Hemisphere.[5] All sterling accruing to the American account countries was freely convertible into United States dollars on demand and freely transferable to other accounts.

The creation of the transferable account system was the most important modification effected to meet Britain's obligations under the provisions of the Anglo-American financial agreement. Through this device, Britain attempted to fulfill the convertibility obligation while fostering the use of sterling as an international currency in order to minimize the drain resulting from the restoration of sterling convertibility. Countries for whom transferable accounts were established undertook to accept sterling unconditionally from all sources in payment for current transactions and were required to maintain a sufficiently comprehensive and workable exchange control to preclude the transfer of sterling on capital accounts. The fulfilling of these prerequisites before obtaining transferable account status meant in effect that the transferable account countries

agreed to use and *hold* sterling as an international currency. First they agreed to accept sterling from all countries in payment for exports or for any other current purpose. Second, they agreed to retain the sterling they earned until

[5] See Table 46. The American accounts were established in July, 1945, by merging the United States account and the Central American accounts.

such time as they needed to use it for buying imports or making other current payments. In effect, therefore, they committed themselves to sterling both as a means of international payments and as an international store of value.[6]

Transferable account countries were allowed free and automatic transferability of sterling to virtually all accounts,[7] including the American accounts. Since sterling in the latter accounts was freely convertible into dollars, transferable account countries enjoyed, in effect, convertibility privileges with respect to all currently earned sterling required to discharge obligations on current accounts.

The implementation of the convertibility obligation with respect to the resident account (sterling area) countries involved the elimination of the discriminatory aspects of the dollar pool. It should be noted, however, that Britain did not commit herself to the dissolution of the dollar pool per se. It was noted above that even in the prewar period countries on the sterling standard customarily sold their excess foreign exchange earnings to London. As long as this practice did not lead to discrimination it was not outlawed by the Anglo-American Financial Agreement, which sought to ban only the discriminatory aspects of dollar pooling.

There remained a miscellaneous group of countries that for one or another reason was not accorded transferable account status by July 15, 1947. This group can be subdivided into three parts. One consisted of Switzerland and the occupied countries Germany and Japan that refused to acquiesce to Britain's demand that sterling be freely acceptable on current account as a prerequisite to achieving transferable account status. These countries received the right of direct convertibility of currently earned sterling subject to the provisions of the prevailing bilateral monetary agreements. A second group consisted of countries with whom Britain was unable to reach a satisfactory agreement by July 15. Britain obtained United States permission to postpone temporarily the date of implementation of the convertibility agreement with these countries. The third group consisted of countries which were deprived of transferable account status because of their inability to maintain sufficiently comprehensive and workable exchange controls. These countries were granted the right of administrative transferability.

The accompanying table shows the composition of the various accounts during the brief convertibility period.

[6] Tew, *International Monetary Cooperation, 1945–1952*, p. 132.

[7] The sole exception to this concerned the right of transferability to some countries in the miscellaneous group discussed below.

TABLE 46

STERLING ACCOUNTS IN THE PRECONVERTIBILITY PERIOD

RESIDENT ACCOUNTS (Sterling Area)
The British Commonwealth except
  Canada and Newfoundland)
Faroe Islands
Iceland
Iraq
Ireland
Palestine
Transjordan

AMERICAN ACCOUNTS
Bolivia
Chile
Colombia
Costa Rica
Cuba
Dominican Republic
Ecuador
El Salvador
Guatemala
Haiti
Honduras
Mexico
Nicaragua
Panama
Peru
Philippine Islands
United States and dependencies
Venezuela

TRANSFERABLE ACCOUNT COUNTRIES
Argentina
Belgium and monetary area
Brazil
Canada and Newfoundland
Czechoslovakia
Egypt and Sudan
Ethiopia
Finland
Iran
Italy
The Netherlands and monetary area
Norway
Portugal and monetary area
Spain
Sweden
Uruguay

Source: *Midland Bank Review.*

OTHER ACCOUNTS
Countries that refused to accept
  sterling unconditionally
Germany (occupation authorities)
Japan (occupation authorities)
Switzerland
Countries unable to maintain suf-
  ficiently comprehensive ex-
  change control systems
Afghanistan
Albania
Korea
Liberia
Nepal
Saudi Arabia
Tangier
Countries with which Britain failed
  to reach agreements by July
  15, 1957
Austria
Bulgaria
China
Denmark
France and monetary area
Greece
Hungary
Paraguay
Poland
Rumania
Siam
Turkey
U.S.S.R.
Yugoslavia

Restoring sterling convertibility at a time of a general dollar shortage was a fiasco, and the events immediately following the restoration demonstrated clearly the wisdom of Britain's earlier policy in endeavoring to remove the dollar from non-American trade. Far from expanding trade, as the adherents of convertibility had argued, the restoration of convertibility resulted in an intensification of import and currency restrictions as dollar-short countries attempted to increase their earnings of convertible sterling.[8] The ability to earn convertible sterling was frequently not evidence of superior efficiency but rather of a restrictive commercial policy. This resulted in a huge drain on Britain's reserves. The accompanying table shows the amount of sterling selected countries managed to convert during the brief convertibility period.

TABLE 47
CONVERSION OF STERLING INTO DOLLARS,
JANUARY TO AUGUST 31, 1947
(*In millions of pounds*)

	Jan.–June, 1947	July–Aug., 1947	Total
Argentina	18.7	23.3	42.0
Belgium and monetary area	18.3	34.4	52.7
Brazil	5.0	7.5	12.5
Finland		2.8	2.8
Italy	1.3	1.3	2.6
Netherlands and monetary area	1.1	2.7	3.8
Portugal and monetary area	4.7	2.9	7.6
Other countries	0.2	0.9	1.1
Total (pounds)	49.3	75.8	125.1
Total (dollars)	197.2	303.2	500.4

Source: Hansard, V, 443, c. 219–20 (written reply).

The drain on Britain's reserve during the period of convertibility and the almost complete exhaustion of the American credit necessitated the suspension of the convertibility arrangements.

Britain's Payments Machinery from the Suspension of Convertibility to the Establishment of the Intra-European Payments Schemes. The suspension of convertibility following the precipitous drain on the reserves necessi-

---

[8] Currency restrictions were imposed in Argentina, Belgium, Chile, Czechoslovakia, Holland, Norway, Spain, Syria, Peru, Lebanon, Uruguay, Brazil, and Mexico. The object of these restrictions was to reduce the value of imports from the sterling area in order to earn convertible sterling. Many of the countries which levied restrictions of one sort or another against sterling area goods were in surplus with the sterling area even before the restrictions were imposed. See *The Economist*, August 9, 1947, p. 253, and United Nations, ECE, *Economic Conditions and Prospects of Europe*, p. 105.

tated important modifications in Britain's payments machinery. Between the suspension of convertibility and the establishment of the Intra-European Payment Schemes, Britain effected two major modifications in the payments machinery. One concerned the degree of transferability and convertibility attached to different accounts; the other, composition of the accounts.

The rights and privileges of the American account and resident account countries remained virtually unchanged in the postconvertibility period. All sterling accruing to American accounts remained fully convertible into dollars; the only modification, and one of little importance, was that sterling accruing to American accounts was no longer automatically transferable to the bilateral accounts.

Theoretically, sterling area countries continued to have free access to the dollar pool, although in practice this freedom was moderated in two ways: the rights of some sterling area countries to draw on the pool was limited by negotiated agreements [9] and, perhaps of greater importance, the discriminatory aspects of the dollar pool were reintroduced.[10]

The degree of transferability attached to the transferable account countries was drastically modified. Automatic transferability was limited in the postconvertibility period to the transfer of sterling to resident accounts, to other transferable accounts, and to a residual group of countries; the right of automatic transfer to either American account or bilateral account countries was withdrawn.

Three countries in the bilateral group, Argentina, Canada, and Iran, enjoyed virtually full convertibility privileges. To other bilateral countries, however, the right of automatic transferability was limited to the transfer of sterling to the resident accounts. All other transfers were governed by the principle of administrative rather than automatic transferability. The prevailing monetary agreements with their stipulated "swings" (gold points) determined the degree of convertibility for the bilateral countries.

In addition to modifying the degree of transferability attached to the different accounts, the United Kingdom effected important changes in the composition of the accounts, with the intent of minimizing the loss of dollars to third countries. Chile and Peru, which had American account status during the convertibility period, were transferred to other groups— Peru to the bilateral account group and Chile to the transferable account

9 See above, p. 126.
10 See above, p. 88.

group.   Six countries—Argentina, Brazil, Canada, Uruguay, Belgium, and
Portugal—were moved from the transferable account group to the bilateral
account group.   Seven countries—Austria, Denmark, Greece, Poland,
Siam, the U.S.S.R., and West Germany—which had been in the miscellaneous group during the convertibility period, were accorded transferability account status.

TABLE 48
STERLING ACCOUNTS IN THE POSTCONVERTIBILITY PERIOD
AMERICAN ACCOUNTS
As above on page 165 except for the removal of Chile and Peru.

TRANSFERABLE ACCOUNTS

Anglo-Egyptian Sudan	Greece
Austria [a]	Italian monetary area
Chile [d]	Netherlands monetary area
Czechoslovakia	Norway
Denmark [a]	Poland [a]
The Faroe Islands and	Spanish monetary area
Greenland [c]	Sweden
Egypt	Thailand [a]
Ethiopia	U.S.S.R. [a]
Finland	Western Zones of Germany [a]

BILATERAL ACCOUNTS

Argentina [b]	Lebanon [a]
Belgium monetary area [b]	Paraguay [a]
French Somaliland [a]	Peru [d]
French franc area [a]	Portuguese monetary
Brazil [b]	area [b]
Bulgaria [a]	Rumania [a]
Canada [b]	Switzerland [a]
China [a]	Syria [a]
Formosa [a]	Tangier [a]
Hungary [a]	Turkey [a]
Iran [b]	Uruguay [a]
Israel [c]	Vatican City
Japan [a]	Yugoslavia

RESIDUAL GROUP

Afghanistan	Liberia
Albania	Nepal
Andorra	Saudi Arabia
Eritrea	Yemen

[a] Formerly "other account" countries, see p. 165.
[b] Formerly transferable account countries.
[c] Formerly resident account.
[d] Formerly American account.

The rationale behind these changes was to accord transferable account status to only those countries that were prepared to accept and hold sterling. The authorities were reluctant to grant transferable account status to countries which were persistently in surplus or in deficit on sterling accounts. The granting of transferable account status to persistent creditors might lead to a loss of dollars from an accumulation of sterling by the creditors in excess of the "swings" established in the bilateral monetary agreements. The granting of transferable account status to persistent debtors would have intensified these countries' difficulties in effecting payment to sterling area countries.

The modifications of Britain's payments machinery in the postconvertibility period were not designed to limit the transfer of sterling but rather to preclude the loss of gold and dollars to third countries. Indeed, the authorities tended to encourage the maximum degree of transferability compatible with the preservation of the reserves. Table 49, which shows the amount of sterling transferred automatically and administratively in 1948 and 1949, suggests that the authorities broadly interpreted the concept of administrative transferability.

TABLE 49

TRANSFER OF STERLING, 1948 AND 1949

(*In millions of pounds*)

	1948	1949
Automatic	88	144
Administrative	152	125
Total	240	269

Source: Bank of England, *Report for the Year Ending February 28, 1951*, p. 6.

Britain and the European Regional Payment Schemes. Though the bilateral monetary agreements of the early postwar period were instrumental in expanding trade over the level that would otherwise have been achieved, developments with respect to intra-Europan trade were far from satisfactory. The major defects of the postwar monetary agreements were that they fostered an expansion of trade along bilateral lines and that they provided for an inadequate margin of credit. It was apparent fairly early in the postwar period that a regional approach to Europe's payments problem offered the best means to increase intra-European trade.

Establishing a regional payments scheme was hindered by persistent creditors and debtors. The extreme shortage of goods and dollars that existed in the early postwar period precluded the indefinite extension of credit. The creditors were reluctant to accumulate "soft" currencies which could not be used to discharge payments in areas from which essential imports could be obtained. The debtors were equally reluctant to undertake the conversion of their currencies into precious gold or dollars. The postwar regional payments schemes occurred within the framework of this basic conflict of interests.

The first regional payments scheme that attempted to obviate the necessity for a rigid bilateral equalization of accounts was the result of a multilateral compensation agreement involving Belgium, France, Italy, the Netherlands, and the Bizone as full members and Denmark, Norway, Sweden, the United Kingdom, Greece, Portugal, and the French Zone of Germany as occasional members. The agreement, which was signed in November, 1947, and came into operation in January, 1948, did not supersede the existing bilateral monetary agreements. The aim of the multilateral agreement was "to provide a means whereby credit and debit balances arising under the payments agreements may be mutually offset . . . to reduce the necessity for gold transfers in settlement of these balances and restore credit margins for purposes of further trade financing." [11]

This agreement was important mainly because it laid the groundwork for the Intra-European Payments Scheme. The operation of the regional scheme which resulted from the multilateral agreement and the problems to which it gave rise were identical in all respects to those which resulted from the operation of the Intra-European Payments Schemes and are best discussed in that context.

The Intra-European Payments Schemes (IEPS). The Intra-European Payments Schemes were established to facilitate and increase intra-European trade by tying drawing rights extended by prospective creditors to prospective debtors to the dollar aid provided by the United States through the ERP program.[12] The stimulation of intra-European trade was considered a prime necessity if Europe were ultimately to reduce her dependence on American aid. In the early postwar years western Europe's dollar shortage was accentuated by the low levels of production and the failure of intra-European trade to revive. By 1948, despite notable strides toward the restoration of production, intra-European trade continued to lag.[13] It

[11] United Nations, ECE, *Economic Situation and Prospects of Europe,* p. 100.

[12] Other provisions to facilitate intra-European trade were concerned with trade liberalization measures.

[13] See United Nations, ECE, *Economic Survey of Europe in 1948,* p. 134, and OEEC, *European Recovery Program, Second Report of the OEEC,* Paris, February, 1950, p. 33.

became evident that, among other things, a new payments machinery was necessary to encourage an expansion of trade, and the first Intra-European Payments Scheme was designed to accomplish this objective.

The negotiations leading to the Intra-European Payments Scheme revealed once more the strong British desire to eliminate the dollar as much as possible from non-dollar trade. The American position in the negotiations was that the Intra-European Payments Scheme should be regarded as a first step toward the restoration of full convertibility of European currencies. Accordingly, the Americans argued that the drawing rights made available by the prospective creditors should be freely transferable. This position was shared by the prospective debtor countries, which wanted maximum freedom in using the drawing rights, and Belgium, the leading prospective creditor, who foresaw the possibility of earning hard currency through the accumulation of European currencies beyond the gold points of the bilateral monetary agreements.[14] It was precisely for this reason, however, that Britain objected to the American scheme.[15] Sir Stafford Cripps argued for almost complete bilateralism with respect to the utilization of the drawing rights, tempered with a degree of administrative transferability. Britain's refusal to participate in any Intra-European Payments Scheme that would increase the risk of gold and dollar losses to third countries ultimately led to the acceptance of her position.

In the final draft, the first Intra-European Payments Scheme provided for two types of compensations made possible by the extension of drawing rights from prospective creditors to prospective debtors; first category compensations were to be effected automatically by the agent [16] while second category compensations required the prior approval of the parties concerned. First category compensations could occur in either of two ways. The first consisted of the utilization of the drawing rights by the debtor to discharge a direct debt to the extender of the drawing rights. This type

[14] The Intra-European Payments Scheme was constructed on the foundations of the bilateral monetary agreements. Thus an accumulation of currency by, for example, Belgium beyond the bilateral gold point would lead to gold outflows to Belgium.

[15] Cripps stated the case clearly before the House of Commons. "If [transferable drawing rights were allowed] . . . it would inevitably involve us in payment of gold to those European countries whose currency is hard, and we clearly can not accept such a possibility . . . . The whole purpose of the payments scheme is to enable European trade to be carried on without recourse to gold or dollar payments . . . . We have made our position quite clear in OEEC and we can not depart from it." Hansard, V, 456, c. 263–4.

[16] The Bank for International Settlements was established as the agent for the Intra-European Payments Schemes.

of compensation resulted in the "decrease in one or more debit balances against an equivalent decrease in one or more credit balances." [17]   The second type of first category compensations consisted of the utilization of a drawing right to discharge a debt with a country that, in turn, was in deficit with the extender of the drawing right.   The common denominator of these two types of first category compensations was that in neither case could the compensation lead to an accumulation of the prospective creditor's currency by another country that, in turn, was a creditor of the extender of the drawing right; the utilization of drawing rights could not lead to a loss of gold and dollars.   Second category compensations consisted of the utilization of drawing rights to discharge deficits with third countries that were, in turn, creditors to the extender of the drawing rights.   Since the utilization of drawing rights in this fashion could lead to an outflow of gold from the country extending the drawing rights, it could be effected only with the prior approval of all parties.

Total drawing rights established under the first Intra-European Payments Scheme amounted to 805 million dollars, with Britain extending 334 million dollars and receiving a drawing right against Belgium equal to 30 million dollars.   In addition the United Kingdom allowed some participating countries to draw down their accumulated sterling balances by 150 million dollars to discharge current account deficits with the sterling area.

Though the operation of the first Intra-European Payments Scheme enabled an expansion of intra-European trade, the payments plan had many defects.   The expansion in European trade was mainly along bilateral lines; second category compensation in the year 1948–49 amounted to but 5 million dollars.[18]   The existence of over-all creditors and over-all debtors precluded the possibility of effecting important multilateral compensations as long as the prior consent of the participants was required. The payments scheme not only failed to achieve a significant expansion in intra-European multilateral trade but it tended to encourage the extension of bilateralism.   The establishment of the drawing rights on a bilateral basis set up a rigid pattern of trade which, with the passage of time, did not necessarily conform to the underlying economic conditions.

The debtor countries received drawing rights on particular countries and used these drawing rights even though it in effect meant that they bought their imports from high price sources.   Because the imports they got from the country

[17] *Agreement for Intra-European Payments Scheme,* Cmd. 7456, p. 4.
[18] ECA, *Fifth Annual Report to Congress,* 1949, p. 13.

extending drawing rights were in effect free, considerations of price were of secondary importance. This tended to put Europe's trade into a straitjacket, the rigidity of which was ensured by the fact that the drawing rights were not transferable.[19]

Finally, the payments scheme failed to provide deficit countries with sufficiently strong incentives to remove the disequilibrium.

These defects emanated in large part from the fact that a payments scheme that would have allowed a greater degree of flexibility would also have exposed some countries to the possibility of losing gold to other participating members. The outstanding lesson of the brief convertibility experiment was that the introduction of the dollar into non-American trade at a time of a general dollar shortage would inevitably lead to a contraction rather than expansion of non-dollar trade.

Britain's intent to avoid this motivated her position in the negotiations leading to the first Intra-European Payments Scheme and was equally important in the renegotiation of the second payments scheme in the spring of 1949. In these negotiations the United States, with the support of Belgium, proposed that the drawing rights be made freely transferable and convertible into dollars.

The ECA advised the OEEC that it attached great importance to the encouragement of multilateral trade and intensification of competition and that the new agreement should be designed to contribute to this end. . . . The ECA favored the greatest possible transfer of drawing rights among particular countries, with some possibility of the holders of drawing rights to convert them into dollars for expenditure elsewhere. It was felt that these provisions would enable European buyers to choose more freely among competing sellers. Intensification of competition would stimulate a downward adjustment of cost and prices and contribute to the increase of European production and improvement of European ability to earn dollars.[20]

The United Kingdom was the most vociferous opponent of this plan. Cripps argued that the introduction of the dollar would inevitably lead to a contraction of European trade, that American competition in Europe would tend to reduce the effectiveness of American aid,[21] and that, in view

[19] *The Economist,* February 15, 1949, p. 249. Also see United Nations, ECE, *Economic Survey of Europe in 1948,* pp. 141–145.

[20] ECA, *Fifth Annual Report to Congress,* p. 14.

[21] Cripps's argument was that with a given amount of dollar aid an increase in the dollar imports of commercially stronger countries must necessarily be accompanied by a reduction in the dollar imports of the commercially weaker countries. This arrangement was thus likely to lead to the importation, by Europe as a whole, of less essential goods.

of the fact that Britain was the largest extender of drawing rights, the ability to use these drawing rights multilaterally would expose her to the greatest danger of losing gold. Cripps proposed in lieu of the American plan the extension of the first Intra-European Payments Scheme for another year.

The revised Intra-European Payments Scheme, which came into effect in July, 1949, and which was to run for one year, represented a compromise between the British and the American views. Twenty-five percent of the drawing rights was extended multilaterally while the remainder was extended on a bilateral basis. Other provisions that affected Belgium's position in the Intra-European Payments Scheme,[22] assuring greater flexibility [23] and increasing incentives,[24] were incorporated into the revised agreement. Basically, however, the revised payments scheme, like the original one, reflected, in large part, Britain's desire to minimize the risks of gold and dollar losses from intra-European trade. And while Britain's adamant stand led to some rigidities and distortions, it was, all things considered, the wisest course to follow under the circumstances. In 1949 the dollar was becoming scarcer, and the restoration of even partial convertibility, as advocated by the ECA, would undoubtedly have led to a reduction in the over-all volume of trade.

The European Payments Union (EPU). The compromise embodied in the revised Intra-European Payments Scheme was not satisfactory to the advocates of greater multilateralism and convertibility. Moreover, as the time approached for the cessation of American aid many advocates of schemes designed to expand intra-European trade had misgivings concerning a payments arrangement, the efficient operation of which was con-

---

[22] Belgium, an over-all creditor, was induced to extend long-term credit to her debtors to help finance part of her intra-European surplus. This arrangement was necessitated by the fact that Belgium's prospective surplus with the OEEC countries was expected to exceed Belgium's dollar deficit by some 200 million dollars with the result that even if drawing rights were extended equal to her dollar deficit part of her European surplus would remain uncovered.

[23] Greater flexibility was introduced through the provision calling for a periodic review of the plan and for possible revision of the schedule of drawing rights.

[24] Several provisions were inserted in the new intra-European payments scheme to increase incentives. Thus a creditor could complain against the "abnormal use of the multilateral drawing rights established in favor of any of its debtors," while a debtor could complain if the extension of the drawing rights resulted in efforts by the creditor to perpetuate the deficits. These provisions were at best ambiguous. Cf. *Agreement for Intra-European Payments and Compensations for 1949–1950,* September 7, 1949; Diebold, *Trade and Payments,* p. 70 ff.; ECA, *Ninth Report to Congress,* p. 21 ff.

tingent upon the continued existence of American aid. Accordingly, by the time the second Intra-European Payments Scheme expired, considerable sentiment developed for the establishment of machinery that would allow for a greater degree of multilateralism than did the payments scheme and that was not as dependent on the continued extension of American aid. The European Payments Union was the outgrowth of this climate of opinion.

The fundamental aim of the European Payments Union was the restoration of full transferability between European currencies and partial convertibility of these currencies into dollars.

Under the Union, each country's surpluses or deficits with every OEEC country were set off against one another, leaving it with a single net surplus or deficit with the European Payments Union. Debts less than a certain amount were completely covered by an automatic grant of credit. If the debt exceeded the credit grant part of it was covered by credits and part by payments of gold and dollars. These arrangements made the European Payments Union a flexible and largely automatic system capable of clearing up a much larger proportion of intra-European debts than the earlier agreements. The successful working of the Union assumed a certain degree of balance in intra-European trade; the sliding scale of dollar payments helped produce a balance by giving debtors an incentive to reduce their deficits.[25]

The negotiations leading up to the European Payments Union reveal the extent to which the British approach to the payments problem was still motivated by the fear of losing dollars. Initially, the British refused to join the proposed union because of the special position of sterling as a world currency. Specifically, the British argued that the existing wide transferability of sterling would enable the European Payments Union countries to earn sterling from third countries and would involve Britain in a loss of gold.[26] The British were also concerned lest the accumulated sterling balances held by the OEEC countries which amounted to 378 pounds in June, 1950, be presented for clearance through the European Payments Union machinery and thus become partially converted into gold. The British proposed, in lieu of the original plan, that she be given a special status in the Union whereby, as a quid pro quo for the retention of her complex bilateral monetary arrangements, the United Kingdom would agree to extend credit to the European Payments Union members to enable them to finance their sterling deficits, while Britain would forego the right

[25] Diebold, *Trade and Payments,* p. 87.
[26] Cf. Sargent, *Britain and Europe,* in Worswick, *British Economy.*

to borrow from the European Payments Union. This plan proved un-
acceptable to the United States and to the other participating countries.[27]

Even after Britain acquiesced to become a full member of the Union,
she argued for stronger guarantees against the loss of gold, and proposed
that the credit margins be widened and the gold payment obligations nar-
rowed.   Furthermore, the British insisted that the Charter of the European Payments Union sanction the right to discriminate in favor of any
participating country which became a debtor to the Union and to discriminate against persistent creditors.   The British insistence on the inclusion
of these principles almost led to the withdrawal of Belgium from the
negotiations.[28]

The actual agreement did not accord Britain special status, although
the inclusion of several provisions allayed her fears that participation in
the European Payments Union would result in an extraordinarily large
drain of gold emanating from the special position of sterling in world trade
and the existence of a large volume of sterling balances.   Each member
country was assigned a quota approximating 15 percent of her trade and
payments with other member countries in 1949.[29]   These quotas were
the bases used to compute gold payments due the Union or gold receipts
from the Union in accordance with a predetermined schedule.   Thus a
country that incurred a net deficit with the Union amounting to 20 percent
or less of its quota automatically received a credit from the Union covering
that deficit.   Likewise, a country that earned a net surplus with the Union
equal to or less than 20 percent of the initial quota automatically extended
credit to the Union to cover the surplus.   Deficit or surplus positions ex-
ceeding 20 percent of the initial quotas were financed partially through additional credits and partially through gold.   The accompanying table shows

[27] At this stage of the negotiations the British conceived the European Payments
Union as a lender of last resort rather than as a mechanism to replace the postwar
bilateral monetary agreements.   The British wanted the European Payments Union
to help finance payments deficits after countries had exhausted the credit margins
established under these bilateral agreements.   Cf. *The Economist,* March 5, 1950,
p. 690, and Diebold, *Trade and Payments,* p. 101.

[28] For an account of the negotiations leading to the establishment of the European Payments Union see Hirschman, "The European Payments Union; Negotiations
and Issues," *The Review of Economics and Statistics,* February 15, 1950.

[29] Britain's quota amounted to 1,060 million dollars and was based on the whole
sterling area's trade with the European Payments Union countries in 1949.   For this
purpose, however, the sterling area is defined exclusive of Ireland which had its own
quota.

TABLE 50

ORIGINAL SCHEDULE FOR FINANCING OF DEFICITS AND CREDITS
UNDER THE EUROPEAN PAYMENTS UNION

| | PAYMENTS | | RECEIPTS | |
Percent of Quota	*Gold*	*Credits*	*Gold*	*Credits*
1st 20		20		20
2nd 20	4	16	10	10
3rd 20	8	12	10	10
4th 20	12	8	10	10
5th 20	16	4	10	10
Total	40	60	40	60

Source: OEEC, *A European Payments Union and the Rules of Commercial Policy to Be Followed by Member Countries,* Paris, 1950, p. 7.

the proportion of deficits and surpluses financed in the two ways discussed above.[30]

The European Payments Union attempted to solve the vexing problem posed by the existence of persistent creditors and debtors by assigning to the prospective creditors initial debit positions and to the prospective debtors initial credit positions. The United Kingdom, a prospective creditor of the Union, was assigned an initial debit of 150 million dollars.

The United Kingdom failed to subordinate the European Payments Union to the bilateral payments machinery which had been laboriously constructed in the postwar period. The British proposal that the European Payments Union be a lender of last resort was rejected, although a generalized option was incorporated into the charter enabling creditors to hold particular currencies instead of the European Payments Union credits. The credits that could be advanced under the bilateral agreements, however, could not exceed

the creditor's cumulative surplus with its partners or the amount the creditor would have to advance to the European Payments Union under the regular provisions of the agreement. Bilateral credits received in this way are deducted

[30] The different schedules for payments and receipts necessitated a working capital fund which was supplied by the ECA. This fund, which amounted to 350 million dollars, was supplied out of the foreign aid funds. In 1952, a threat arose that the dollars would not suffice with the result that the schedule for debtors was changed. Beginning in July, 1952, a debtor country received complete credit only for deficits equal to 10 percent of its quota. Deficits equal to 20 percent of its quota had to be discharged partially in gold. There was also a steepening of gold payments for the early parts of the quota and a reduction in later parts. There was no change, however, in the over-all ratio of gold payments to credits. A change in schedule in July, 1955, resulted in deficit countries discharging 75 percent of their debts in gold.

from the total credits which a debtor country may get from the European Payments Union (or which a creditor must advance to it). In other words, a country may substitute bilateral credits for its credits to or from European Payments Union, but by doing so it may not increase, or decrease, or alter its creditor or debtor position within the group of participating countries.[31]

Thus the generalized option allowing countries to hold their credits in the form of particular member currencies rather than in the form of European Payments Union credits, in no way altered the fundamental payments machinery established under the European Payments Union.

The British likewise failed to gain acceptance of the principle of discrimination in favor of persistent debtors and against persistent creditors, although the OEEC code of trade liberalization did include some broad statements which lend themselves to such an interpretation. Thus the OEEC was authorized to consider changes in policy to rectify a disequilibrium if a creditor's surplus balance with the Union exceeded 75 percent of its quota and to recommend any action "it deems necessary . . . to relieve the payments position of extreme debtors." The possibility of relaxing some of the trade liberalization measures and allowing the debtors to impose import restrictions are specifically mentioned as the type of action the European Payments Union might recommend to rectify a persistent disequilibrium. A debtor country may not apply discriminatory import restrictions unilaterally, however.

The British did succeed in eliminating the danger that she might lose gold and dollars through the use of the accumulated sterling balances in European Payments Union clearings. The ECA agreed to compensate the United Kingdom for any loss of gold and dollars resulting from the use of these balances.[32]

The participation of the United Kingdom in the European Payments Union deprived the complex payments machinery which had developed since the war of much of its significance as far as OEEC countries were concerned. Accordingly, Britain announced that any European Payments Union country could obtain transferable account status on request. While some European Payments Union countries failed to utilize this right, the automatic transferability of OEEC countries' currencies was ensured by the

---

[31] Diebold, *Trade and Payments,* p. 101.

[32] The OEEC countries that held the largest balances were Portugal (80 million pounds), Italy (60 million pounds), France (28 million pounds), and Sweden (22 million pounds).

European Payments Union and thus deprived the transferable accounts system of its original significance.[33]

The analysis of Britain's payments machinery in the postwar period serves as a background against which the sterling area's dollar payments to non-dollar countries can be examined. The accompanying table shows

TABLE 51

NET GOLD AND DOLLAR RECEIPTS FROM (+) OR PAYMENTS TO (−) NON-DOLLAR COUNTRIES, 1946–51

(*In millions of dollars*)

	1946	1947	1948	1949	1950	1951	Total
Western hemisphere countries	− 60	− 233	− 14	− 7	+27	+ 4	− 283
OEEC countries	+ 274	− 503	− 199	− 178	− 21	− 105	− 732
Other non-sterling countries	− 4	− 56	− 74	− 102	− 17	− 60	− 313
Nonterritorial organizations	− 28	− 212	− 30	− 6	− 3	− 4	− 283
Total	+ 183	− 1004	− 317	− 293	− 14	− 165	− 1610

Source: *United Kingdom Balance of Payments, 1946–1953*, Cmd. 8976, Table 20.

the manner in which these payments were incurred.

DOLLAR PAYMENTS TO WESTERN HEMISPHERE COUNTRIES

The heavy dollar drain to the non-dollar Western Hemisphere countries in the early postwar period reflects, in large part, their increased dependence on dollar imports.[34] This produced a rather severe dollar shortage which these countries hoped to correct through dollar earnings from third sources. The importance of exports from the non-dollar Western Hemi-

[33] A substantial modification in Britain's payments arrangements was effected in March, 1954, with the virtual abolition of the bilateral accounts. The five types of sterling accounts which remained were the American accounts, the resident accounts, the transferable accounts, the registered accounts, and the blocked accounts. With two unimportant exceptions, bilateral account countries were given transferable account status. Moreover, the two conditions which formerly had to be satisfied before a country was given transferable account status—the general acceptability of sterling and the obligation not to transfer sterling except as a counterpart of bona fide commercial operations—were no longer applicable. The registered accounts were created as a result of the reopening of London's gold market. Traders outside the sterling and dollar areas can trade on the London gold market with these accounts. The accounts, however, are established only against the proceeds of gold sales or against United States and Canadian dollars. The blocked accounts consisted of the proceeds of sales of certain kinds of sterling assets.

[34] Two factors were primarily responsible for this development: the severe reduction of imports from non-dollar sources during the war and the ambitious industrialization schemes undertaken by Latin and Central American countries, which increased their demand for capital goods.

sphere countries permitted their demand that trade deficits incurred with them be partially liquidated in gold and dollars. Thus even in 1946, before the convertibility agreement was implemented,[35] the sterling area was subject to a loss of gold and dollars to the non-dollar countries of the Western Hemisphere. In 1947, after the implementation of the convertibility agreement and the achievement of transferable account status by the more important non-dollar Western Hemisphere countries, the drain on the sterling area's reserves was accentuated by the heavy conversions made by these countries; Argentina and Brazil alone contrived to convert approximately 220 million dollars between January and September, 1947.

After the convertibility crisis the United Kingdom made a determined effort to reduce dollar payments to non-dollar Western Hemisphere countries by negotiating trade agreements designed to achieve a bilateral balance of payments with the more important of the non-dollar Western Hemisphere countries. The success Britain achieved is reflected in the relatively small dollar payments made to these countries after 1947.

DOLLAR PAYMENTS TO OEEC COUNTRIES

In 1946 the sterling area was the net recipient of 275 million dollars from the OEEC countries. The heavy receipt reflects the generally low levels of production in OEEC countries, and, more particularly, the large deficit France incurred with the sterling area. Indeed, dollar payments by France accounted for a large part of the dollar payments of the OEEC countries to the sterling area in 1946.

The heavy dollar payments the sterling area made to the OEEC countries between 1947 and 1949 is attributable almost wholly to the dollar payments made to Belgium, Switzerland, and the Bizone. In 1947 the sterling area made dollar payments to Switzerland equal to 70 million dollars and to Belgium equal to 270 million dollars.[36] In 1948 gold and

[35] It should be noted that the Anglo-Argentine agreement of September, 1946 (Cmd. 6671), gave Argentina the right to dispose for payment on current transactions all currently earned sterling. Since this provision applied to transfers to the American account countries, Argentina's net sterling earnings were convertible into dollars as early as September, 1946.

[36] United Nations, ECE, *Economic Survey of Europe in 1948,* p. 138. The gold losses to Switzerland are attributable to the deficits of the rest of the sterling area. The United Kingdom had a favorable balance on current account with Switzerland in 1947. The gold losses to Belgium were occasioned, in large part, by the repatriation of Belgian capital and accumulated income, military payments, and the transfer of sterling to Belgium by non-dollar, non-sterling countries.

dollar losses to Belgium amounted to approximately 120 million dollars,[37] while gold and dollar losses to Switzerland and the Bizone continued to be heavy. During the life of the first Intra-European Payments Scheme (between October, 1948, and June, 1949) the United Kingdom made dollar payments to Belgium equal to 115 million dollars, to Switzerland equal to approximately 30 million dollars, and to the Bizone [38] equal to approximately 20 million dollars.[39] During the second year of the Intra-European Payments Scheme, dollar payments made to OEEC countries were severely reduced and amounted to 53 million dollars.[40] The absence of information, official or unofficial, precludes the possibility of dividing this total net dollar payment into the component parts. It is probable, however, that dollar payments to Belgium and, to a smaller extent, Switzerland and the Bizone were responsible for the outflow of gold and dollars to the OEEC countries.

Britain's participation in the European Payments Union broke down the distinction between the different OEEC currencies. Since the European Payments Union supplanted the bilateral monetary agreements, net losses (gains) of gold and dollars to (from) European Payments Union countries could result only from an over-all deficit (surplus) with the OEEC countries rather than from deficits (surpluses) with specific countries, as was the case under the Intra-European Payments Scheme. In the first year of European Payments Union, coinciding as it did with the primary product boom, the sterling area earned an "accounting" [41] surplus equal to 423 million dollars. This surplus was covered by the United Kingdom's extension of a 317 million dollar credit to the Union and by the receipt from the Union of an amount of gold equal in value to 106 million dollars.[42]

The results of the second year of the operation of the European Payments Union were less salutary. The collapse of primary product prices accompanied by the huge increase in sterling area imports from the OEEC

---

[37] *Banker,* June, 1949, p. 159.

[38] The figure for the Bizone is for the period to May, 1949.

[39] Hansard, V, 465, c. 2311 (written reply), and *The Economist,* August 13, 1949, p. 376.

[40] *United Kingdom Balance of Payments* (Cmd. 8065), Table 10, p. 25.

[41] The "accounting" surplus was equal to the net surplus minus the use of "existing resources" by the EPU countries and the initial debit of the United Kingdom.

[42] *Balance of Payments of the United Kingdom, 1946–52,* Cmd. 8666, Tables 12 and 13.

countries resulted in a drastic deterioration of Britain's European Payments Union account. Between the first and second halves of 1951 Britain's current transactions account with the OEEC countries deteriorated by 381 million dollars while the current accounts of the rest of the sterling area with the OEEC countries deteriorated by 582 million dollars.[43] While some improvement was effected in the first half of 1952, it did not suffice to stay the drain on Britain's reserves. In the second half of 1951 the United Kingdom incurred a 985 million dollar accounting deficit with the European Payments Union which was financed through the receipt of credit from the Union equal to 781 million dollars and the outflow of gold equal to 204 million dollars.[44] In the first half of 1952 the accounting deficit of the United Kingdom was reduced to 534 million dollars, of which 361 million dollars was financed through gold outflows and 173 million dollars through the receipt of credit by the European Payments Union. The huge loss of gold to the European Payments Union in the second half of 1951 and the first half of 1952 were important factors in the 1951 payments crisis.

The huge gold losses to the OEEC countries necessitated a retreat from the liberalization measures which Britain had undertaken as part of the Intra-European Payments Schemes and the European Payments Union.[45] It was the desire to avoid developments of this kind that prompted Cripps to urge the elimination of the dollar from intra-European trade. In the face of a drain on the reserves, the introduction of the dollar left Britain with no alternative but to treat the OEEC as a hard currency area, which, indeed, it was after the establishment of the European Payments Union.

DOLLAR PAYMENTS TO OTHER NON-STERLING COUNTRIES

Reference to the table on page 179 reveals that the sterling area made net payments of dollars to other non-sterling countries in every year between 1946 and 1951. These dollar payments are attributable to the hard currency releases made to Egypt and to the dollar payments made to Iran occasioned by Britain's oil operations. Aside from these the sterling

---

[43] *Ibid.*, Table 11. The rest of the sterling area surplus of 680 million dollars was converted to deficit of 246 million dollars.

[44] *Ibid.*, Table 13.

[45] On June 30, 1951, 90 percent of Britain's private trade was liberalized. By June 30, 1952, the proportion was reduced to 46 percent.

area's gold and dollar losses to other non-sterling area countries were negligible.

CONCLUSIONS

Despite Britain's attempts in the postwar period to remove the dollar from third-country trade, the dollar drain to non-dollar countries accounted for a substantial portion of the sterling area's dollar deficit. This drain was a reflection of the world-wide dollar shortage that resulted from the deep-seated structural changes in the world economy. In this view, the dollar drain to third countries is not to be considered an additional factor inducing the dollar shortage. Rather, it is to be regarded as a measure of the success third countries enjoyed in shifting the burden of the shortage to the sterling area.

Britain's policy in the postwar period was motivated by the desire to encourage the maximum amount of non-dollar trade. The British government believed that success along these lines would make a significant contribution toward the solution of the dollar problem. The government further believed that the removal of the dollar from third-country trade was a prerequisite for the expansion of non-dollar trade, and this attitude explains, in large part, Britain's position in the negotiations leading up to the establishment of the postwar European regional payments schemes. Given the severe and pervasive dollar shortage which characterized this period, it is submitted that the British insistence upon removing the dollar from third country trade constituted a positive contribution toward the solution of the disequilibrium and laid the groundwork for an ultimate restoration of convertibility and abandonment of discriminatory trade practices.

VIII Current State of the Dollar Problem

THE THREE PRECEDING chapters were concerned with the factors responsible for the emergence and severity of the sterling area's dollar problem between 1946 and 1951. Between the middle of 1952, when the drain on the reserves was stayed, and the middle of 1954, sterling staged a remarkable recovery. The gold and dollar reserves which amounted to but 1,685 million dollars on June 30, 1952, rose to 3,017 million dollars on June 30, 1954. More important, perhaps, was the fact that the biennial cycle which characterized the sterling area's balance of payments between 1947 and 1951 appeared to be broken. These developments gave rise to expressions of hope that the dollar problem was at last resolved. These hopes, however, were short-lived—beginning in mid-1954, the sterling area's payments position deteriorated. Between June, 1954, and December, 1955, the area's reserves declined by 897 million dollars and the end of the drain was not yet in sight. The specter of the dollar shortage reappeared. The purpose of the present chapter is to sketch the major factors responsible for these developments. The 1951–52 payments crisis is reviewed briefly to serve as a backdrop against which the subsequent developments can be studied.

The precipitous drain on sterling area reserves which commenced in the third quarter of 1951 and which continued through the second quarter of 1952 [1] was induced by several adverse developments. The more important of these were: (a) the collapse of primary product prices from the high levels attained following the outbreak of the Korean War, leading to a severe decline in the dollar earnings of the overseas sterling area countries: (b) a lagged increase in the volume of imports into the overseas sterling area countries, induced in large part by their high earnings during the commodity boom; (c) a substantial increase in the volume of imports into the United Kingdom, due in large part to the necessity of repairing the stockpiles which had been depleted during 1950; (d) Britain's ex-

[1] During this brief period the sterling area's reserves declined from 3,270 million dollars to 1,685 million dollars.

panded rearmament program, which had an adverse effect on her imports as well as on her exports; and (e) the deterioration of Britain's invisible accounts, which resulted from the Iranian seizure of the Abadan oil properties as well as from the necessity of meeting the first installment on the postwar American and Canadian loans.

The drain on reserves was finally stayed by intensifying restrictions against imports and by reducing the level of domestic capital formation. The introduction of a hard money policy also helped by discouraging investment in working capital. Because the drain of hard currencies to third countries was particularly heavy during the crisis, the import restrictions were intensified in a nondiscriminatory manner; imports from the EPU countries, for example, were restricted to the same extent as were imports from the dollar area. Some overseas sterling area countries, acutely short of sterling as a result of their import boom, also restricted imports from the United Kingdom.

The success of these measures in staying the drain on the reserves is evident from an examination of the sterling area's dollar balance of payments between the first half of 1952 and the first half of 1953. Between these periods Britain converted a current account deficit with the dollar area equal to 394 million dollars into a surplus equal to 81 million dollars. The rest of the sterling area's dollar surplus was increased from 47 million dollars to 230 million dollars, and a loss of 336 million dollars to third countries was replaced by dollar and gold earnings from these sources equal to 149 million dollars. The net effect of these developments was to transform a sterling area dollar deficit of 648 million dollars in the first half of 1952 into a dollar surplus of 521 million dollars in the first half of 1953.

Although the recovery of the sterling area's dollar accounts between these two periods was spectacular, it should not be overlooked that the major factor responsible for this recovery was the severe reduction in the value of sterling area imports. Thus of the 475 million dollar improvement in Britain's current account, 279 million dollars was accounted for by the decline in Britain's dollar imports. British exports to the dollar area increased by but 46 million dollars while her invisible dollar exports increased by 126 million dollars. The improvement in the rest of the sterling area's dollar accounts was likewise due to a reduction in the value of dollar imports rather than to an expansion of exports to the dollar area. Indeed, dollar exports in the first half of 1953 were some 75 million dollars less than in the first half of 1952.

The developments which were mainly responsible for the improvement in the sterling area's dollar accounts following the payments crisis in 1951–52 continued through mid-1954. Table 52 reveals that the dollar imports of the sterling area continued to decline along with the area's dollar exports. The fact that the improvement in the sterling area's dollar accounts was due largely to the decline in the value of imports indicates where the underlying factors responsible for this improvement must be sought.

TABLE 52

STERLING AREA DOLLAR ACCOUNTS

(*In millions of U.S. dollars*)

	Jan.–June, 1952	Jan.–June, 1953	Jan.–June, 1954
United Kingdom			
Merchandise imports	991	712	673
Invisible imports	211	180	183
Total debits	1202	892	856
Merchandise exports	560	606	573
Invisible exports	86	212	274
Total credits	646	818	857
American defense aid	162	155	68
Current account balance	− 394	81	59
Capital account balance	34	62	78
Total United Kingdom balance	− 360	143	137
Rest of sterling area			
Colonies			
Imports	105	84	78
Exports	285	215	187
Other transactions (net)	33	39	42
Gold sales to Britain	6		8
Colonies' balance	219	171	159
Other sterling area			
Imports	725	501	504
Exports	400	394	375
Other transactions (net)	14	78	48
Gold sales to Britain	139	87	179
Other sterling area balance	− 172	59	98
Rest of sterling area balance	47	230	257
Sterling area transactions with non-dollar countries	− 336	149	104
Total sterling area dollar balance	− 648	521	499

Sources: 1952 data from *United Kingdom Balance of Payments, 1946–1953,* Cmd. 8976; 1953–54 data from *United Kingdom Balance of Payments, 1946–1954,* Cmd. 9291.

The decline in the value of sterling area dollar imports between the first half of 1952 and the first half of 1954 is attributable largely to three factors: the intensification of import restrictions; the improvement in Britain's terms of trade, especially vis-à-vis the dollar area; and the decline in the sterling reserves of some important overseas sterling countries, leading to an intensification of their import restrictions. While it is not possible at this point to isolate with any precision the extent to which the decline in imports may be attributed to any of these factors, the data suggest that all were important.

The significance of the intensified import restrictions in reducing the volume of imports into the United Kingdom is suggested by the accompanying table, which shows the volume of British imports between 1952 and the first half of 1954 by quarters.

TABLE 53
VOLUME OF UNITED KINGDOM IMPORTS
(1950 = 100)

Quarters	Total	From Sterling Area	From Dollar Area
1952, First	112	114	132
Second	106	117	134
Third	94	112	104
Fourth	99	124	97
1953, First	106	132	93
Second	116	140	123
Third	112	131	145
Fourth	114	131	123
1954, First	113	141	104
Second	114	137	116

Source: *Board of Trade Journal*, August 6, 1955.

The volume of imports Britain derived from the dollar area declined markedly between the first and the second halves of 1952. Moreover, in view of the fact that Britain's imports from the dollar area generally increase in the second half of the year, the actual decline was even greater than that suggested by the data. Although the volume of imports Britain derived from the dollar area tended to increase in 1953 and the first half of 1954, it was still considerably below the January–June, 1952, level. There can be little doubt that the reduction in the volume of British dollar imports was due in large part to the intensification of the import restrictions. It is possible, however, that part of the reduction may also have been due to the increased availability of goods—especially in the sterling area—from other sources, which provided Britain with a substitute for dollar imports.

As important as the intensification in the import restrictions was in reducing the value of Britain's dollar imports between 1952 and 1954, it was not the only factor responsible for this development. Perhaps of equal, if not greater, importance was the improvement in Britain's terms of trade vis-à-vis the dollar area. Unfortunately, official data referring to Britain's dollar terms of trade are not available on a quarterly basis. The annual data shown in the accompanying table can be used, however, as an indication of the magnitude of the change.

TABLE 54

BRITAIN'S TERMS OF TRADE WITH THE DOLLAR AREA

(1950 = 100)

	Average Value of Dollar Imports	Average Value of Dollar Exports	Terms of Trade with Dollar Area [a]
1951	124	120	103
1952	128	123	104
1953	109	119	91
1954	105	117	89

[a] Terms of trade are measured as the ratio of import average values over export average values. A decline signifies an improvement.

Source: *Board of Trade Journal*, August 6, 1955, p. 324.

Between 1951 and 1954 Britain's terms of trade vis-à-vis the dollar area improved by approximately 15 percent. This improvement resulted from a more rapid decline in the average value of Britain's imports than of her exports. The gain to Britain as a result of this improvement in the terms of trade was greater, therefore, than if the same improvement had occurred as a result of an unequal *increase* in the average value indexes of imports and exports. It should be noted, however, that the improvement in Britain's terms of trade between 1951 and 1954 did little more than restore the terms of trade that existed in 1947. Even in 1954 Britain's terms of trade vis-à-vis the dollar area was considerably less favorable than in the prewar period.

In view of the fact that the improvement in the sterling area's dollar accounts was largely due to a decline in the value of dollar imports rather than to an expansion in the value of dollar exports, the recovery of sterling was more apparent than real. This is especially true if the decline in imports was due to factors which could not, in the circumstances, be sustained, and developments since the middle of 1954 tend to confirm this. The basic factor responsible for the deterioration of the sterling area's dollar accounts since the middle of 1954 was the perceptible increase in imports, especially from dollar sources. At the time of writing, the available data do not permit a full analysis of the factors responsible for this development. It is clear, however, that it was due mainly to an expansion in the domestic demand for goods and services which exceeded the increase in domestic production and which brought about an increase in imports. In short, since mid-1954 Britain's basic difficulties stem from overt inflationary pressures.

The Conservative party's victory in November, 1951, signaled a return to "orthodox" economic policies. The "dash for freedom" to which the Conservative government was committed could not be put into effect immediately, however, because of the severe payments crisis in 1951–52; it was noted that the drain on reserves in 1952 was reversed by relying on essentially the same methods employed by the Labor government in 1947 and 1949. With the improvement in sterling accounts, however, the process of liberalizing the economy gained momentum. In short order, many of the controls which characterized the war and early postwar periods were removed. Price controls and rationing were abandoned; state trading was severely reduced; the commodity markets were reopened; monetary policy, long in abeyance, became the cornerstone of the government's anti-inflationary program, and subsidies designed to restrain the rise in the price of "wage goods" were scaled down.

When there is an approximate balance between the supply of and the demand for goods and services at high levels of income and employment, a substantial case can be advanced for the desirability of eliminating specific controls and other impediments to the operation of market forces. Economists have long demonstrated that these controls, to the extent that they are successful, tend to misallocate resources and hence reduce the level of economic welfare. The conditions necessary for the successful removal of controls and the return to a free market economy were not present in postwar Britain. The existence of strong inflationary pressures was one of the legacies of the war, and, though the Labor government did much to prevent these pressures from resulting in a severe misallocation of resources, very little was done to remove them. To do so would have required the introduction of policies which would not have been consistent with the maintenance of a high level of income and employment. This neither the Labor government nor the Conservative government after 1951 was willing to do. Furthermore, in view of the fact that the gold and dollar reserves were at constantly low levels, the inflationary pressures could not be fully "absorbed" by allowing prices to rise. Had the British adopted this approach, there can be little doubt that the pressures on the reserves would have been even greater than they actually were.

In the light of these considerations, the removal of controls in the post-1951 period had an immediately adverse effect on Britain's balance of payments. The level of domestic consumption which had increased moderately between 1947 and 1951 rose substantially between 1952 and 1955. During this period real consumption increased by 11.7 percent. In addition, the removal of controls on building and investment coupled with liberalized investment allowances contributed to an investment boom. The resulting pressure on Britain's resources tended to inhibit exports and to increase imports.

The manner in which the investment boom and the increase in real personal consumption adversely affected Britain's balance of payments can be illustrated by examining the economic situation between 1954 and 1955, the period during which Britain's balance of payments worsened. Between 1954 and 1955, Britain's gross national product increased by 3.5 percent, or by 525 million pounds measured at 1954 factor prices. During the same period, however, total expenditure, including exports, increased by 875 million pounds. The excess of the increase in expenditure over the increase in product was met by an increase in imports which amounted to 350 million pounds. The accompanying table presents the relevant data in succinct form.

TABLE 55

CHANGES IN EXPENDITURE AND SUPPLIES, 1954–55

(In millions of pounds, at 1954 factor cost)

Expenditure	
Consumer expenditures	+ 290
Government expenditure on goods and services	− 55
Gross fixed investment	
New dwellings	− 50
Other fixed investment	+ 225
Investment in stocks and work in progress	+ 210
Exports of goods and services	+ 245
Total change in expenditure	+ 875
Supplies	
Gross domestic product	+ 525
Imports of goods and services	+ 350
Total change in supplies	+ 875

Source: *Economic Survey for 1956,* Cmd. 9728, March, 1956, p. 8.

The increase in consumption, in fixed investment, and in investment in stocks was largely responsible for the total increase in gross national expenditure. It should be noted, moreover, that the increase in these items of expenditure was concentrated largely on the metal goods industries.

For example, the large increase in consumption expenditures was largely for consumer durable goods. The *Economic Survey for 1956* estimated that approximately one-third of the increase in total consumer expenditure between 1954 and 1955 is attributable to the increase in private motoring. The increase in fixed capital formation was concentrated largely in manufacturing and took the form of investment in plant machinery and vehicles in which the metal content is particularly high. Finally, it is estimated that more than one-half of the increase in stocks occurred in the metal using industries. These facts are of great significance in explaining (a) why the volume of imports rose as much as it did, (b) why the increase in Britain's imports was derived largely from dollar sources, and (c) why the increase in the volume of British exports lagged behind that of her major competitors.

Between 1954 and 1955 Britain's industrial production rose by approximately 5 percent. Two-thirds of this increase was accounted for by the increase in production in the metals and metal using industries. Despite this significant increase in output, the increased demand for products of the metal goods industries could not be satisfied from domestic sources. This led to an increase in the volume of imports out of proportion to the increase in output. Between 1953 and 1954, for example, a 4 percent increase in total real product was associated with a 1 percent increase in the volume of imports. By contrast, a 3.5 percent increase in real product between 1954 and 1955 was associated with an 11 percent increase in the volume of imports. The fact that one-third of the increase in imports was accounted for by the increase in the imports of metals and metal materials strongly suggests that the nature of the increase in demand, which occurred between 1954 and 1955, was largely responsible for the disproportionate increase in the volume of imports.

In addition to a more than proportionate increase in the volume of imports, the increase in the domestic demand for metal products also resulted in important changes in the geographical pattern of Britain's imports. Metal goods could be most readily—or only—obtained from dollar sources. Between 1954 and 1955, Britain's imports from dollar sources increased by 36 percent, imports from OEEC countries increased by 17 percent, imports from the rest of the non-sterling world increased by 18 percent, while the increase in imports from sterling countries was only equal to 5 percent.

Finally, the heavy domestic demand for metal goods tended to inhibit the expansion of British exports, especially to the dollar market. Between 1954 and 1955, the volume of British exports increased by approximately

7 percent. Though superficially satisfactory, the performance of British exports left much to be desired. There are several reasons for this. First, the volume of exports in 1955 was inflated somewhat by the carrying over of some goods which, because of the dock strike, could not be shipped in the latter part of 1954. If adjustment is made for this factor, the volume of British exports in 1955 exceeded the 1954 level by slightly more than 4 percent. Second, however, overseas markets were particularly buoyant in 1955, and the expansion of exports was limited largely by the availability of goods. Had the demands on the British metal industries been less intense, British exports could have expanded by much more than they actually did. This is reflected by the fact that the increase in Britain's exports failed to keep pace with the increase in the exports of her major competitors. Between 1954 and 1955, the value of Britain's manufactured exports increased by 7 percent. Between the same years, the increase in the value of Germany's manufactured exports was 18 percent, that of Japan's 27 percent, and that of the United States's 9 percent.

The large increase in the volume of imports and the much smaller expansion in the volume of Britain's exports were the major factors responsible for the worsening of Britain's—and the sterling area's—dollar balance of payments after mid-1954. Given the reasons for these developments, it is obvious that the restoration of international equilibrium necessitated the introduction of measures designed to restrain home demand with the twofold object of reducing imports and diverting a larger proportion of the total output from the domestic to the export market. To achieve these objectives the government placed heavier reliance on monetary policies than had been the case in the earlier years. By a series of steps the bank rate was raised to 5.5 percent, restrictions on consumer loans were restored, and the Chancellor of the Exchequer requested the banks to tighten their loan standards and to effect a reduction in their advances. Tax and expenditure policies were also brought to bear. The purchase tax which had been reduced in April, 1953, was raised again to a level as high as 60 percent on automobiles, television sets, washing machines, and other durable goods. The restrictions on consumption of durable goods were reinforced by efforts to cut back on capital formation. The government announced reductions in capital formation in the nationalized industries, the rate of interest charged by the Public Loans Board to the local authorities was increased, and the liberalized investment allowance scheme was abandoned. In the April, 1956, budget, the Chancellor of the Exchequer made a dramatic appeal for more savings and underlined the seriousness of the problem by announcing a "lottery bond." At the time of writing it is too early to gauge the success of these measures. The Chancellor warned, however, in no uncertain terms, that should these measures fail to restore international equilibrium, he was ready to introduce even more rigorous ones.

In the light of the factors responsible for Britain's most recent payments crisis, there can be little doubt that the government has the power to stay the drain on the reserves. The only problem is whether Britain will be able to restore equilibrium on her international accounts while maintaining a high level of income and employment and making satisfactory provision for the future.

IX *Principles of Trade and the*
Dollar Shortage

THE POSTWAR dollar shortage gave rise to a heated debate on both sides of the Atlantic concerning the principles of trade and payments best adapted to meet the crisis. The American government strenuously advocated return to a system of interconvertibility of currencies, complete and unimpeded adherence to the principle of nondiscrimination in trade, and restoration of a multilateral trade and payments structure. On the other hand, many British economists argued that while the principles advocated by the Americans were admirable under normal conditions, the postwar situation demanded that Britain resort to bilateral trade, actively participate in regional blocs, and judiciously employ trade discrimination.

The American brief for the abolition of currency controls and the adherence to the principle of nondiscrimination in trade was based on two major arguments. First, the Americans viewed the postwar dollar shortage as being due, in large part, to inefficient methods of production and to the failure of the dollar-deficit countries to restrain inflationary pressures. The operation of these factors led to uneconomic price levels, which were perpetuated by the continued reliance on discriminatory trade practices and the maintenance of inconvertible currencies. The only way in which the dollar-deficit countries could be made to effect the necessary adaptations was to subject their economies to blasts of competition emanating from the United States. Second, the Americans argued that continuing discriminatory trade practices and maintaining inconvertible currencies were injurious to their commerce. Secretary Vinson, testifying before the House Committee on Banking and Currency concerning the Anglo-American Financial Agreement of 1946, did not conceal his distress over this:

If sterling cannot be converted into dollars, England and the sterling area countries must concentrate on their trade with each other not because their goods are better, but because of monetary impediments. It will mean that Egyptian and India cotton will replace American cotton; Rhodesian and near eastern tobacco will replace American tobacco; and British automobiles and machinery will replace American automobiles and machinery. In half the trade area of the world, American products would be at a severe disadvantage in competition with the products of the sterling area countries. Our trade with Britain and the sterling area would become a mere trickle.

American exporters ask no special advantages in trading with foreign countries. They do ask that no discrimination be directed against them. Our producers are perfectly willing to sell their products in competition with the products of other countries, provided the buyer has a fair choice to select American goods on the basis of quality and price.[1]

Formally, if not always in practice, American foreign economic policy in the postwar period was motivated by the desire to restore a multilateral trading structure based on the principle of the interconvertibility of currencies and adherence to the nondiscriminatory trade principle. The first clear statement of American ideals appeared as Article VII of the Mutual Aid Agreement between the United Kingdom and the United States, signed on February 23, 1942. The article committed the two countries to a course of action

directed to the expansion, by appropriate international and domestic measures, of production, employment and the exchange and consumption of goods, which are the material foundations of the liberty and welfare of all peoples; to the elimination of all forms of discriminatory treatment in international commerce, and to the reduction of tariffs and other trade barriers.

To implement this agreement, the United States sponsored the International Monetary Fund and the International Trade Organization and insisted that the United Kingdom undertake to restore sterling convertibility and adopt the nondiscriminatory principle as a quid pro quo for an American line of credit.

The International Monetary Fund was designed to establish a financial framework for the restoration of multilateral trade and the removal of discriminatory practices. This goal was to be achieved by establishing a fund for lending the necessary foreign exchange to member countries temporarily suffering from balance of payments disequilibria. The need for a fund of this sort was demonstrated in the interwar period, when countries faced with a temporary disequilibrium on international accounts and unable to obtain short-term loans were forced to deflate, impose import restrictions—frequently in a discriminatory fashion—and devalue their currencies. Resort to these policies to correct a temporary disequilibrium

[1] *Hearings before the House Committee on Banking and Currency,* House of Representatives, 79th Congress, Second Session, Vol. 23, p. 4.

was frequently deflationary [2] and, when countries discriminated against retaliated, also tended to reduce the volume of trade.[3]

In return for the privilege of borrowing from the Fund, member countries agreed to devaluate currency beyond 10 percent only by authority of the Fund, to outlaw restrictions on current payments and discriminatory currency practices, and to work for the restoration of currency convertibility with respect to current transactions. Recognition that balance of payments difficulties might prevent adherence to these principles led to the inclusion in the Fund's charter of the "scarce currency clause" whereby member countries, on the declaration of the Fund that the currency of any member is in scarce supply, may "temporarily impose limitations on the freedom of exchange operations in the scarce currency." Moreover, in view of the deep-seated nature of the postwar disequilibrium, the charter of the Fund specified a five-year transition period during which the members were allowed to discriminate and to maintain inconvertible currencies if these were dictated by balance of payments considerations.

The financial code of ethics embodied in the charter of the International Monetary Fund was supplemented by a commercial code in the charter of the International Trade Organization. The charter was, in large part, a reaffirmation of the principles of trade advocated by the Americans with special emphasis placed on the desirability of adherence to the nondiscriminatory principle and the elimination of trade restrictions. For the purpose at hand the most important provisions in the charter were those that pledged all members to accept the unconditional, most-favored-nation clause; to abandon the use of quantitative restrictions for protective purposes; and to adhere to the nondiscriminatory principle. The charter, however, contained many exemptions to these general principles and provided for a "transition period" during which members suffering from

[2] This can be seen by examining the following case. A country pursues an expansionary policy at a time when the world is depressed. This expansion results in a balance of payments deficit which, if reserves are inadequate, leads either to the abandonment of the expansionary policies or to the resort to one of the policies mentioned in the text. The pursuit of any of these policies will prevent the foreign countries from enjoying the expansionary effects of her policies.

[3] The valid theoretical distinction between the use of currency devaluation and import restrictions as defensive measures and their use as "beggar thy neighbor" policies is in practice likely to be overlooked. The United States, for example, feeling the impact of Britain's restrictive international policies may resort to retaliation despite the fact that these policies were introduced as defensive measures and did not reduce the level of American trade.

balance of payments difficulties were not obligated to adhere to the nondiscriminatory principle and could employ quantitative restrictions for purposes of protection.

The charters of the International Monetary Fund and the International Trade Organization represented compromises between principles and expediency. The principles of trade and finance cherished by the United States State Department were present, but the exceptions were sufficiently broad to placate outspoken critics of these principles. Indeed, one supporter of the State Department's philosophy of trade characterized the charter of the International Trade Organization as an "economic Munich." [4]

No similar criticism can be made of the provisions embodied in the Anglo-American Financial Agreement. In this document the principle of nondiscrimination and the restoration of convertibility were elevated from articles of faith to operational guides. Moreover, the American government made no secret of the fact that the line of credit was being established largely to secure Britain's adherence to these principles.

The Anglo-American Financial Agreement extended to Britain a line of credit of 3,750 million dollars which could be drawn upon between the effective date of the agreement and December 31, 1951. The credit was established to assist Britain in her transitional difficulties and to render the financial aid necessary for the almost immediate restoration of currency convertibility and adherence to the nondiscriminatory principle. Provision was made for repaying the loan in fifty annual installments commencing in December, 1951. Interest on the credit was set at 2 percent with the proviso that the interest could be waived in any year if Britain's overseas earnings did not suffice to enable her to purchase a quantum of imports equivalent to the 1936–38 average level. A rather vague provision specified that the credit might not be used to discharge capital obligations to other countries.

The United Kingdom undertook, as a quid pro quo, to make sterling receipts from current transactions freely available for current use in any currency area without discrimination, to forego the use of exchange controls to restrict payments to the United States for importable goods or services, to refrain from restricting payments and transfers on current account one year after the effective date of the agreement, and to employ import restrictions only in a nondiscriminatory fashion. In addition, the agreement

[4] Courtney, *Economic Munich.*

provided the conditions of release of the sterling balances; the United Kingdom undertook to reach accords with the various creditors to provide for the immediate release of part of the balances, temporary blocking of some balances, and the scaling down of the remainder. The United States indicated the amount of annual sterling releases it thought it would be propitious to make by stipulating that annual releases of up to 43 million pounds could be considered current expenditure in computing Britain's eligibility to waive the annual interest payment.[5]

The publication of the agreement provoked a great debate in England. The government, though sponsoring the measure, did so reluctantly,[6] and Keynes, the British representative at the negotiations leading up to the accord, made an eloquent plea for its acceptance on the grounds that, harsh as some of the terms appeared to be, it was the best that could be obtained under the circumstances.[7]

Hostility toward the accord was at times so great that certain responsible critics recommended rejection of the loan despite the overwhelming need for American aid. Some of the criticism was directed at the financial terms of the agreement. It was argued that the credit was too small and that the rate of interest was too high. Many Britons believed the United States should have approached the agreement as a post hoc attempt to equalize war burdens, whereas the United States approached it in a quasi-commercial spirit.[8] There is really little to be said about this criticism; dissatisfaction must inevitably develop between lender and borrower in the negotiation of a loan required, in large part, to heal wounds of partners in a battle. It is doubtful whether tempers would have flared, however, were the financial provisions of the loan the only source of contention. Differences concerning the financial terms became significant primarily because of the existence of more fundamental points of disagreement.

The British objections to the loan were largely concerned with principle and centered around the advisability of restoring currency convertibility so soon after the war and the wisdom of adhering to nondiscrimination

[5] *Text of the Anglo-American Financial Agreement*, Cmd. 8708.

[6] See Hansard, V, 417, c. 439.

[7] See Keynes's speech before the House of Lords delivered December 18, 1945, and reprinted in Harris, *New Economics*, pp. 380–95.

[8] It would, perhaps, be more correct to say that the administration was aware that Congressional approval would not have been forthcoming for an interest-free loan or grant. This, at any rate, was Keynes's interpretation. *Ibid.*, p. 387.

at a time of general dollar shortage. Some critics questioned American motives. Sir Hubert Henderson, a leading critic of the accord, claimed that

the essential characteristic of the Anglo-American Financial Agreement, taken as a whole, is that it is designed not to help the correction of the disequilibrium in the balance of payments but to forbid attempts to correct it, if these should seem injurious to American export trade. Hence the emphasis on non-discrimination, which is tantamount to a demand that the flow of international trade must not be influenced by balance of payments considerations.[9]

Other critics disagreed with the American diagnosis of the dollar problem and argued, with Balogh, that "the restoration of equilibrium in the world economy in an expansionist fashion requires a permanent rechanneling of trade by discriminatory methods and complex preferential arrangements."[10]

NONDISCRIMINATION

The critics of nondiscrimination rarely attack the principle, per se. They argue, however, that blind adherence to the principle of nondiscrimination frequently frustrates the attainment and maintenance of international equilibrium at the highest level of trade. *The Economist,* for example, though opposed to the nondiscrimination clause of the Anglo-American agreement, argued that this opposition should not be construed as "a desire to scrap the doctrine of nondiscrimination entirely." The doctrine is "in general . . . admirable . . . one of the things that prevents international trade from degenerating into mere cut throat chaos." Adherence to the doctrine is absurd, however, when it causes countries "to refrain from buying each other's goods in circumstances when they could not in any case buy American goods." [11] Henderson's plea for discrimination in international trade is likewise based on the argument that "with large scale disequilibrium in the international balance of payments to be corrected, insistence on non-discrimination is likely to prove a contractionist influence of great potency." [12] Even Balogh, one of the most vociferous advocates of discrimination, was not opposed to the principle of nondis-

[9] Henderson, "The Anglo-American Financial Agreement," *Bulletin of the Oxford University Institute of Statistics,* January, 1946, p. 13.

[10] Balogh, "Discrimination," *Bulletin of the Oxford University Institute of Statistics,* August, 1948, p. 223.

[11] *The Economist,* July 10, 1948, p. 45.

[12] Henderson, "Implications of Marshall's Speech," *Bulletin of the Oxford University Institute of Statistics,* August, 1948, p. 224.

crimination when adherence to this principle resulted in an expansion of trade. In the postwar period, however, he felt that the application of the principle of nondiscrimination would lead to a contraction of the level of world trade.[13]

Since both the adherents of the principle of nondiscrimination and its critics accepted as the desideratum the maximizing of trade at a level consonant with maintaining international equilibrium, the question resolves itself into which principle, nondiscrimination or discrimination, was most likely to lead to the realization of this ideal in the postwar period.

The critics of the principle of nondiscrimination frequently adduced the following model to substantiate their position. Assume three countries, the United States, the United Kingdom, and France, carrying on trade with each other at a time of a general dollar shortage. Adherence to the principle of nondiscrimination would compel the United Kingdom to cut her imports from France whenever the dollar shortage dictated a reduction of imports from the United States. This restriction of imports from France, moreover, would have to occur despite the availability of French francs. Under these circumstances judicious discrimination on the part of the United Kingdom against dollar goods while maintaining the level of trade with France would result in a higher level of trade than would result from a blind adherence to the principle of nondiscrimination.[14]

The argument embodied in the model has a great deal of cogency, especially in view of the fact that the model appears to be a reasonable, though simplified, construct of the real world in the postwar period. There

[13] Balogh, "Discrimination—Britain's Trade Problem and the Marshall Plan," *Bulletin of the Oxford University Institute of Statistics,* July–August, 1948, p. 224.

[14] An important literature has grown up around the best way in which a country can impose import restrictions. See Frisch, "On the Need for Forecasting a Multilateral Balance of Payments," *American Economic Review,* September, 1947, pp. 535–51; Hinshaw, "Professor Frisch on Discrimination and Multilateral Trade," *Review of Economics and Statistics,* November, 1948; Hirschman, "Disinflation, Discrimination and the Dollar Shortage," *American Economic Review,* December, 1948; Polak, "Balancing International Trade, A Comment on Professor Frisch's Paper," *American Economic Review,* March, 1948; Meier, "The Trade Matrix: A Further Comment on Professor Frisch's Paper," *American Economic Review,* September, 1948; Meade, *Theory of International Economic Policy,* chap. 30; Kindleberger, *The Dollar Shortage,* p. 288 ff.; Fleming, "On Making the Best of Import Restrictions," *Economic Journal,* 1951. Part of this literature attempts to prove not only that import restrictions levied in a discriminatory fashion are likely to reduce trade by less than import restrictions applied in a nondiscriminatory fashion but also that the resultant decline of trade is likely to be less than that resulting from either exchange adjustments or deflation.

is an implicit assumption in the model, however, which, on examination, may vitiate the policy conclusions that flow from it.   The assumption is that the United States, though the target of discriminatory treatment, will not resort to retaliatory action.   If this is an unrealistic assumption and the United States does indeed retaliate then it may very well be that discrimination will result in a greater contraction of world trade than adherence to the principle of nondiscrimination even under the circumstances postulated in the model.

It may appear strange that the United States might resort to retaliation when discrimination is employed under the stress of a dollar shortage.   It can be argued that in the last analysis her trade position would be no more affected than if the dollar-short country reduced American imports as part of a general nondiscriminatory reduction of imports.   This argument appears to place too much reliance on rational behavior and not nearly enough on irrational actions.   United States exporters are likely to regard a reduction in their exports differently if it is due to general import restrictions imposed by foreign countries than if the reduction is attributable to a particular action aimed against them.   In the first instance the exporters maintain their relative position in world markets, whereas in the second instance their relative share of the world trade is reduced.

These considerations may not, at that, be wholly irrational.   Discrimination against the exporters of particular countries may result in a ruthless severing of trade connections built up over many years; new trade connections are developed which may, in particular cases, outlast the dollar shortage.   Price is not the only determinant of the direction of international trade any more than it is in domestic trade.[15]

Thus, if the United States should resort to retaliatory action when it is made the target of discriminatory treatment, the models which purport to show that the judicious use of discrimination tends to maximize trade under conditions of a general dollar shortage lose a good deal of cogency. Resort to discrimination will maximize trade under these circumstances only if the United States acquiesces.   While the best of possible worlds in the postwar period would have been that which allowed the United Kingdom to discriminate without fear of American reprisal, if the United States failed to sanction this arrangement Britain would have been left with no practical alternative but to accept the American conditions.   Fortunately,

---

[15] MacDougall, "British and American Exports: A Study Suggested by the Theory of Comparative Costs," *Economic Journal,* September, 1952, p. 501.

as was noted above, adherence to the principle of nondiscrimination in the early postwar period did not adversely affect Britain's international position. When world supply conditions eased and adherence to the principle of nondiscrimination might have hampered recovery, the United States, while not assenting to the use of discrimination, did not object to it. Indeed, the underlying philosophy of the European Recovery Program concerning self-aid and American support of the European Payments Union, were negative sanctions for the use of discrimination. Judging from actual postwar developments with regard to the problem of discrimination, it can be said, without fear of contradiction, that the American bark was worse than its bite.

MULTILATERALISM VERSUS BILATERALISM AND REGIONAL BLOCS

The restoration of a multilateral trade and payments structure was the second major tenet of the American government's postwar trade philosophy. The British critics of this tenet relied on three major arguments: (1) that maintaining international equilibrium at a high level of employment would be jeopardized by Britain's participation in a multilateral trade and payments structure in which an unstable United States would inevitably play a major role; [16] (2) that only through resort to bilateralism coupled with the judicious use of discrimination could the United Kingdom hope to balance her accounts at a high level of international trade; [17] and (3) that the growth of American productivity necessitated the formation of regional blocs in order to enable the United Kingdom, and indeed the rest of the developed countries of Western Europe, to compete successfully with the United States.[18] In addition to these arguments, many hoped that the United Kingdom could, in the absence of a multilateral trade and payments structure, use her bargaining position to improve her terms of trade.[19]

Full Employment and Multilateralism. Theoretical and practical developments in the interwar period lend substance to the first argument against joining a multilateral structure in which the United States would play a leading role. The income approach to economic problems and its

---

[16] Kalecki, "Multilateralism and Full Employment," *Canadian Journal of Economics and Political Science,* August, 1946, pp. 322–27.

[17] Einzig, "The Case for Bilateralism," *The Banker,* October, 1947.

[18] Cf. Balogh, "Discrimination—Britain's Trade Problem and the Marshall Plan," *Bulletin of the Oxford University Institute of Statistics,* July–August, 1948, and *Dollar Crisis,* passim.

[19] See p. 213.

application to international trade theory clearly explained the international propagation of business cycles. Since the main outlines of this theory are well-known, a summary statement will suffice at this point. A decline in income in a leading country adversely affects this country's trading partners in several ways: industrial imports into the depressed country are immediately reduced, while the decline in income induces a decline in consumption which affects its nonindustrial imports as well. The impact of an income decline in a leading country on the income and employment of her trading partners is determined, in part, by the marginal propensities to consume and import, the acceleration coefficients, and the income elasticities of demand for imports in the depressed country and in the rest of the world. In addition, a fall in income in a leading country may result in a reduction in capital exports. To the extent that the economies of the trading partners were geared to the receipt of these foreign loans, their cessation may induce an additional wave of deflation. The literature abounds in mathematical and quasi-mathematical models designed to show the manner in which business cycles are propagated under varying assumptions.[20] Since we are here concerned with the main outlines of the theory rather than with its refinements and curiosa, it is not necessary to reproduce these models. The main conclusion is sufficiently clear: the instability of a leading economy in a multilateral trade and payments system is transmitted to the other partners and thus increases their difficulties of maintaining full employment. This difficulty is especially marked if the international reserves of the partner countries are at such low levels that they cannot cushion even temporarily any but the smallest deficits.

The structure of her economy, the composition of her exports, and the direction of her trade make the United Kingdom especially vulnerable to cyclical fluctuations in the United States. Britain specializes in the production and export of capital goods and high standard of living consumer goods, for which international demand is characterized by a high income elasticity. A decline in the level of world income from a depression in the United States is thus likely to have particularly severe effects on Britain's exports.

It should be noted, moreover, that the adverse effects of an American recession on Britain's trade is not limited to the decline in her exports to

---

[20] See, among others, Harrod, *International Economics;* Paish, "Banking Policy and the Balance of Payments," *Economica,* November, 1936; Salant, "Foreign Trade Policy in the Business Cycle," *Readings in the Theory of International Trade,* pp. 201–26.

the United States. Britain sells a large proportion of her exports to the rest of the sterling area, which places a heavy reliance on the export of primary products to the United States. In view of the importance of the United States as an importer of primary products, a serious depression in the United States is likely to have a doubly adverse effect on the exports and incomes of the outer sterling area countries: first, the volume of sterling area exports to the United States is almost certain to decline; and second, the decline in American demand is likely to be sufficient to result in a sizable decline in primary product prices. An American recession is thus likely to have an important adverse effect on the incomes of primary producers with a consequent reduction of their imports from all industrial suppliers. Should the American recession be associated with a decline in capital exports as well, the foreign exchange receipts of the primary producers may be even further reduced.

The dangers emanating from the participation in a multilateral system in which an unstable United States plays a dominant role cannot be dismissed cavalierly. It should be noted, however, that these dangers are greater in what may be called, in the absence of a better term, a laissez faire multilateral system than in one with "built-in" safeguards against the propagation of business fluctuations. Professor Meade has demonstrated that in practically all cases it is possible to prevent the international propagation of business cycles if proper policies are pursued.[21] An understanding of the difficulties an inherently unstable economy imposes on her trading partners and the manner in which these difficulties can be avoided or minimized will do much to offset the objections to participating in a multilateral trade and payments system with the United States. Until the United States is prepared to commit herself to these policies, however, members of a mulilateral trading structure may be subject to periodic dollar shortages resulting from the instability of the American economy.

Multilateralism and International Equilibrium. The British critics of multilateralism argue that the United Kingdom can balance her accounts at a level of trade sufficiently high to provide her with the necessary imports to feed her population and industrial machine only by resorting to a series of bilateral agreements with her major trading partners. Reliance on a multilateral trading structure with all the vicissitudes to which such a structure is subject is, in the view of these critics, much too dangerous a course for a country as dependent upon imports as is the United Kingdom. Under

[21] *Theory of International Economic Policy,* Vol. 1, part 3. A good analysis of what actually happened in the 1930s can be found in a Department of Commerce study, *The United States in the World Economy.*

the circumstances, the United Kingdom should take advantage of the fact that she is an important importer to push her exports in the markets of her leading suppliers.

This argument for bilateralism has a great deal of merit especially for periods characterized by wide-scale dislocations as in the postwar period. In fact, there is little doubt that the bilateral agreements into which Britain entered in the postwar period contributed significantly to the expansion of trade.[22] The exposure of the European economy to multilateralism supported by the principle of nondiscrimination and interconvertibility of currencies in the early postwar period would have been disastrous, as indeed it almost was as far as the United Kingdom was concerned during the convertibility period.[23]

To recognize the merit in the argument is not to admit the case for a permanent abandonment of multilateralism for bilateralism. Bilateral trade arrangements are peculiarly suited for the economically weak; they provide a breathing period during which the fundamental weaknesses of the economy can be corrected. If bilateralism is resorted to in lieu of more positive measures to correct the weakness, however, the structural maladjustments will be perpetuated. In these circumstances, it is probably better that bilateralism not be used at all and the economy be subjected immediately, as unprepared as it is, to the blasts of competition resulting from participation in a multilateral trading structure.

Insistence upon restoring a multilateral trading structure before the economic dislocations caused by the war were rectified must be considered one of the major weaknesses of the Anglo-American Financial Agreement. It provided those who want bilateralism as a permanent way of trade with arguments which their basic position does not warrant. The bilateralists found no difficulty in demonstrating that the early restoration of multilateralism coupled with the interconvertibility of currency and adherence to the principle of nondiscrimination were not in the best interests of the United Kingdom and from this they argued for a permanent bilateral trading system. Moreover, every failure of the multilateral experiment, in conditions under which it could not possibly succeed, encouraged the bilateralists to urge the adoption of a permanent bilateral structure as Britain's sole salvation. Given the postwar circumstances, it would have been wiser for the advocates of multilateralism to recognize the need for

[22] See above, Chapter IV.
[23] See above, p. 166.

bilateral arrangements while proclaiming multilateralism as the eventual goal.[24]

The Growth of American Productivity and a Multilateral Trading Structure. Some advocates of bilateralism and regional blocs have argued that the growth of American production and the apparent tendency toward an increasing disparity between productivity in the United States and the rest of the world have made it increasingly difficult for the rest of the world to maintain international equilibrium while maintaining membership in a multilateral trade and payments structure. According to these economists a resort to bilateralism or the formation of regional blocs is a necessary prerequisite for reestablishing international equilibrium at a viable level of trade. Since the basic premises of this argument have been questioned by many competent students, it is necessary to enquire whether disparate rates of growth of productivity can induce balance of payments disequilibria.

Balogh, a leading advocate of this thesis, argued that "there is a peculiar recurrence of the dollar shortage due to the basic structural unbalance between the rates of dynamic growth whenever the discrepancy in productivity has become too great to be managed by minor manipulations." [25] Harris substantially agreed with this argument when he wrote that "so long as the gains from the competitive position of the United States . . . continue at a rate rapid enough to more than neutralize the corrective effects of gold flows and exchange movements, so long will the dollar remain scarce." Mrs. Croome was even more explicit.

Let a large group or Area A for any reason establish a considerable absolute lead in productivity per head, giving rise to corresponding considerable superiority in its margin available for investment which will mean a progressive widening of the absolute level etc.; then the reduction of costs to that area when translated into lower export prices will exert an unremitting deflationary pressure on the rest of the world, which can benefit from A's low priced exports only at the cost, first of continuous downward adjustment of its own price level (inimical to full employment) and secondly, of structural unemployment during the adaptations forced by concurrent changes in comparative advantage.[26]

The question thus arises: "Will not a widening of the American productivity levels, the more rapid growth of the giant, make all adaptations obsolete even before it can possibly be completed and re-open the need for siege discipline—or rather, in practice, make it impossible for that discipline

---

[24] This is the position the British government adopted after the suspension of convertibility. See Hansard, V, 441, c. 1560.

[25] Balogh, *Dollar Crisis,* p. 149.

[26] Croome, "The Dollar Siege," *Lloyds Bank Review,* July, 1950, p. 37.

ever to be relaxed?" [27] In other words, will not the relative increase of American productivity lead to a chronic dollar shortage?

To a large group of economists the answer to this question is a categorical no. Haberler, in reference to this argument, lamented that "even in the land of Adam Smith, Ricardo, Marshall and Keynes it is necessary to point out again and again that trade is governed by comparative not by absolute costs." [28] This appeal to the doctrine of comparative advantage is not decisive, however. In general, the advocates of the thesis that the increasing disparity between America's and the rest of the world's productive efficiency is a factor responsible for the emergence of the dollar shortage do not question the validity of the doctrine, properly stated,[29] but rather its application to short-run dynamic problems. Specifically, the classical theory assumes that wage rates will rise *pari passu* with productivity increases. Under these circumstances it can be demonstrated that a uniform increase in productivity in the more progressive economy is not likely to have adverse effects on the less progressive trading partners. Should wage rates fail to rise concomitantly with productivity, however, a more rapid increase of productivity in the progressive economy may create difficulties. Haberler, writing in the interwar period, stated the classical position lucidly:

Suppose that productivity per head increases in the United States but remains constant in Europe. Unless the total amount of money increases, there must be a change in the international distribution of gold if the gold parity is to be maintained. In the United States prices fall, exports increase, imports diminish, gold flows in and prices rise again. In European countries, the amount of money has to fall *although conditions at home do not call for a deflation.* This would be avoided if the quantity of money in the United States was increased from the start.[30]

Though Haberler's statement is predicated on the equilibrating character of gold flows, the situation would not be substantially different if the gold-flow

[27] *Ibid.,* p. 30.

[28] Haberler, "Dollar Shortage," in Harris, ed., *Foreign Economic Policy of the United States,* p. 436.

[29] Professor Viner states with care that the doctrine of comparative advantage maintains that "if trade is left free each country *in the long run* tends to specialize in the production of and to export those commodities in whose production it enjoys a comparative advantage in terms of real costs, and to obtain by importation those commodities which could be produced at home only at a comparative disadvantage in terms of real costs, and that such specialization is to the mutual advantage of the countries participating in it." *Studies in International Trade,* p. 438.

[30] Haberler, *Theory of International Trade,* p. 47. (Italics added.)

theory were replaced with a more modern theory. The important thing is that those economists who argue that disparate rates of growth in productivity may create payments difficulties for the less progressive partners deny the existence of automatic forces which effect the requisite changes in the levels of money income and prices when productivity increases.

It is not sufficient to state that disparate rates of growth can create payments difficulties. It is important to know the circumstances under which payments difficulties will be created. To analyze this problem, several cases must be distinguished. An economy A may be uniformly more progressive than an economy B, or the relative increase in productivity in A may be limited to her export industries, or, finally, the relative increase in A's productivity may be confined to those industries that compete with imports. It is necessary to inquire which of these three cases is more likely to induce balance of payments difficulties in the less progressive trading partner.

The literature concerned with this aspect of the problem has contributed to a great deal of confusion. For even among those economists who maintain that disparate rates of growth in productivity can create balance of payments difficulties there is very little agreement concerning the circumstances under which these difficulties will result. Harrod, for example, has suggested that a relative increase in productivity in the export sectors of the more progressive economy will create difficulties for her trading partners.[31] Hicks, on the other hand, has argued that a relative increase in productivity in the export sectors is almost certain to be to the advantage of the less progressive economies while import-biased increases in productivity are likely to injure them.[32] Balogh disagrees with both Hicks and Harrod and has maintained that it is random increases in productivity in the more progressive economy which are likely to have an adverse effect on her trading partners.[33] Finally, Williams has argued that a uniform increase in productivity in the more progressive economy is all that is necessary to impose difficulties on the less progressive partners.[34]

In view of these disagreements, it is necessary to examine the different cases in some detail. In the analysis that follows it is assumed that produc-

[31] Harrod, *Toward a Dynamic Economy,* p. 109.
[32] Hicks, "An Inaugural Lecture," *Oxford Economic Papers,* June, 1953, pp. 127–28.
[33] Balogh, "The Dollar Problem Revisited," *Oxford Economic Papers.*
[34] Williams, *Economic Stability,* p. 13.

tivity increases in the more progressive economy A and remains stationary in the less progressive economy B.

Uniform increase in productivity in A with an incomplete wage adjustment.—When productivity increases uniformly in A and wages rise by less than the increase in productivity, A's price level will, in the absence of a profit inflation, decline and her income level will increase.[35] Two factors will thus be operating to affect A's trade balance: first, the decline of prices of both exports and import substitutes will tend to stimulate exports and reduce imports; second, however, the increase in A's income may induce an increase in imports and in domestic consumption of exportable goods. The net effect of these movements on A's trade balance will depend upon the relative importance of the substitution and the income effects. If the substitution effects are more important than the income effect, a uniform increase in productivity in A will inflict payments difficulties on B. If, on the other hand, the income effect is quantitatively more important than the substitution effects, a uniform increase in productivity in A may lead to an improvement in B's trade balance.

Uniform increase in productivity in A with complete wage adjustment.—If wages in A increase *pari passu* with a uniform increase in its productivity, A's balance of trade is likely to deteriorate. In this case, the increase in productivity will not affect A's price levels and therefore the substitution effects will not be operative. A's level of income will increase, however, and this will probably induce an increase in imports as well as in domestic consumption of exportables leading to a worsening of A's trade balance.

Export-biased increases in productivity and imperfect wage adjustment.—When the increase in productivity in A is limited to her export industries and wages do not rise concomitantly, A's export price level will decline. Whether this will lead to an improvement of A's trade balance will depend on B's price elasticity of demand for A's exports. If B's price elasticity of demand for A's exports is 1, the value of A's exports to B, expressed in A's currency, will remain constant, although her barter terms of trade will deteriorate. If, on the other hand B's price elasticity of demand for A's exports is greater than 1 or less than 1 the value of A's exports to B will increase or decline respectively, and A's barter terms of trade will deteriorate.

[35] It is assumed throughout that the increase in productivity is not associated with a decline in employment in any form.

The income effect will also be operative if wages in A rise although by less than the increase in productivity. This effect is likely to lead to a deterioration of A's trade balance by inducing an increase in imports and an increase in domestic consumption of exportables. Combining the price and income effects, it is not possible to say a priori how an export-biased increase is likely to affect the trade balances of A and B.

Export-biased increases in productivity and perfect wage adjustment.— If the increase in productivity is limited to A's export industries and if there is a perfect wage adjustment, A is likely to suffer a deterioration in her trade balance. A's export price level will be unaffected and hence there will be no stimulus to exports. A's incomes will have risen, however, and if the income elasticity is positive A's imports will increase.

Import-biased increases in productivity and imperfect wage adjustment.—An increase in productivity in A's import substitute industries accompanied by a less than perfect wage adjustment has an uncertain effect on A's trade balance. On the one hand, the reduction in the prices of import substitutes may result in a decline of imports to A. On the other hand, the increase in A's income may induce an increase in imports and in domestic consumption of exportables. If the substitution effect is more important than the income effect, A's balance of trade will improve. If the income effect is more important than the substitution effect, A's trade balance will deteriorate.

Import-biased increases in productivity with complete wage adjustment.—Should wages rise *pari passu* with an increase in productivity in the import substitute industries, A's trade balance is likely to deteriorate. In this case, A's price levels will be unaffected and hence the substitution effect will not be operative. The income effect, however, is likely to induce an increase in imports as well as an increase in domestic consumption of exportable goods.

The preceding analysis of the possible effects on the trade balance resulting from disparate rates of productivity growth has indicated that relative increases in productivity in one country may have adverse as well as beneficial effects on the trade balances of her trade partners. In the absence of specific information concerning the relevant elasticities, it is not possible to arrive at hard and fast conclusions. Certainly the view that the more rapid rate of productivity growth in the United States must impose payments difficulties on her trade partners is premature. It is equally possible to argue that one of the chief ways to avoid a permanent dollar shortage is through continued rapid progress in the United States.

There is one aspect of the problem which has not as yet been discussed and which may be significant. Progress may manifest itself in increases in productivity in old, established industries or it may manifest itself in technological developments leading to entirely new industries, producing new products which bring in their train new demands. In such a case, progress in one country may be associated with important shifts in international demand which may disturb the old pattern of trade. It was suggested above that the shift of international demand away from the nineteenth century staples, in the production of which Britain excelled, to new commodities, in the production of which the United States and Germany enjoyed a competitive advantage, was an important factor responsible for Britain's difficulties in the interwar period. Should the United States continue to assume the role of the innovator while the economies of other countries lag, the less progressive countries may be adversely affected.

Even if it is granted that membership in a multilateral trading structure with a highly progressive economy may exert deflationary pressures on the less fortunate countries, the basic question remains of whether resort to bilateralism or the formation of regional blocs is the best corrective. Since both a less than perfect multilateral structure [36] and a resort to bilateralism or the formation of regional blocs will result in a lower real income than participation in an ideal multilateral structure, the question posed above can be resolved from the economic point of view by inquiring into which system—an imperfect multilateral structure, bilateralism, or regional blocs— will result in a greater reduction of income. Unfortunately, a priori, it is not possible to come to any definitive conclusion. A great deal will depend on whether the economy of the less progressive country under consideration is competitive with or complementary to the economy of the more progressive country; the more competitive the two economies are the greater will be the deflationary pressures exerted on the less progressive economy by participation in a multilateral system.

It should not be overlooked that even if it could be proved that the

[36] An ideal multilateral structure is one which is consistent with the maintenance of full employment in all the member countries without deflationary pressures exerted on any one originating from the economics of the other members. An imperfect multilateral system is one in which some members are subject to deflationary pressures arising from the instability of other members or from disparate rates of productivity growth.

resort to bilateralism or the formation of regional blocs will result in a smaller reduction in real income than participation in an imperfect multilateral trading system, all other things equal, the desirability of a regional bloc scheme can still be doubted. The United States may not passively permit the rest of the world to form regional blocs to the detriment of her exports. An analysis of regional blocs which fails to consider the possible retaliatory action of the excluded country is as faulty as an analysis of a perfect oligopolistic market situation that predicates passivity by one of the oligopolists when the others lower their prices or invade his market.

The fact that the United States did not retaliate in the postwar period against the sterling area bloc, for example, is no indication that the United States will not in the future resort to such tactics. Under Secretary of State Clayton, referring to the discriminatory aspects of the dollar pool, stated the case succinctly:

I think there is no question that if Britain goes on in her international trade by the device of the sterling bloc . . . we in the United States will be compelled to set up a dollar economic bloc because we cannot sit here and see these pooling agreements . . . channelling trade between Britain and these countries. We cannot sit here and see our trade generally declining, as it certainly will, and we will be compelled to adopt that course ourselves.[37]

Nor is it certain that if the United States should resort to retaliatory action, she will emerge second best. Most countries will relinquish the benefits of inexpensive exports reluctantly and will seize an opportunity to enjoy these exports provided the terms are not too onerous. The threat of forming economic blocs with the exclusion of the United States will provide Americans with sufficient incentives to offer acceptable terms. Moreover, it should not be overlooked that the United States is potentially the most important capital exporting nation and that with the increased tempo of industrialization in underdeveloped areas, many countries will seek to strengthen their ties with the United States, even should this mean a weakening of ties with the United Kingdom. As was indicated above, there is evidence to suggest that this consideration is likely to be important even with respect to some sterling area countries. The hard and unpleasant fact seems to be that the formation of regional blocs as a permanent solution to Britain's difficulties is contingent upon America's sanctioning such blocs. It is not probable that the United States will acquiesce to an arrangement of this kind permanently.

[37] *Hearings before the House Committee on Banking and Currency,* p. 195.

Bilateralism and the Terms of Trade. Some critics of the restoration of a multilateral trading structure in which the United Kingdom would participate have argued that the organization of trade along bilateral lines would enable Britain to improve her terms of trade, and would thus help redress the unbalance between the new and old worlds. Balogh argued that if the United Kingdom can "induce countries to enter into long term agreements with [her], and because of [Britain's] giving them security, grant [the United Kingdom] better terms than those available on the free market," the welfare of both Britain and her suppliers would increase.[38] It would be absurd, Balogh continued, for the United Kingdom to sacrifice one of her most valuable economic weapons—the fact that she is one of the world's leading importers—in order to participate in a multilateral trading structure.

Undoubtedly, particular countries can improve their terms of trade by exerting pressure on their trading partners;[39] the history of the interwar period furnishes ample evidence of the "success" achieved by employing trade as an adjunct of politics and diplomacy. It remains to inquire, therefore, whether the bargaining position of the United Kingdom is sufficiently strong to warrant pursuing this course of action.[40]

There is near unanimity that in the short run the United Kingdom can improve her terms of trade by exerting pressure on her trading partners, although there is some disagreement concerning the long run when the unfortunate trading partners have had a chance "to extricate themselves from such a bad bargaining position."[41] Even the unanimous feeling concerning the short run is predicated on the assumption that the United States will not retaliate. This assumption is not wholly warranted, however. It must not be overlooked that Britain's attempt to improve her terms of trade through the negotiation of bilateral agreements is likely to have an adverse effect on American exports. It is thus necessary to inquire whether Britain's bargaining position is sufficiently secure to withstand a trade war with the United States.

MacDougall studied the relative bargaining power of the United States

[38] Balogh, "Discrimination—Britain's Trade Broblem and the Marshall Plan," *Bulletin of the Oxford University Institute of Statistics,* July–August, 1948, p. 226.

[39] Cf. De Scitovszky, "A Reconsideration of the Theory of Tariffs," *The Review of Economic Studies,* Summer, 1942. Reprinted in AEA, *Readings in the Theory of International Trade,* p. 378.

[40] The question whether it is desirable to use trade as an adjunct of diplomacy can not be treated here.

[41] Meade, *Planning and the Price Mechanism,* p. 95.

and the United Kingdom in the interwar period and his conclusions are not favorable to the bilateralists. He found that the United States was almost as important an importer of commodities as the United Kingdom, was a more important importer of services, and wielded tremendous influence as a result of her ability to extend loans. He concluded that, all things considered, the United States's bargaining power was superior to Britain's.[42]

MacDougall also examined the absolute bargaining power of the United Kingdom emanating from her position as a leading importer and concluded that though impressive, it was exaggerated by the bilateralists. In the interwar period Denmark, Eire, and New Zealand were the only important countries that sold over half their exports to Britain.[43] About 70 percent of the countries supplying Britain in the interwar period sold less than 30 percent of their total exports in the British market.[44] Moreover, by correlating the sources from which the United Kingdom received her imports with the markets in which she sold her exports in 1938, MacDougall concluded that only about half of the British exports was sold in exploitable markets; the other half was sold in markets which were, in the main, unexploitable.[45] He concluded that this analysis "serves as a salutary reminder that a large part of our trade is done with countries that do not greatly depend on our market and a larger share with countries where the pull of the United States market is greater than our own." [46]

Thus, though the United Kingdom could improve her terms of trade in the short run by relying on a network of bilateral arrangements, the attempt to do so in the face of American opposition would probably be disastrous. The gains that Britain could derive from bilateralism are contingent upon receiving, if not the sanction, at least the assurance that the United States would not resort to retaliatory action.

An analysis of the various arguments that can be adduced to support a resort to bilateralism or the creation of regional blocs as a solution of Britain's difficulties has revealed both their strengths and weaknesses. It may be concluded that, on the whole, the advantages that Britain can

[42] MacDougall, "Britain's Foreign Trade Problem," *Economic Journal*, March, 1947, p. 99.

[43] MacDougall, "Britain's Bargaining Power," *Economic Journal*, March, 1946, p. 31.

[44] *Ibid.*, p. 28.

[45] MacDougall defined an exploitable country as one which sold 20 percent or more of her total exports on the British market. *Ibid.*, p. 31.

[46] *Ibid.*, p. 32.

derive from the adoption of these schemes as a permanent way of life are more than offset by their inherent disadvantages.

CURRENCY CONVERTIBILITY AND THE DOLLAR PROBLEM

The restoration of sterling convertibility on current transactions was the third major plank in America's postwar trade and payments program. The desirability of interconvertibility of currencies under normal circumstances is so manifest that here again few criticized the principle. The critics of the restoration of sterling convertibility argued simply that the circumstances in the postwar period were not propitious and that an attempt to free the pound would inevitably lead to a contraction of trade, as dollar-short countries would almost inevitably apply import restrictions against sterling goods. The events during the brief convertibility period more than substantiated this contention.

With a general dollar shortage, sterling convertibility can be maintained only if measures are devised to preclude a wholesale switch from sterling to dollar goods. It was not possible in the postwar period to effect the necessary safeguards without depriving convertibility of most of its operational significance.

The most important consideration is to prevent a contraction of trade. The outstanding moral that can be drawn from the experience of the postwar period is that the introduction of the dollar into the trade of third countries is likely, as long as the dollar remains scarce, to lead to a contraction rather than to an expansion of trade. Under the circumstances, the most advisable course for Britain to follow would be to maintain sterling inconvertibility, while allowing the maximum freedom of transferability consistent with the protection of the reserves. The aim of Britain's policy should be to move cautiously toward the restoration of convertibility, but to resist pressures toward restoring convertibility before there is reasonable assurance that it can succeed. In the interim, the maintenance of a moderate degree of discrimination [47] and the tempering of the disadvantage of inconvertibility with the maximum degree of "safe" transferability, appear to be the policies best designed to facilitate the expansion of non-dollar trade and hence to mitigate the dollar problem.

[47] Assuming, that is, that the continued use of discrimination does not result in a trade war with the United States.

X Some Proposed Solutions:
A Critical Examination

A LARGE PART of this study has been devoted to examining the factors responsible for the emergence of the sterling area's postwar dollar problem. In this chapter some of the more frequently proposed solutions for the sterling area's dollar problem are examined. Attention is focused, in turn, on the possibility of developing sterling area sources of supply, the contribution that can be expected from revision of American commercial policies, the desirability of an upward revaluation of the price of gold, and the probable effectiveness of an increase of American foreign investment in alleviating the sterling area's dollar problem.

THE DEVELOPMENT OF STERLING AREA SOURCES OF SUPPLY

In view of the fact that the necessity of placing heavier reliance on the dollar sources of supply in the postwar period was a major contributory factor in the sterling area's dollar problem, it is not surprising that in formulating long range schemes for the correction of the dollar problem prime emphasis should be placed on the possibility of displacing American imports by developing non-dollar sources of supply. The sterling area was acutely aware of this necessity. The communiqué issued at the end of the Commonwealth Economic Conference of December, 1952, noted:

Throughout the Commonwealth there is a wide scope for expanding production of essential supplies. . . . This development of the basic essentials has on occasion been impeded by other developments of a less sound and permanent kind, which has overtaxed the countries' resources and has failed to contribute to the building of economic strength. The conference agreed that in sterling area countries development should be concentrated on projects which directly or indirectly contribute to the improvement of the area's balance of payments with the rest of the world.[1]

One of the most pressing problems facing the sterling area is that of increasing the production of food and raw materials. This will enable the

[1] Communiqué issued at the end of the Commonwealth Economic Conference, London, December 11, 1952. Reprinted in British Information Service, *Labor and Industry in Britain,* December, 1952, p. 168.

rest of the sterling area to reduce its dependence on dollar sources of supply and allow the United Kingdom to substitute sterling sources for dollar sources. The expansion of primary production in the sterling area has accordingly become one of the main targets of the area's development schemes. The Colombo Plan,[2] for example, places prime emphasis on the production of foodstuffs in the southeast Asian Commonwealth countries. This plan, begun in 1951 and expected to be completed in six years, contemplates a total expenditure of 1,868 million pounds of which more than 635 million pounds or 34 percent of the total is to be used for expanding primary production. It is expected that as a result of these expenditures India's production of food grains will increase by 3 million tons, cotton by 195,000 tons, jute by 375,000 tons, and oil seeds by 1.5 million tons. Pakistan is expected to increase her production of cereal and pulses by 2.5 million tons, oil seeds by 792,000 tons, sugar cane by 71,300 tons, jute by 98,000 tons, and cotton by 52,000 tons. Substantial increases are also expected in primary production in Malaya and Ceylon.

Other sterling area countries are actively engaged in projects designed to increase primary production. Australia is currently engaged in a program designed to increase her wheat acreage to 13.7 million in 1957–58. New Zealand likewise is aiming at significant increases in wool and cattle production. Plans to increase the production of fertilizers are currently under way in Australia, New Zealand, the Union of South Africa, India, Pakistan, and Ceylon.[3]

The heavy dependence of the sterling area on foreign sources for steel, coal, copper, zinc, aluminum, and oil has led to attempts to increase their production in the sterling area. Australia, India, and the Union of South Africa are currently according high priority to steel production. Australia and the Union of South Africa are actively engaged in increasing coal production, and Australia's target is to transform a coal deficit into a coal surplus. Australia is also aiming at increasing lead and zinc production, copper production, and aluminum production to a level that would make her self-sufficient with respect to these commodities. Development projects in the colonies are designed to increase production of copper (Northern Rhodesia), bauxite (Gold Coast), and aluminum.[4] Important proj-

[2] See Rao, "The Colombo Plan for Economic Development," *Lloyds Bank Review,* July, 1951.

[3] See "Development Projects in the Commonwealth," *Labor and Industry in Britain,* March, 1953, pp. 22–31.

[4] See, for example, *Volta River Aluminum Scheme,* Cmd. 8702.

ects to reduce the need for imports are planned for Australia, the Union of South Africa, India, and Aden. Finally, ambitious schemes to increase the production of paper (New Zealand), chemicals (Ceylon and the Union of South Africa), locomotives and rolling stock (India), and textile goods (Pakistan) are currently being executed.[5]

In addition to the specific projects cited above, many sterling area countries are making a conscious effort to remove the serious impediments to production resulting from the rather severe shortages of transportation and power facilities. The completion of these projects should enable an expansion of production and exports necessary for the correction of the sterling area's payments difficulties.

The success of these projects is contingent, in large part, upon restraining inflation in the rest of the sterling area, increasing domestic savings,[6] and abandoning many projects which are not designed to rectify the balance of payments difficulties. The success achieved in these directions will largely determine whether the postwar payments difficulties can be corrected without too drastic a decline in the standards of living of the affiliated members of the sterling area.

AMERICAN COMMERCIAL POLICIES

Reference was made above to the obstacles presented by American commercial policy to the expansion of sterling area exports to the United States. These obstacles take the form of continued high tariffs, especially on manufactured imports; custom procedures designed to frustrate imports and create uncertainty; subsidies to shipping; "Buy American" acts, and so forth. From an economic vantage point the existence of these obstacles to an expansion of American imports is indefensible. The elimination of the dollar shortage necessitates either an increase in American imports or a reduction in American exports.[7] It can be demonstrated, moreover, that

[5] See "Development Projects in the Commonwealth," *Labor and Industry in Britain,* March, 1953, pp. 22–31.

[6] The communiqué issued at the end of the Commonwealth Economic Conference in December, 1952, stressed that the major portion of the "finance" necessary for the execution of these projects would, inevitably, have to be provided by domestic savings. See section 10 of the communiqué reprinted in *Labor and Industry in Britain,* December, 1952, p. 158.

[7] It is assumed that it is not probable that the proceeds of dollars resulting from an increase in American foreign lending will suffice to fill the gap. See below, p. 223 ff., for a discussion of this proposition.

from the welfare point of view it is more desirable for the adjustment to be effected through an expansion of imports than through a reduction of exports.

In this regard, the sterling area's welfare coincides with that of the United States. If, as a result of the Americans' refusal to adopt policies designed to increase their own imports, the adjustment is effected largely through a reduction in the level of imports the sterling area derives from dollar sources of supply, the standard of living of the sterling area countries must inevitably decline. This conclusion is valid even should the sterling area succeed, after the passage of sufficient time, in substituting soft currency sources for the dollar area.[8] Attaining equilibrium through the expansion of imports by the United States, on the other hand, will enable the sterling area countries to enjoy a higher standard of living and will allow a progressive relaxation of import restrictions which have been dictated by balance of payments considerations. This latter development, in turn, will enable a larger volume of trade than would otherwise be possible and thus a greater enjoyment, by the whole trading community, of the gains resulting from the expansion of international trade.

If the pursuit of policies designed to frustrate the expansion of American imports is indefensible on economic grounds, it is, unfortunately, not politically feasible to reverse. It would be unrealistic to believe that the United States will, in the foreseeable future, pursue policies that will inflict perceptible damage on those industries whose existence is contingent upon the maintaining of protective barriers. For while it is true that the failure to pursue policies designed to increase imports must inevitably result in a decline in American exports,[9] the political impact of this method of effecting adjustment is likely to be less severe than that resulting from the liberalization of trade. In the latter case the direct relationship between trade policies and their effects on the American economy is manifest, while in the former case the responsibility for the adverse effects can be more readily ascribed to the trade policies pursued by foreigners.[10]

Given these powerful political considerations, it is unlikely that the

---

[8] The substitution of soft currency sources for the dollar area, if carried beyond a certain point, must inevitably result in increasing the cost of these imports.

[9] Unless other methods are utilized to supply dollars to the rest of the world.

[10] Indeed, the failure to liberalize trade, by necessitating that adjustment be effected through a decline of exports, may even appear as a justification for the Americans to increase trade barriers.

United States will liberalize trade policies enough to make a significant contribution toward correcting the sterling area's dollar problem. Any program designed to correct the postwar dollar problem that places heavy reliance on this improbable development must be rejected as unrealistic. The most the sterling area and other dollar-short countries can hope for is a continued expansion of American income unaccompanied by any raising of trade barriers.[11]

THE UPWARD REVALUATION OF THE PRICE OF GOLD

The failure of the dollar price of gold to rise in the postwar period was a factor in the sterling area's dollar problem. Had the price of gold risen *pari passu* with the price level of internationally traded goods, the rest of the sterling area would have made a net contribution to the central dollar pool in every postwar year other than 1947, all other things equal.[12] Realizing the importance of the failure of the price of gold to rise in terms of dollars in the sterling area's postwar dollar problem, some observers have advocated an upward revaluation of the dollar price of gold as an effective solution to the dollar problem.

In assessing the desirability of this solution,[13] it is necessary to distinguish between the effects of an upward revaluation of the price of gold on the dollar (or equivalent) earnings of the United Kingdom and the effects on the dollar value of the sterling area gold reserves. The failure to distinguish between these two effects has led to faulty analysis.

A priori, it is difficult to come to any definitive conclusions concerning the effects of an upward revaluation of the price of gold on the dollar (or equivalent) earnings of the United Kingdom. An upward revaluation of the price of gold in terms of sterling and the dollar will result in a deterioration of Britain's and the United States's terms of trade vis-à-vis the gold producing countries. The purchasing power of the gold producing countries, relative to the exports of both the United States and the United Kingdom, will increase, while the relative competitive position of both of these

---

[11] It should be noted that the postwar inflation in the United States tended to reduce the real burden of the tariff.

[12] It is probable, however, that under these circumstances, the dollar expenditure of the rest of the sterling area would have increased.

[13] It is assumd that the price of gold is revalued in terms of sterling as well as the dollar. A revaluation of gold in terms of the dollar alone will result in an appreciation of the pound vis-à-vis the dollar, a development that is not likely to be in Britain's interests.

countries in the gold producing countries will remain the same. The factor that will determine whether the dollar earnings of the United Kingdom will increase or not will be the degree to which the availability of supplies in the United Kingdom will enable an expansion of exports of the type the gold producing countries wish to purchase with their increased purchasing power. Given the ability to expand exports, there is no reason why the United Kingdom should not earn the same proportion of the newly mined gold as before the upward valuation of the price of gold. Under these circumstances the dollar (or equivalent) earnings of the United Kingdom will rise. Even should Britain earn a smaller proportion of the gold, the dollar equivalent earnings may still rise if the upward revaluation of the price of gold results in an increase in its production, or if the increased dollar value of a smaller proportion of gold exceeds the dollar value of the larger proportion of gold that was earned before the revaluation.

Fortunately, the case for an upward revaluation of the price of gold in terms of sterling and dollars is not contingent upon arriving at definitive conclusions concerning Britain's ability to expand exports to the gold producing countries. By far the most important effect of an upward valuation of the price of gold in terms of dollars is on the dollar value of Britain's gold reserves. The postwar sterling area's difficulties were intensified by a shortage of reserves, which deprived the area of an important buffer and tended to transform into crises [14] what otherwise might have been regarded as passing disturbances. Any action, therefore, that increases the dollar value of the sterling area's gold reserves must be regarded as beneficial.

America's refusal to revalue the dollar price of gold upward was based on four arguments: that raising the price of gold (1) would tend to encourage essentially useless production; (2) would result in an increase in American foreign expenditure, without an increase in the importation of consumable goods; (3) would lay the groundwork for an inflationary expansion of credit; and (4) would undermine confidence in the dollar.[15] Though there is some substance in the first two objections, it is submitted that the latter two, which are by far the more significant, are groundless.

Modern banking techniques are sufficiently refined to prevent an inflationary expansion of credit resulting from an increase in the value of

[14] The 1949 crisis, in terms of the drain on the reserves, was less severe than the 1937–38 crisis which Britain weathered, largely because of the availability of larger reserves.

[15] See *The Banker*, February, 1953, pp. 90–93.

the gold base should this expansion be undesirable. In the interwar period neutralization of gold flows, designed and undesigned, resulted in the central bank's international and domestic assets moving more frequently in the opposite than in the same direction.[16] In the American banking system the increase in the gold base can be prevented from exercising an inflationary effect by the simple expedient of raising the Federal Reserve's gold requirement. Alternatively, the revaluation "profits" can be immobilized in a specially created fund in much the same manner that the "profits" resulting from the 1934 devaluation were immobilized. Because of the effective weapons at the disposal of the modern central banker, the argument that an increase in the gold base must result in an unwanted inflationary expansion of credit is without much merit.

The argument that an upward revaluation of the price of gold will result in a loss of confidence in the dollar is even less tenable. An upward revaluation of the price of gold in terms of all the major currencies will not disturb the international value of the dollar. The increase of purchasing power at the disposal of the gold producing countries is likely to exert some inflationary pressure in the American market. It is inconceivable, however, that this would lead to "a flight of capital" or cause investors "to have nothing more to do with United States government bonds" or "threaten the very existence of . . . colleges, hospitals, churches, foundations etc." [17] Arguments of this type are predicated on the fundamentally wrong assumption that the value of a currency derives from its gold backing and that any change in the gold backing must lead to a loss of confidence. This assumption has been thoroughly discredited by events in the interwar and war periods.

The conclusion that emerges is that an upward valuation of the price of gold in terms of the major currencies is one of the more inexpensive ways by which the United States can improve the international liquidity position of the sterling area.[18] The existence of deep-seated prejudices against "tampering" with the monetary base is likely to remain a chief obstacle to alleviating the sterling area's difficulties in this relatively painless manner.

[16] See League of Nations, *International Currency Experience,* p. 68.

[17] See The National City Bank, *Monthly Newsletter,* February, 1953.

[18] It should be indicated, however, that the fortuitous manner in which gold reserves are distributed is an argument against using this method to increase international liquidity.

UNITED STATES INTERNATIONAL INVESTMENT AND THE STERLING AREA'S
DOLLAR PROBLEM

A study of the manner in which international equilibrium was attained
and maintained during Britain's supremacy in the nineteenth century [19]
has led many economists to advocate the pursuit of similar policies by the
United States to eliminate the dollar shortage. Recognition of the political unfeasibility of increasing imports to an amount that would supply the
rest of the world with a sufficient supply of dollars has prompted these
economists to urge an expansion of American foreign investment.

In discussing the effectiveness of an increase of American *private* [20]
foreign investment as a solution to the dollar problem, it is necessary to
consider the areas in which Americans are likely to invest, the type of investments the Americans are likely to make, and the benefits that are
likely to accrue to the sterling area from these investments.

An examination of American private foreign investment in the postwar
period, which serves as a guide in this analysis, reveals that the investment
was, with the exception of the development of oil sources in the Near
East, predominantly in neighboring countries,[21] that it was predominantly
direct investment,[22] that these direct investments were, almost exclusively,
"hard currency oriented," [23] and that the indirect benefits derived by the

[19] The maintenance of international equilibrium in the nineteenth century and the
avoidance of a sterling shortage is attributable to a concatenation of favorable
circumstances. Among the more important of these were the huge and growing
market for food and raw material imports in the United Kingdom and the relative
scarcity of investment opportunities at home. This latter factor, combined with a
relatively high propensity to save, resulted in foreign investments which in the period
before World War I amounted to no less than 50 percent of the annual savings.
See Viner, "America's Aims and the Progress of Underdeveloped Countries" in *The
Progress of Underdeveloped Areas* (University of Chicago Press, 1952), p. 181.

[20] American grants that are prompted by the existence of the dollar shortage must
be separated, in this context, from private investment that is not induced by the
dollar shortage.

[21] In 1950 approximately 70 percent of American direct investment was concentrated in Canada and Latin America. Department of Commerce, *Foreign Investments of the United States*, 1953, p. 2.

[22] Between 1946 and 1953 direct investment abroad increased by 9,000 million
dollars while portfolio investment increased by but 800 million dollars. Department
of Commerce, *Survey of Current Business*, May, 1954, p. 10.

[23] By hard currency oriented investment we mean investment in enterprises resulting in hard currency earnings either through the sale of the company's product to the
United States or to other hard currency areas. See Bloch, "Foreign Investment and
the Dollar Shortage," *Review of Economics and Statistics*, May, 1953, p. 156.

rest of the world from these investments were exceptionally small. These developments are extremely important in assessing the effectiveness of an increase in American foreign investment as a solution to the sterling area's dollar problem.

The fact that American private investment in the postwar period was predominantly in neighboring countries is important. Since these countries have close ties with the United States, American investments eventuated in an increase of American exports to these countries. This tendency was reinforced by the large concentration of American investment in American subsidiaries operating abroad. Thus, though the investment resources made available by American private investors were not contractually tied to American exports, the end result was the same. As is indicated below, the proportion of American investment dollars expended in third countries was discouragingly low in the postwar period.

The likelihood that the pattern of American foreign investment will be transformed in the foreseeable future is not strong. The deep aversion by the American investor for portfolio investments dates to the interwar period when the losses incurred on portfolio account exceeded those incurred on direct investment account. Moreover, the inconvertibility of currencies in the postwar period, resulting in "transfer" problems, and the political uncertainty existing in many of the underdeveloped areas have tended to reinforce the American preference for neighboring countries as an outlet for their investment dollars and for investments that are "hard currency" oriented.[24]

---

[24] This tendency was already noticeable in the 1930s after the breakdown of the multilateral structure of trade and payments and the emergence of transfer difficulties. "The international commercial warfare of the 1930's . . . had a direct bearing on foreign investments during this period. While discouraging such investments in general, and particularly those depending on triangular and multilateral trade for the transfer of returns, the effects of this warfare on direct investments were more diverse. It was least harmful to investments in enterprises exporting goods to the creditor country, particularly if not only the production but also the trade of the venture were in the hands of the enterprises concerned. In such cases, unless the trade was interfered with by the country in which the investment was made, no monetary transfer of payments was involved. Even when the goods were sold to a third country, the sale was likely to take place in the creditor country and to be invoiced in its currency. Conditions thus tended to favour investments in, or by enterprises with head offices in the creditor countries." United Nations, *International Capital Movements During the Interwar Period*, p. 49.

This tendency to concentrate foreign investment in hard currency oriented concerns owned by the investors has continued into the postwar period. "At the present time [postwar] . . . the great bulk of the investment appears to be of [this] type . . . .

The adverse effects of these tendencies on the ability of "third countries" to earn dollars made available by American investment activity is reflected in a study by the Department of Commerce which shows the manner in which the supply of dollars made available to foreign countries by American foreign investment in 1950 was utilized. According to this study, the supply of dollars to foreign countries resulting from the American investment abroad and the sale of products by American companies operating abroad to the United States amounted to 2.9 billion dollars. Of this amount 1.2 billion dollars were remitted to the parent firm in the form of profits and fees and 1.5 million dollars were expended directly for United States exports. The remaining 200 million dollars were expended in the rest of the world.[25] It is manifest that if 1950 is a representative year, the dollars the rest of the world may earn from American foreign investment activity are not likely to make a significant contribution toward the solution of the dollar problem.

American private investment can make an indirect contribution to the solution of the dollar problem, however, by enabling an increase in the production of those commodities which were in desperately short supply in the postwar period. For this reason any increase in the level of private investment is to be welcomed. It is quite another matter, however, to argue that an increase in foreign investment in the form that it is likely to take in the foreseeable future can effect an equilibrium between the dollar and sterling areas.

While investment of the older type may have been more conducive to economic development in the capital receiving countries and were, in addition, of great importance to the countries involved in triangular trade between debtor and creditor countries, the more recent type of investment is, it appears, *the only one which is able to attract private capital* on a large scale in foreign ventures. This is due to the risk to which foreign investments are exposed at a time when international economic relations are out of balance, when financial transfers are subject to control, currencies are not freely convertible and mutilateral trade is greatly reduced." *Ibid.*, p. 50. (Italics added.)

[25] Pizer, "Income on International Investments of the United States," *Survey of Current Business*, October, 1951, p. 12.

XI *Conclusions and Policy Proposals*

THE STERLING AREA'S dollar problem is symptomatic of deep-seated changes in the structure of world production, trade, and payments, which had their origins in the interwar period but which were accentuated by war and postwar developments. In this study an attempt has been made to analyze the more important factors responsible for the emergence and the severity of the dollar problem.

Though many factors contributed, in one manner or another, to the postwar disequilibrium, the preceding analysis has shown that six were of prime importance. These were: the precipitous rise in the American export price level between the pre- and postwar periods; the dominant position of American companies in the world petroleum industry; the inadequacy of primary production in the non-dollar countries in the early postwar period; the increased tempo of industrialization in some overseas sterling area countries; the failure of the dollar price of gold to rise; and the failure of the United Kingdom to make the necessary adaptations to the basic changes that occurred in the structure of the world economy. Examination of these factors reveals the superficiality of those analyses that assign the most important roles to inappropriate policies pursued on either or both sides of the Atlantic or to transitory adverse developments. It also indicates that the problem of assigning blame—a problem that has unfortunately occupied the attention of many observers—is not a meaningful one. The dollar problem is not primarily the result of ignorance, of wilful policies, or of a low level of economic statesmanship; it is, rather, the resultant of basic forces which have transformed the nature of the world economy, thrust the United States into a position of economic leadership, and precluded adequate adjustment to these developments by the rest of the western world.

An analysis of the basic reasons for the emergence and severity of the dollar shortage indicates the avenues of escape. It is necessary to distinguish, however, between long-run and short-run solutions. In the analysis that follows, attention is focused first on the prerequisites for a long-run solution to the dollar shortage and then on the policies necessary to mitigate the interim problem.

PREREQUISITES FOR A LONG-RUN SOLUTION

An effective solution to Britain's dollar problem is contingent upon the restoration of a multilateral payments structure which would enable the United Kingdom to earn sufficient dollars from third sources to offset her own direct dollar deficits. The collapse of the multilateral payments structure was due primarily to (a) the increase in Britain's direct dollar deficits, induced by the rise in the American export price level; (b) the failure of primary production in non-dollar sources to expand sufficiently, which compelled the rest of the sterling area to place heavier reliance on dollar sources of supply for essential imports; (c) the increased tempo of industrialization in some sterling area countries, which induced an increase in capital goods imports obtainable in large part only from the dollar area; (d) the geographic shift in the sources of American imports, which resulted in an increase in dollars accruing to countries with close economic ties with the United States; and (e) the direction of American capital exports to the Western Hemisphere. It is evident that the reestablishment of a workable multilateral payments structure requires policies designed to halt and reverse some of these tendencies.

Reducing the sterling area's dependence on dollar sources of supply is obviously a first prerequisite. To achieve this, however, non-dollar sources of supply must be developed for primary products and for capital goods which the former dollar earners want to purchase in increasing quantities.

The possibility of developing non-dollar sources of supply for primary products is greatly dependent upon the policies the western world is prepared to initiate to ensure that primary producers will not be deprived of the fruits of economic progress, as in the past. The trend toward industrialization, which was the most important factor responsible for the relative decline of non-dollar primary production in the postwar period, was symptomatic of deep dissatisfaction on the part of the primary producing countries, whose economic structure precluded significant increases in real income and subjected them to uncontrollable, severe fluctuations. Exhortations to the primary producers to increase production are not likely to bear fruit, unless the western world is prepared to introduce policies designed to guarantee that primary production will not permanently ensure a state of poverty. The minimum program must include commodity stabilization schemes designed to eliminate the more violent fluctuations in primary product prices [1] and to establish an international fund prepared to extend loans to primary producers on a counter-cyclical basis. Given basic stability and reasonable assurances that they will share equitably in the fruits of economic progress, there is no reason why the primary producing countries should not expand production sufficiently to enable a reduction of imports from dollar sources of supply.[2]

It would be unrealistic to expect that the introduction of these schemes would completely reverse the trend toward industrialization, nor would this be entirely desirable even should it occur. It need not be assumed, however, that this development must continue to have adverse effects on Britain's economy. Whether it will or not depends, in large part,

upon the way in which the [United Kingdom] reacts to the . . . situation. The balance of advantage or disadvantage can be influenced decisively by the wisdom or unwisdom of the policy followed by its business enterprises, its organizations of workers and its government. The key to the situation is industrial adaptability. Leading industrial countries can retain their lead and move on to still higher standards of living as other areas develop if they succeed in being adaptable, that is, if they shift labor and capital into lines of production where rising world income is bringing more rapid expansion of demand than of supply and out of lines of production where new supply is increasing faster than new demand. If established industrial areas react adaptively in this way, their own business opportunities, employment, and standards of living are likely to be raised by the development of new regions. If they react non-adaptively or anti-adaptively, then the net effect may be bad for them.[3]

The United Kingdom reacted "non-adaptively or anti-adaptively" to the industrialization of overseas areas in the interwar period. As was noted above, Britain's policy during this period was to secure for herself as large a market in the older export lines as was possible, while allowing the United States and Germany to obtain the lion's share of the new markets. This policy was partially responsible for the antiquated structure of Britain's economy in the post-1945 period and hence for her inability

---

[1] The communiqué issued at the end of the Commonwealth Economic Conference on December 11, 1952, pledged the Commonwealth to support commodity stabilization schemes. "The conference agrees that violent fluctuations and an uneconomical level of prices for primary commodities were against the interests of the consumers as well as the producers. All commonwealth countries are therefore ready to cooperate in considering, commodity by commodity, international schemes designed to ensure stability of demand and prices at an economic level" (Section 15). Reprinted in *Labor and Industry in Britain,* December, 1952.

[2] The programs undertaken recently to increase primary production in the sterling area were discussed above. See p. 216 ff.

[3] Staley, *World Economic Development,* p. 23.

to supply the rest of the sterling area countries with the capital goods which they desperately wanted and which, as a result, were derived from the dollar area. This development can be reversed if the United Kingdom pursues policies designed to effect the modifications in her economy which the structural changes in the world economy necessitate. Undoubtedly, the process will be painful and difficult; existing equities will have to be sacrificed, a high level of capital formation maintained, and workers and resources diverted from some areas of the economy to others. The stakes, however, are high. Should Britain again fail to adapt, her traditionally high standard of living will be irrevocably lowered.

There can be no assurance, of course, that a workable multilateral payments structure will emerge even should primary producers be induced to increase production and the British economy succeed in adapting to the new circumstances. One thing, however, is certain: the failure to effect these two developments will surely preclude the emergence of a workable multilateral trade and payments structure. And under such circumstances, it will be virtually impossible to correct Britain's dollar problem.

An increase in non-dollar primary production and the adaptation of the British economy to the altered circumstances are, in the nature of the case, costly and, perhaps of even greater importance for the problem at hand, time consuming. It is necessary, therefore, to inquire into the nature of the policies that can mitigate the problem in the interim.

SHORT-TERM CORRECTIVES

The object of interim policies should be to maintain trade at a viable level, while providing a breathing space to effect the required developments discussed above. Every policy that contributes to this end is ipso facto desirable, whereas any policy that impedes the achievement of this should be eschewed. Regarded in this manner, many desirable interim policies become evident. It is convenient in the analysis that follows to examine these policies in accordance with whether their implementation is contingent upon action taken by the United Kingdom, the United States, or both.

The policies Britain can undertake to mitigate the dollar problem before an ultimate solution is evolved are manifest. First, a determined effort must be made to maintain economic stability. Though reduced, the dangers of an inflationary breakthrough have by no means disappeared. In view of the fact that an inflationary spiral may not only jeopardize Britain's competitive position in world markets (already weakened somewhat by the return of Germany and Japan as exporters) but may also preclude the implementation of the requisite capital formation program, the whole arsenal of weapons Britain resorted to in the postwar period to contain the inflationary pressures must be kept in a state of constant preparedness. Second, effective safeguards must be erected to prevent as large a drain as occurred in the immediate postwar period as a result of capital exports to the rest of the sterling area, sterling balance releases, and the relatively free access which the rest of the sterling area had to the resources of the dollar pool. The modifications necessary to effect these safeguards may result in the destruction of the sterling area, at least as it operated in the postwar period. This consequence may be lamented, but the fear of it should not be allowed to impede these changes; Britain simply cannot carry the burden of "unrequited exports" to the extent that she did in the immediate postwar period. Indeed, it would not be unreasonable to insist that, under the circumstances, Britain should carefully screen capital exports to the sterling area and should allow only those that contribute either to the legitimate development programs or to the restoration of international equilibrium. Finally, the government's industrial policies should be designed to facilitate the transfer of labor and resources to industries whose products have a high international demand and where an increased production at competitive prices and delivery dates will allow the United Kingdom to replace successfully the dollar area in third markets.

Whether the dollar problem is mitigated before an ultimate solution is evolved will depend, in large part, on the policies pursued by the United States as well as on those pursued by the United Kingdom. As in the case of Britain, some of the policies the United States can initiate are evident; others, however, are subject to controversy. First, it is essential that the United States maintain a high level of employment and income. The evidence of the interwar and the postwar periods clearly shows that even slight fluctuations in the level of American industrial activity can have deleterious effects on Britain and the rest of the sterling area. Second, it is equally essential that the United States reduce tariff barriers and simplify custom procedures. Though the American tariff has been reduced over the past two decades, it is still extremely high. Furthermore, recent findings concerning the probable American price elasticity of demand for imports lend strong support to the view that tariff reductions applied in a nonselective manner can induce a considerable increase in American imports and hence can make a significant contribution toward solution of the dollar problem. The Americans must be made to realize that, in the long run, the level of exports is a function of the value of imports and other dollar outflows and that, in accordance with the law of comparative costs, welfare will be increased if uncompetitive import-substitute industries are sacrificed rather than the more efficient export industries. Third, a good case can be made for the continuance of American foreign aid programs in one form or another, at least until significant progress is made in laying the groundwork for a new multilateral payments structure. One extremely valuable form of American aid is that enabling the expansion of primary production in non-dollar sources of supply, and otherwise contributing to the development of the underdeveloped areas. To make the maximum contribution, however, it is essential that aid should not be tied to American exports. It need hardly be added that the need for extraordinary aid programs from the point of view of the dollar problem will vary directly with the nature of America's commercial policies. A reduction in tariff barriers and a simplification of customs procedures will obviate the need for as large an aid program as would be necessary to maintain trade at a viable level should American tariffs be maintained or increased. Finally, the United States can increase international liquidity by the simple expedient of raising the dollar price of gold. It was noted above that, all things considered, this would be a desirable policy.

One major problem remains to be considered: the principles of trade to which the United Kingdom should adhere in the interim period before the emergence of a new multilateral structure which would enable the normal balancing of sterling-dollar accounts. In the postwar period, the United States government worked relentlessly for the restoration of convertibility and adherence to the principle of nondiscrimination. It was maintained above that in general these principles are admirable and are designed to prevent international trade from becoming chaotic. In the postwar period, however, adherence to the nondiscriminatory principle would undoubtedly have contributed to a reduction of trade, as countries would have had to levy import restrictions against non-dollar goods whenever a shortage of dollars dictated the imposition of import restrictions against dollar goods. Recognizing this problem, the United States has allowed countries to discriminate in the postwar period. Indeed, in her sponsorship of the ERP with its underlying philosophy of self-aid, and her approval of the EPU, the United States has, in effect, sanctioned a degree of discrimination against dollar goods. These decisions were wise, and it is submitted that the United Kingdom and other dollar deficient countries should be allowed to continue to discriminate as long as the dollar shortage remains a major problem.

It is recognized, of course, that continued use of discrimination involves dangers, in that it may prevent the required adaptations. It must be emphasized that the view that Britain can solve her balance of payments difficulties by sponsoring regional blocs based on the principle of discrimination is here categorically rejected. The Americans have clearly stated that they cannot countenance a trading bloc of this kind on a permanent basis without resorting to retaliatory action, and there is absolutely no reason for believing that in a trade war the United States will not emerge victorious. The proposal for a limited and temporary continuance of discrimination is not advanced as a substitute for the basic adaptations that Britain must effect. Rather it is designed to give Britain a breathing spell during which the requisite adjustments can be made. Hence, justification for the continued use of discrimination must be found in the type of policies Britain pursues to effect an international equilibrium.

The same considerations are applicable to the American insistence on the restoration of currency convertibility. Interconvertibility of currencies is so manifestly desirable that it cannot be opposed on principle. It must be realized, however, that maintaining currency convertibility is contingent upon the existence of a rough equilibrium in the foreign exchange markets. An attempt to restore currency convertibility under conditions of dollar scarcity is likely to lead to a contraction of the level of trade and hence would impede adjustment. Britain's long-run policy should certainly be to restore sterling convertibility, a policy to which she is committed. It is essential, however, if currency convertibility is to be maintained, to postpone action until there is reasonable assurance that the freeing of sterling will not lead to a precipitous drain on the reserves, thus necessitating the abandonment of convertibility itself. Fewer policies are better designed to destroy the possibility of an eventual restoration of convertibility than one which would lead to a repetition of the 1947 episode. The inability to maintain sterling convertibility in the postwar period reflected sterling's basic weakness; the successful restoration of convertibility is contingent upon the removal of those factors responsible for this weakness.

The dollar problem was produced by basic changes in the structure in the world economy over which no nation had control. This, however, does not make it an insoluble problem. Given a high degree of economic statesmanship, international cooperation, and mutual understanding, the conditions necessary for a solution can ultimately be achieved. In the interim, the pursuit of proper policies can do much to mitigate its effects.

Bibliography

OFFICIAL SOURCES

The official publications used in the preparation of this study are too numerous to cite individually. The following list includes only the more basic of these publications and those which were specifically cited in footnotes.

CANADIAN SOURCES

Dominion Bureau of Statistics. Canadian Balance of International Payments (annual).
—— Canadian Year Book (annual).
—— Review of Foreign Trade.

UNITED KINGDOM PUBLICATIONS

Board of Trade. Accounts Relating to Trade and Navigation of the United Kingdom (monthly).
—— *Board of Trade Journal* (monthly).
—— Working Party Reports (Reports on British industries prepared by experts at the direction of the Board of Trade. See especially the Working Party Reports on cotton, wool, and heavy clothing.)
British Information Service. *Labor and Industry in Britain* (quarterly).
—— British Record (biweekly).
Bureau of Customs and Excises. Annual Statement of the Trade of the United Kingdom with British and Foreign Countries (annual).
Central Statistical Office. *Monthly Digest of Statistics.*
—— National Income and Expenditure (annual).
Command Papers. Anglo-American Financial Agreement, 1946, Cmd. 8708.
—— Coal Mining: Report of the Technical Advisory Committee (Reid Report), 1945, Cmd. 6610.
—— Economic Survey for 1947, Cmd. 7046.
—— Economic Survey for 1948, Cmd. 7344.
—— Economic Survey for 1949, Cmd. 7647.
—— Economic Survey for 1950, Cmd. 7915.
—— Economic Survey for 1951, Cmd. 8195.
—— Economic Survey for 1952, Cmd. 8509.

—— Economic Survey for 1953, Cmd. 8800.

—— Economic Survey for 1954, Cmd. 9108.

—— Economic Survey for 1955, Cmd. 9412.

—— National Income and Expenditure of the United Kingdom, 1938–1945, Cmd. 7099.

—— Present Position and Future Development of the Iron and Steel Industry (1937), Cmd. 5507.

—— Statistical Material Presented to the Washington Conference, Cmd. 6707.

—— Papers on Trade, Payments and Monetary Agreements of the United Kingdom with Foreign Countries (Individual citations are not feasible; there were dozens of such agreements in the postwar period.).

—— United Kingdom Balance of Payments, 1946–1953, Cmd. 8976.

—— United Kingdom Balance of Payments, 1946–1954, Cmd. 9291.

—— United Kingdom Balance of Payments, 1946–1955, Cmd. 9585.

—— Volta River Aluminum Scheme, Cmd. 8702.

—— White Paper on Personal Incomes, Cmd. 7321.

Hansard. Debates of the House of Commons.

—— Debates of the House of Lords.

U. K. Treasury. Bulletin for Industry.

UNITED STATES

Board of Governors, Federal Reserve System. *Federal Reserve Bulletin* (monthly).

Economic Cooperation Administration. Reports to Congress.

Department of Commerce. Annual Abstract of Statistics.

—— The Balance of International Payments of the United States.

—— Foreign Investments of the United States, 1953.

—— Foreign Trade Reports.

—— International Transactions of the United States During the War. Washington, 1948.

—— *Survey of Current Business* (monthly).

—— The United States in the World Economy. Washington, 1943.

United States Government Printing Office. Congressional Record.

INTERNATIONAL AGENCIES

Bank for International Settlements. Annual Reports.

—— The Sterling Area. Geneva, 1952.

International Bank for Reconstruction and Development. Annual Reports.

International Monetary Fund. Annual Reports.

—— Annual Reports on Exchange Restrictions.

—— Balance of Payments Year Books.

—— *International Financial Statistics.*

League of Nations. Balance of Payments, 1938.
—— Industrialization and Foreign Trade. Geneva, 1945.
—— International Currency Experience. Geneva, 1944.
—— Network of World Trade. Geneva, 1942.
Organization for European Economic Cooperation. Annual Reports.
—— Statistical Bulletins (monthly).
United Nations. International Capital Movements During the Interwar Period. New York, 1949.
—— Postwar Price Relations in Trade between Underdeveloped and Industrialized Countries. Geneva, 1949.
—— A Study of Trade Between Latin America and Europe. Geneva, 1953.
—— World Economic Reports (annual).
—— A Survey of the Economic Situation and Prospects of Europe. Geneva, 1948.
—— Economic Survey of Europe in 1948. Geneva, 1949.
—— Economic Survey of Europe in 1949. Geneva, 1950.
—— Economic Survey of Europe in 1950. Geneva, 1951.
—— Economic Survey of Europe in 1951. Geneva, 1952.
—— Economic Survey of Europe Since the War. Geneva, 1953.
United Nations Economic Commission for Asia and the Far East. Annual Reports.
United Nations Economic Commission for Europe. Economic Bulletin (quarterly).

NEWSPAPERS AND MAGAZINES

I found the following newspapers and magazines particularly useful for accounts of developments affecting the international economic position of Britain and the sterling area:
The Banker (monthly)
The Economist (weekly)
British Information Service, Labor and Industry in Britain (quarterly)
The Manchester Guardian
National City Bank, Monthly Newsletter
The New York Times
The Times (London)

OTHER PUBLISHED SOURCES

Adler, J. H. "The Postwar Demand for United States Exports," *Review of Economic Studies,* February, 1946.
—— "United States Import Demand During the Interwar Period," *American Economic Review,* June, 1945.

Adler, J. H., E. R. Schlesinger, and E. Westerborg. The Pattern of United States Import Trade Since 1923. New York, Federal Reserve Bank of New York, 1952.

Ala'i, H. "The Liquidity Crisis Abroad," *American Economic Review*, December, 1947.

Akerman, J. "The Problem of International Balance in Progressive Economies," *Economia Internazionale*, May, 1951.

Allen, G. C. British Industries and their Organization. London, Longmans Green, 1935.

—— "Economic Progress, Retrospect and Prospect," *Economic Journal*, September, 1950.

Allen, R. G. D. "Mutual Aid between the United States and the British Empire," *Journal of the Royal Economic Society*, Part 111, 1946.

American Economic Association. Readings in the Theory of International Trade. Philadelphia, Blakiston, 1949.

—— "The International Trade Charter and the Principle of Non–Discrimination," *Economia Internazionale*, August, 1950.

—— "Productivity in Manufacturing and Real Income per Head in Great Britain and the United States," *Oxford University Papers*, November, 1947.

Balogh, T. "The Abolition of the Food Subsidies," *Bulletin of the Oxford University Institute of Statistics*, November, 1948.

—— "Britain and the General Tariff Agreements," *Bulletin of the Oxford University Institute of Statistics*, December, 1947.

—— "The British Balance of Payments," *Bulletin of the Oxford University Institute of Statistics*, July, 1947.

—— "The British Balance of Payments and Domestic Economic Policy," *Bulletin of the Oxford University Institute of Statistics*, February, 1951.

—— "Britain's Foreign Trade Problem," *Economic Journal*, March, 1948.

—— "Britain, O.E.E.C. and the Restoration of a World Economy," *Bulletin of the Oxford University Institute of Statistics*, February and March, 1949.

—— "The Concept of a Dollar Shortage," *Manchester School of Economics and Social Studies*, May, 1949.

—— "Discrimination—Britain's Trade Problem and the Marshall Plan," *Bulletin of the Oxford University Institute of Statistics*, July–August, 1948.

—— The Dollar Crisis; Causes and Cures. Oxford, Blackwell, 1950.

—— "The Dollar Problem Revisited," *Oxford Economic Papers*, September, 1954.

—— "Exchange Depreciation and Economic Adjustment," *Review of Economics and Statistics*, November, 1948.

—— "European Unification and the Dollar Problem," *Quarterly Journal of Economics*, February, 1951.

—— "Investment in Britain and the United States," *Bulletin of the Oxford University Institute of Statistics*, June, 1952.

—— "Notes on the Dollar Shortage," *American Economic Review*, June, 1951.

—— "The United States in the World Economy," *Bulletin of the Oxford University Institute of Statistics,* October, 1946.

Bareau, P. "Britain's Invisible Exports," *The Banker,* April, 1948.

—— "The Future of the Sterling Area," *Lloyds Bank Review,* January, 1952.

—— "The New Bilateralism," *The Banker,* February, 1948.

Barker, H. P., and R. F. Kahn. "Home and Export Trade," *Economic Journal,* June, 1951.

Barna, T., E. A. G. Robinson, and C. F. Carter. "The Economic Position of the United Kingdom in 1947," *London and Cambridge Economic Service,* May 12, 1947.

Beame, R. W. "European Multilateral Clearing," *Journal of Political Economy,* October, 1948.

Benham, F. "Full Employment and International Trade," *Economica,* August, 1946.

—— Great Britain Under Protection. London, Macmillan, 1941.

Bernstein, E. M. "British Policy and a World Economy," *American Economic Review,* December, 1945.

—— "Multilateral Trade in an Unbalanced World," *Canadian Journal of Economics and Political Science,* August, 1950.

Bloch, E. "Foreign Investment and the Dollar Shortage," *Review of Economics and Statistics,* May, 1953.

Bloomfield, A. I. United States Capital Imports and the Balance of Payments. Chicago, Chicago University Press, 1950.

Booker, H. S. The Problem of Britain's Overseas Trade. London, Staples Press, 1948.

Brady, R. Crisis in Britain. Berkeley, University of California Press, 1950.

Brown, A. J. "International Equilibrium and National Sovereignty under Full Employment," *International Affairs,* October, 1949.

Brown, W. A. American Foreign Assistance. Washington, Brookings Institute, 1953.

—— The International Gold Standard Reinterpreted. New York, National Bureau of Economic Research, 1940.

—— The United States and the Restoration of World Trade. Washington, Brookings Institute, 1950.

Buchanan, N. S. International Investment and Domestic Welfare. New York, Henry Holt, 1945.

Burn, D. L. Economic History of Steel Making. Cambridge, Cambridge University Press, 1939.

Cairncross, A. "Saving and Investment Since the War," *Westminster Bank Review,* February, 1955.

Carter, C. F. "Index Numbers of the Real Product of the United Kingdom," *Journal of the Royal Statistical Society,* 1952.

Carter, C. F., and T. C. Chang. "A Further Note on the British Balance of Payments," *Economica,* August, 1947.

Carter, C. F., W. B. Reddaway, and R. Stone. The Measurement of Production Movements. Cambridge, Cambridge University Press, 1948.

Chandler, L. V.   Inflation in the United States, 1940–1948.   New York, Harpers, 1951.

Chang, T. C.   Cyclical Movements in the Balance of Payments.   Cambridge, Cambridge University Press, 1951.

—— "A Statistical Note on the World Demand for Exports," *Review of Economics and Statistics,* May, 1948.

Chester, D. N., ed.   Lessons in British War Economy.   London, Cambridge University Press, 1951.

Clark, C.   The Conditions of Economic Progress.   London, Macmillan, 1946.

—— The Economics of 1960.   London, Macmillan, 1942.

Clay, H.   "Britain's Declining Role in World Trade," *Foreign Affairs,* April, 1946.

—— "The Place of Exports in Britain's Industry after the War," *Economic Journal,* June–September, 1942.

Cole, G. D. H.   Why Nationalize Steel?   London, New Statesman and Nation pamphlet, 1948.

Committee for Economic Development.   Britain's Economic Problem and Its Meaning for America.   New York, 1953 (Mimeographed).

Conan, A. R.   "Changes in the Dollar Pool," *Canadian Journal of Economics and Political Science,* February, 1950.

—— The Sterling Area.   London, Macmillan, 1952.

Copeland, D.   "Australia's Economy," *Lloyds Bank Review,* October, 1950.

—— "The Dollar Gap and the Commonwealth," *Foreign Affairs,* July, 1950.

Courtney, P.   The Economic Munich.   New York, Philosophical Library, 1949.

Crick, W.   "Free Trade and Planned Economies," *South African Journal of Economics,* March, 1947.

Croome, H.   "The Dollar Siege," *Lloyds Bank Review,* July, 1950.

Crossland, C.   "Movement of Labor in 1948," *Bulletin of the Oxford University Institute of Statistics,* May, 1949, and July–August, 1949.

Crowley, N. G., and C. P. Haddon-Cave.   "The Regulation and Expansion of World Trade and Employment," *Economic Record,* June, 1947.

Dacey, W. M.   "Inflation and Its Aftermath," *Lloyds Bank Review,* July, 1946.

Davies, E.   National Capitalism.   London, Gollancz, 1939.

Day, A. C.   "Devaluation and the Balance of Payments," *Economica,* November, 1950.

Dennison, S. R.   "Industrial Productivity," *Lloyds Bank Review,* January, 1949.

—— "Wages in Full Employment," *Lloyds Bank Review,* April, 1950.

De Vegh, T.   "Can Western Europe Help Itself," *Political Science Quarterly,* December, 1949.

Devons, E.   "British Industrial Production," *Lloyds Bank Review,* April, 1948.

—— "Some Aspects of United Kingdom's Export Trade," *Lloyds Bank Review,* July, 1952.

Diebold, W.   Trade and Payments in Western Europe: A Study in Economic Cooperation.   New York, Harpers, 1952.

Economic Cooperation Administration.   The Sterling Area: An American Analysis.   Washington, United States Government Printing Office, 1951.

Ellis, H.   The Economics of Freedom.   New York, Harpers, 1950.

Ellis, H.   "The Dollar Shortage in Theory and Fact," *Canadian Journal of Economics and Political Science,* August, 1948.

Einzig, P.   "The Case for Bilateralism," *The Banker,* October, 1947.

Enke, S., and V. Salera.   International Economics.   New York, Prentice-Hall, 1947.

Feis, H.   "The Conflict over Trade Ideologies," *Foreign Affairs,* January, 1947.

Fels, R.   "Regional Multilateral Clearing," *Journal of Political Economy,* August, 1948.

Ferguson, J. H.   "The Anglo-American Financial Agreement and Our Foreign Economic Policy," *Yale Law Journal,* August, 1946.

Fisher, A.   International Implications of Full Employment in Great Britain. London, Royal Institute of International Affairs, 1946.

Flanders, A.   "Wage Policy and Full Employment in Britain," *Bulletin of the Oxford University Institute of Statistics,* July–August, 1950.

Fleming, J. M.   "On Making the Best of Balance of Payments Restrictions," *Economic Journal,* March, 1951.

—— "Regional Organization of Trade and Payments," *American Economic Review, Papers and Proceedings,* May, 1952.

Franklin, N. R.   "South Africa's Balance of Payments and the Sterling Area, 1939–1950," *Economic Journal,* June, 1951.

Frisch, R.   "On the Need for Forecasting a Multilateral Balance of Payments," *American Economic Review,* September, 1947.

—— "Outline of a System of Multicompensatory Trade," *Review of Economics and Statistics,* November, 1948.

Garmany, J. W.   "South Africa and the Sterling Area," *South African Journal of Economics,* December, 1949.

Garmany, S.   "Post-War Exchange Rate Parities," *Quarterly Journal of Economics,* November, 1945.

Gibson, R.   "Devaluation and the Dollar Gap," *Current Economic Comment,* February, 1952.

Gordon, L.   "European Recovery Program in Operation," *Harvard University Business Review,* March, 1949.

Gordon, M. S.   Barriers to World Trade.   New York, Macmillan, 1941.

—— "International Aspects of American Agricultural Policy," *American Economic Review,* June, 1946.

Graham, F. D.   Causes and Cures of a Dollar Shortage.   Princeton, Essays in International Finance, No. 10, Princeton University Press.

Haberler, G.   "Causes and Cures of Inflation," *Review of Economics and Statistics,* February, 1948.

—— "Currency Depreciation and the International Monetary Fund," *Review of Economics and Statistics,* August, 1944.

—— "Economic Aspects of a European Union," *World Politics,* July, 1949.

—— "Some Economic Problems of the European Recovery Program," *American Economic Review,* September, 1948.

—— The Theory of International Trade. New York, Macmillan, 1937.

Hall, M. "The United Kingdom after Devaluation," *American Economic Review,* December, 1950.

Halpern, D. "European East-West Trade and the United Kingdom's Food Supply," *Economic Journal,* March, 1951.

Hancock, W. K., and M. M. Gourny. British War Economy. London, His Majesty's Stationery Office, 1949.

Hargreaves, J. A. "United States Import Propensities since the War," *Bulletin of the Oxford University Institute of Statistics,* January–February, 1950.

Harris, S. E. "Dollar Scarcity: Some Remarks Inspired by Lord Keynes' Last Article," *Economic Journal,* June, 1947.

Harris, S. E., ed. Essays in Economic Reconstruction. New York, McGraw-Hill, 1949.

——, ed. The European Recovery Program. Cambridge, Harvard University Press, 1948.

——, ed. Foreign Economic Policy for the United States. Cambridge, Harvard University Press, 1948.

——, ed. The New Economics. New York, Knopf, 1948.

——, ed. Postwar Economic Problems. New York, McGraw-Hill, 1943.

Harrod, R. F. The Dollar. London, Macmillan, 1953.

—— "Imbalance of International Payments," *International Monetary Fund Staff Papers,* April, 1953.

—— International Economics. London, Pitman, 1947.

—— The Life of John Maynard Keynes. London, Macmillan, 1951.

—— And So It Goes On. London, Hart-Davis, 1951.

—— Are These Hardships Necessary? London, Hart-Davis, 1947.

—— The Pound Sterling. Princeton, Essays in International Finance, Princeton University Press, 1952.

—— Towards a Dynamic Economy. London, Macmillan, 1949.

Hawtrey, R. G. The Balance of Payments and the Standard of Living. London, Royal Institute of International Affairs, 1950.

—— "The Function of the Exchange Rates," *Oxford Economic Papers,* June, 1949.

—— "The Gold Standard and the Balance of Payments," *Economic Journal,* March, 1926.

——"Monetary Aspects of the Economic Situation," *American Economic Review,* March, 1948.

—— Western European Union: Implications for the United Kingdom. London, The Royal Institute of International Affairs, 1949.

Henderson, H. D. "Anglo-American Financial Agreement," *Bulletin of the Oxford University Institute of Statistics,* January, 1946.

—— "Cheap Money and the Budget," *Economic Journal*, September, 1947.

—— "A Criticism of the Havana Charter," *American Economic Review*, June, 1949.

—— "The Function of Exchange Rates," *Oxford Economic Papers*, January, 1949.

—— "The Implications of the Marshall Speech," *Bulletin of the Oxford University Institute of Statistics*, August, 1947.

—— "The Moral of the British Crisis," *Review of Economics and Statistics*, November, 1949.

—— "The Problem of Retrenchment," *Lloyds Bank Review*, January, 1950.

Hicks, J. R. "The Empty Economy," *Lloyds Bank Review*, July, 1947.

—— "An Inaugural Lecture," *Oxford Economic Papers*, June, 1953.

—— "World Recovery after the War: A Theoretical Analysis," *Economic Journal*, June, 1947.

Hinchliffe, A. "The United Kingdom Export Drive and the Future," *International Affairs*, July, 1948.

Hinshaw, R. "Currency Appreciation as an Anti-Inflationary Device," *Quarterly Journal of Economics*, November, 1951.

—— Professor Frisch on Discrimination and Multilateral Trade," *Review of Economics and Statistics*, November, 1947.

Hinshaw, R., and L. Metzler. "World Prosperity and the British Balance of Payments," *Review of Economic Statistics*, November, 1945.

Hirschman, A. O. "Devaluation and the Trade Balance: A Note," *Review of Economics and Statistics*, March, 1949.

—— "Disinflation, Discrimination and the Dollar Shortage," *American Economic Review*, December, 1948.

—— "The European Payments Union: Negotiations and Issues," *Review of Economics and Statistics*, February, 1951.

—— "Industrial Nations and the Industrialization of Underdeveloped Areas," *Economica Internazionale*, November, 1951.

—— "International Aspects of a Recession," *American Economic Review*, December, 1949.

—— "Types of Convertibility," *Review of Economics and Statistics*, February, 1951.

Hoffman, M. L. "European Payments," *Lloyds Bank Review*, July, 1952.

Holzman, F. D. "Dollar Capital Outflows in the South African Balance of Payments," *South African Journal of Economics*, September, 1950.

Iversen, C. Aspects of the Theory of International Capital Movements. London, Oxford University Press, 1936.

—— "Postwar Economic Problems in Denmark," *Lloyds Bank Review*, October, 1948.

Jenks, L. H. The Migration of British Capital to 1875. New York, Knopf, 1927.

Jewkes, J. "Is British Industry Inefficient?" *The Manchester School of Economics and Social Studies*, January, 1946.

—— Ordeal by Planning. London, Macmillan, 1948.

Kahler, A.   "The British Devaluation," *Social Research,* December, 1949.

Kahn, A. E.   "The British Balance of Payments and Problems of Domestic Economy," *Quarterly Journal of Economics,* May, 1947.

—— Great Britain in the World Economy. New York, Columbia University Press, 1946.

Kahn, R. F.   "A Possible Intra-European Payments Scheme," *Economica,* November, 1949.

Kaldor, N.   "Employment Policies and the Problem of International Balance," *Review of Economic Studies,* Vol. XIX (I), No. 48, 1950–51.

Kalecki, M.   "Multilateralism and Full Employment," *Canadian Journal of Economics and Political Science,* August, 1946.

Katz, S.   "Leads and Lags in Sterling Payments," *Review of Economics and Statistics,* February, 1953.

Kent, T. W.   "Devaluation One Year Later," *Lloyds Bank Review,* October, 1950.

Keynes, J. M.   "The Balance of Payments of the United States," *Economic Journal,* June, 1946.

—— The General Theory of Employment, Interest and Money. New York, Harcourt Brace, 1936.

—— "A Reply to Sir William Beveridge," *Economic Journal,* December, 1923.

—— A Treatise on Money. London, Macmillan, 1930.

Kindersley, R.   "Britain's Overseas Investments," *Economic Journal* (annual paper) 1928–1938.

Klein, L. R.   "A Scheme of International Compensation," *Econometrica,* April, 1949.

Kleiner, G.   "Present Status of the World Dollar Shortage," *Current Economic Comment,* November, 1950.

Knapp, J. G., and F. M. Tamagna.   "Sterling in Multilateral Trade," *Federal Reserve Bulletin,* September, 1947.

Koo, A.   "Income Elasticity of Demand for Imports," *American Economic Review,* September, 1949.

—— "A Note on Professor Frisch's Trade Matrix and Discriminatory Restrictions of Imports," *Review of Economics and Statistics,* September, 1949.

Koopmans, T.   "The Dynamics of Inflation," *Review of Economic Statistics,* May, 1942.

Lerner, A. P.   The Economics of Control. New York, Macmillan, 1946.

Lucas, A.   Industrial Reconstruction and the Control of Competition: The British Experiment. London, Longmans Green, 1937.

Lutz, F. L.   The Marshall Plan and European Economic Policy. Princeton, Essays in International Finance, Princeton University Press, 1948.

MacDougall, G. D. A.   "Britain's Bargaining Power," *Economic Journal,* March, 1946.

—— "Britain's Foreign Trade Problem," *Economic Journal,* March, 1947.

—— "British and American Exports: A Study Suggested by the Theory of Comparative Costs," *Economic Journal*, December, 1951, and September, 1952.

—— "Notes on Britain's Bargaining Power," *Bulletin of the Oxford University Institute of Statistics*, November, 1947.

Maffrey, A. "Prospects for Closing the Dollar Gap," *Lloyds Bank Review*, October, 1952.

Malenbaum, W. "The Colombo Plan," *Department of State Bulletin*, September, 1952.

Martin, K. "The Dollar Gap," *Manchester School of Economics and Social Studies*, May, 1950.

Martin, L. "Indirect Sales of Australian and New Zealand Wool to the United States in 1949," *World Trade in Commodities*, Washington, D. C., Department of Commerce, June, 1950, Part 19.

McCurach, D. "Britain's United States Dollar Problem, 1939–1945," *Economic Journal*, September, 1948.

Meade, J. E. "Bretton Woods, Havana and the United Kingdom's Balance of Payments," *Lloyds Bank Review*, January, 1948.

—— "Financial Policy and the Balance of Payments," *Economica*, May, 1948.

—— Planning and the Price Mechanism. London, Allen & Unwin, 1948.

—— Theory of International Economic Policy: The Balance of Payments. London, Oxford University Press, 1951.

Meir, G. M. "The Trade Matrix: A Further Comment on Professor Frisch's Paper," *American Economic Review*, September, 1948.

Mendershausen, H. "The Pattern of Overseas Economic Development in World War II: The Significance for the Present," *Economica Internazionale*, August, 1951.

Meyer, F. V. Great Britain, the Sterling Area and Europe. Cambridge, Bowes and Bowes, 1952.

Meyer, F. V., and W. A. Lewis. "The Effects of an Overseas Slump on the British Economy," *Manchester School of Economics and Social Studies*, September, 1949.

Mikesell, R. F. "The Determination of Postwar Exchange Rates," *Southern Economic Journal*, January, 1947.

—— "Discrimination and International Trade," *Review of Economics and Statistics*, August, 1950.

—— "International Disequilibrium and the Postwar World," *American Economic Review*, June, 1949.

—— "The International Monetary Fund," *Journal of Political Economy*, October, 1949.

—— "Regional Multilateral Payments Arrangements," *Quarterly Journal of Economics*, August, 1948.

—— "The Role of International Monetary Agreements in a World of Planned Economies," *Journal of Political Economy*, December, 1947.

—— United States Economic Policy and International Relations. New York, McGraw-Hill, 1952.

—— "United States International Financial Policy," *Canadian Journal of Economics and Political Science,* August, 1946.

Morgan, D. "The British Commonwealth and European Economic Cooperation," *Economic Journal,* September, 1949.

Morgan, D., and W. J. Corlett. "The Influence of Price in International Trade: A Study in Method," *Journal of the Royal Statistical Society,* 1951.

Naurocki, Z. "Prospects of Britain's Cotton Industry," *Economic Journal,* April, 1944.

Nurkse, R. Conditions of International Monetary Equilibrium. Princeton, Essays in International Finance. Princeton University Press, 1954.

—— Problems of Capital Formation in Underdeveloped Countries. Oxford, Blackwell, 1953.

Orcutt, G. "Measurement of Price Elasticities in International Trade," *Review of Economics and Statistics,* November, 1950.

Ord, L. Secrets of Industry. New York, Emerson Books, 1945.

Paish, F. "Banking Policy and the Balance of Payments," *Economica,* November, 1936.

—— The Postwar Financial Problem. London, Macmillan, 1950.

Patterson, M. Survey of United States International Finance (annual reports). Princeton, Princeton University Press.

Pizer, S. "Income on International Investments of the United States," *Survey of Current Business,* October, 1951.

—— "The International Investment Position of the United States," *Foreign Commerce Weekly,* April 2, 1951.

—— "Recent Developments in the United States International Investments," *Foreign Commerce Weekly,* April 21, 1952.

Polak, J. J. "Balancing International Trade: A Comment on Professor Frisch's Paper," *American Economic Review,* March, 1948.

—— "Contributions of the September 1949 Devaluation to the Solution of Europe's Dollar Problem," *International Monetary Fund Staff Papers,* September, 1951.

—— "Depreciation and International Monetary Stability," *Review of Economics and Statistics,* August, 1947.

—— "Notes on the Measurement of Elasticities of Substitution in International Trade," *Review of Economics and Statistics,* November, 1950.

Polk, J., and G. Patterson, "The British Loan," *Foreign Affairs,* April, 1946.

—— "The Emerging Pattern of Bilateralism," *Quarterly Journal of Economics,* November, 1947.

Rao, U. "The Colombo Plan for Economic Development," *Lloyds Bank Review,* July, 1951.

Rosenson, A. "The Anglo-American Financial Agreement," *American Economic Review,* March, 1947.

Robbins, L. "The International Economic Problem," *Lloyds Bank Review,* January, 1953.

—— "The Sterling Problem," *Lloyds Bank Review,* October, 1949.

—— "Toward the Atlantic Community," *Lloyds Bank Review,* July, 1950.

Robertson, D. H.   Banking Policy and the Price Level.   London, Staples Press, 1926.

—— "Britain and European Recovery," *Lloyds Bank Review,* July, 1949.

—— "Britain in the World Economy.   London, Allen and Unwin, 1954.

—— "The Economic Outlook," *Economic Journal,* December, 1947.

—— "A Note on the Real Ratio of International Interchange," *Economic Journal,* June, 1924.

—— "The Problem of Exports," *Economic Journal,* December, 1945.

Robinson, E. A. G.   "Britain's Economic Policy," *London and Cambridge Economic Service,* May, 1950.

Robinson, E. A. G., and R. L. Marris.   "The Use of Home Resources to Save Imports," *Economic Journal,* March, 1950.

Robinson, J.   Essays in the Theory of Employment.   Oxford, Blackwell, 1947.

—— "The Pure Theory of International Trade," *The Review of Economic Studies,* Vol. XIV (2) No. 36, 1946–47.

—— The Rate of Interest and Other Essays.   London, Macmillan, 1952.

Rona, F.   "Objectives and Methods of Exchange Control in the United Kingdom during the War and Postwar Transition Period," *Economica,* November, 1946.

Ross, C. R.   "The Food Subsidies and The Budget," *Bulletin of the Oxford University Institute of Statistics,* March, 1952.

Rothbart, E.   "Causes of the Superior Efficiency of United States Industry Compared with British Industry," *Economic Journal,* September, 1946.

Rostas, L.   Comparative Productivity in British and American Industry.   Cambridge University Press, 1948.

—— "Industrial Production, Productivity and Distribution in Britain, Germany, and the United States," *Economic Journal,* April, 1943.

—— "Productivity of Labor in the Cotton Industry," *Economic Journal,* March, 1945.

Rowntree, B. S., and E. R. Laver.   Poverty and the Welfare State.   London, Longmans Green, 1951.

Salant, W. S.   "The Domestic Effects of Capital Exports under the Point Four Program," *American Economic Review, Papers and Proceedings,* May, 1950.

Sargent, J.   "E.P.U. and the Future of Sterling Policy," *Bulletin of the Oxford University Institute of Statistics,* November, 1950.

Sayers, R. S., ed.   Banking in the British Commonwealth.   Oxford, Oxford University Press, 1952.

Schumpeter, J. A.   "English Economists and the State-Managed Economy," *Journal of Political Economy,* October, 1949.

Seers, D.   "The 1947 National Income White Paper," *Bulletin of the Oxford University Institute of Statistics,* July, 1947.

Shannon, H.   "The British Payments and Exchange Control System," *Quarterly Journal of Economics,* May, 1949.

—— "The Sterling Balances and the Sterling Area," *Economic Journal,* September, 1950.

Siegfreid, A.   England's Crisis.   New York, Harcourt Brace, 1931.

Simkin, C.   "Insulationism and the Problem of Economic Stability," *Economic Record,* June, 1949.

Smith, A.   "Evolution of the Exchange Control," *Economica,* August, 1949.

Smith, R. E.   Custom Valuations in the United States.   Chicago, Chicago University Press, 1948.

Smithies, A.   "Devaluation with Imperfect Markets and Economic Controls," *Review of Economics and Statistics,* February, 1950.

—— "European Unification and the Dollar Problem," *Quarterly Journal of Economics,* May, 1950.

Staley, E. V.   World Economic Development; Effects on Advanced Industrial Countries.   Montreal, International Labor Office, 1944.

Steindle, J.   "Reconstruction and Wage Policy," *Bulletin of the Oxford University Institute of Statistics,* September, 1946.

Stern, E.   "Britain's Aid to the Sterling Area," *The Banker,* September, 1949.

Stewart, R. B.   "Instruments of British Policy in the Sterling Area," *Political Science Quarterly,* June, 1937.

—— "Notes on the Dollar Shortage," *American Economic Review,* June, 1950.

Tether, C. G.   "South Africa's Relations with the Sterling Area," *The Banker,* October, 1949.

Tew, B.   International Monetary Cooperation, 1945–1952.   London, Hutchinson's University Library, 1952.

—— "Sterling as an International Currency," *Economic Record,* June, 1948.

Thakeray, F. G.   "Elasticity of Demand for United Kingdom Imports," *Bulletin of the Oxford University Institute of Statistics,* April, 1950.

Tinbergen, J.   "Four Alternative Policies to Restore Balance of Payments Equilibrium," *Econometrica,* July, 1952.

Tyszynski, R.   "World Trade in Manufactured Commodities, 1899–1950," *Manchester School of Economic and Social Studies,* September, 1951.

Urquhart, M.   "Postwar International Trade Arrangements," *Canadian Journal of Economics and Political Science,* August, 1948.

Viner, J.   "An American View of the British Economic Crisis," *Lloyds Bank Review,* October, 1947.

—— Canada's Balance of International Indebtedness.   Cambridge, Harvard University Press, 1924.

—— The Customs Union Issue.   New York, Carnegie Endowment for International Peace, 1950.

—— "International Finance in the Postwar Period," *Journal of Political Economy,* April, 1947.

—— International Trade and Economic Development.   Illinois, The Free Press, 1952.

—— Studies in the Theory of International Trade.   New York, Harper and Brothers, 1937.

Ward, B.   The West at Bay.   New York, Norton, 1948.

Whale, P.   "International Short Term Capital Movements," *Economica,* February, 1949.

—— "International Trade in the Absence of an International Standard," *Economica,* February, 1936.

—— "The Working of the Prewar Gold Standard," *Economica,* February, 1937.

White, H. D.   The French International Accounts, 1880–1913.   Cambridge, Harvard University Press, 1933.

Wilcox, C.   A Charter for World Trade.   New York, Macmillan, 1949.

—— "Trade Policies for the Fifties," *American Economic Review, Papers and Proceedings,* May, 1953.

Williams, J.   "The British Crisis: A Problem in Economic Statesmanship," *Foreign Affairs,* October, 1949.

—— Economic Stability in a Changing World.   New York, Oxford University Press, 1953.

—— "Europe after 1952," *Foreign Affairs,* April, 1949.

—— "International Trade Theory and Policy: Some Current Issues," *American Economic Review, Papers and Proceedings,* May, 1951.

White, H. D.   The French International Accounts.   Cambridge, Harvard University Press, 1933.

Wilson, T., and P. Andrews, eds.   Oxford Studies in the Price Mechanism.   Oxford, Clarendon Press, 1951.

Worswick, G. D. N.   "A Fall in Consumption," *Bulletin of the Oxford University Institute of Statistics,* June, 1948.

Worswick, G. D. N., and P. H. Ady, eds.   The British Economy, 1945–1950.   Oxford, Oxford University Press, 1950.

Wright, K. M.   "Dollar Pooling in the Sterling Area," *American Economic Review,* September, 1954.

Young, J. P.   "Exchange Rate Determination," *American Economic Review,* December, 1947.

Zupnick, E.   "A Note on Variations in the Terms of Trade and a General Dollar Problem," *Review of Economics and Statistics,* May, 1956.

—— The Sterling Area's Central Pooling System Reexamined," *Quarterly Journal of Economics,* February, 1955.

Index

Africa, primary production (1951–52), 39 (*tab.*); *see also* specific countries
Agriculture, in Britain, 12, 42–43, 62 (*tab.*), 64, 133–34
Aircraft industry, Britain's, 22, 69, 70 (*tab.*)
Allen, G. C., 22
Aluminum, 22, 217
American account countries, 163, 165 (*tab.*), 167, 168 (*tab.*), 179*n*
Anglo-American Financial Agreement, 86–89, 108–9, 163, 164, 194, 197–99, 205
Artificial fibers, 137
Attlee, Clement, 87, 88
Australia: and dollar pool, 126; exports from, 84, 94, 95, 131, 134*n*, 140; imports to 113*n*, 131, 133, 135, 136; independent dollar reserves 125*n*; primary production, 217; and sterling area, 125*n*, 156, 157; sterling balance, 35 (*tab.*), 109–10; sterling reserves, 148 (*tab.*); wool trade, 141
Automobile industry, Britain's 22, 43 (*tab.*), 57, 69, 70 (*tab.*), 191
Automobiles: British export, 90*n*; North Amercia's exports to Britain, 82 (tab.); U.S. export prices, 86 (*tab.*)

Balance of payments data, 6
Balogh, T., cited, 61, 199, 206, 208, 213
Baltic countries, in sterling bloc, 122*n*
Bank loans, 47, 51
Bank rate, 46, 49, 192; *see also* Monetary policy
Belgium: and British payments machinery, 165 (*tab.*), 168; conversion of sterling into dollars (1947), 166 (tab.); currency restrictions, 166*n*; dollar drain to, 160; dollar receipts from sterling area (1947–49), 180–81; and EPU, 176; and IEPS, 171–74; monetary agreements with Britain, 162; and regional payments scheme, 170; sterling balance (1945), 35 (*tab.*)

Bilateral accounts countries, 167, 168 (*tab.*)
Bilateralism, 202–14
Bilateral trade, 89–90, 194
Blocked accounts, 109, 179*n*
Britain: bargaining power compared to U.S.'s, 214; Canadian loans to, 34; capital assets, 28–29; as custodian of hard currency reserves, 7; deficit (1938), 38; dependence on imports, 204; dollar deficit, 129; expenditure and supplies, 190; exports, 12, 23–28, 32–33, 58, 68–71, 79 (*tab.*), 99–101, 105–17, 186 (*tab.*), 191–92; government expenditure, 72; imports, 23–26, 32–33, 70, 79 (*tab.*), 82 (*tab.*), 91, 92 (*tab.*), 95, 184, 186 (*tab.*), 187, 191–92; incomes in, 31–32, 44; industrial adaptability, 228–30; international trade relations, 37; and IEPS, 171–74; payments machinery, 161–79; prices, 31, 32–33, 74, 93, 97–99, 100, 130; and regional payments scheme, 170; relations to ISA, 153; relation to U.S. economy, 203; technology in, 13; trade, 23–27, 214; U.S. loans to, 34
Burma: currency agreements with Britain, 126; imports, 131, 133, 134, 135, 136; rice exports, 133; sterling reserves, 148 (*tab.*)
Business cycles, international propagation of, 203; effects of in the United States, 115–16, 157, 202–4
Buy American Act, 117, 218

Canada: aid to Great Britain, 9, 114; and British payments machinery, 165 (*tab.*), 167, 168; exports, 41*n*, 81, 82 (*tab.*); imports, 100–101, 223*n*; loans to Britain, 34; trade with Britain, 80–99
Capital destruction and consumption, British, 28–29, 61
Capital exports: Britain, 26, 108–14, 150–52, 223, 230; and income decline,